Maycie Katherine Southall:

Her Life and Contributions to Education

Dorothy Louise Brown

Published by Dorothy Louise Brown
McMinnville, Tennessee

Printed by McQuiddy Printing Company
711 Spence Lane
Nashville, Tennessee

MAYCIE KATHERINE SOUTHALL:

HER LIFE AND CONTRIBUTIONS

TO EDUCATION

by

Dorothy Louise Brown

Dissertation

Submitted to the Faculty of

George Peabody College for Teachers

of Vanderbilt University

in Partial Fulfillment of the Requirements

for the Degree of

DOCTOR OF PHILOSOPHY

in

Educational Administration

August 1981

William H. Force	_July 23. 1981_
Major Professor	Date
James H. Whitlock	_July 23, 1981_
Second Reader	Date
Ann Alan	_July 23, 1981_
Third Reader	Date
Willis Huntwerger	_July 23, 1981_
Department Chair	Date
Willis Hawley	_8/13/81_
Dean of George Peabody College for Teachers	Date

ii

Dedicated to

Alma

whose caring for education is ever constant.

ACKNOWLEDGMENTS

To all who from various walks of life and diverse geographical areas either directly or indirectly contributed to this research project, appreciation is expressed.

A special note of gratitude is extended to the members of my advisory committee. Just as former students said of Maycie Southall and reported in this study, William Force, chairman, has modeled the role of professional scholar for me. The many learning experiences he provided through classroom endeavors are appreciated, his guidance during my doctoral studies is valued, and his friendship is cherished. For the counsel of James Whitlock and Dale Alam, a note of thanks is also expressed.

Particularly helpful to the development of this study were John Julia McMahan, whose correspondence from New Mexico included many valuable leads to primary sources of contact; O. L. Davis, Jr., who generously sent from Texas recordings of his recent interviews with Maycie Southall in order to eliminate duplication of effort on her part; Jessie Sim, acting executive secretary of The Delta Kappa Gamma Society International, who reviewed Chapter IV for verification of data and who graciously provided copies of official documents requested from the organization's headquarters at

Austin, Texas; and Evelyn Stephenson, a staff member, who rendered assistance, offered suggestions, and gave encouragement during my research in the archives at George Peabody College for Teachers.

Appreciation is extended to the numerous editors and publishers who graciously granted permission for the use of copyrighted material included in this research project. Gratitude is also extended to the numerous authors who kindly allowed use of unpublished material in this study. The source of each quotation or paraphrase is credited in both footnote and bibliography.

Special thanks are expressed to each former student, colleague, and friend of Maycie Southall who responded to my letter of request for information concerning her life and contributions to education. The prompt, generous, and enthusiastic responses were indeed gratifying; certain it is that they denoted a keen interest in the compilation of a permanent record, assembled for posterity, pertaining to the outstanding educational achievements of Maycie Southall.

I did not know Maycie Southall personally prior to the development of this project. The faith that she displayed by allowing me to make a study of her life and contributions to education and use it as my dissertation topic is deeply appreciated. During the progress of the study, I learned to treasure the stimulating interviews held at intervals with Maycie Southall. Her gracious hospitality, interesting reflections, scrupulous verification of facts, kind permission for use of

private files, constructive criticism, and helpful suggestions have blended into educational experiences that will
long be remembered. I value her friendship.

A sincere note of thanks is expressed to the members
of my family for their patience and support throughout this
undertaking. Their understanding and encouragement have
sustained me throughout my educational endeavors.

TABLE OF CONTENTS

1929

MAYCIE SOUTHALL

Doctor of Philosophy
George Peabody College for Teachers

ix

The contributions of Dr. Maycie Katherine Southall to education are measured in her exemplary personal life and dedicated professional life to the end that she represents an era in the progress of educational endeavors in the South and the nation.

William Theo Dalton
Personal letter
February 25, 1980

CHAPTER I

INTRODUCTION

Selection of Topic

Each project has its own history, and perhaps this presentation should be introduced through an explanation of how and why the selection of the topic was made.

Jesse Stuart, poet laureate of Kentucky, reminisced about various educational experiences during his earlier days of graduate work:

> I began to think about a thesis. I had to write one before I could get an M.A., so I must write a thesis. I went to both Vanderbilt University and Peabody College, and looked over the small steel corridors of thin black theses. They were all covered with dust. The only time they were ever used was when a student wanted to see what one was like before he wrote his own. He wanted to look at one for a pattern to cut his by, not for the dry contents, no, no, my heavens, no![1]

Jesse Stuart continued his reverie by describing the dry theses as ". . . dust-covered, happy and contented in their steel corridors on a shelf at Peabody College and Vanderbilt University or anywhere."[2] In conclusion of his soliloquy, the well-known author mused: "Education, you know, is measured on dusty shelves. If you don't believe me, go wipe away

---

[1]Jesse Stuart, To Teach, To Love (New York: World Publishing Co., 1970), p. 155.

[2]Ibid., p. 156.

1

the dust and read for yourself. Don't strike matches around theses or wear tacks in your shoes."[3]

Perhaps the Kentucky author's observations were correct, at least in part, for previous to reading his commentary, this writer had browsed at length among the dissertations in the Education Library at George Peabody College for Teachers; and, yes, this writer was dismayed to find that many of the research efforts have been utilized sparingly if the pocket signature and date-due cards are accurate indicators. Jesse Stuart was, however, ostensibly voicing his own opinion, not necessarily that of others, when he referred to the dryness of the studies. Those dissertations that are biographical in nature held special appeal for this writer and have provided countless hours of reading pleasure. Many of the authors invested immeasurable time and effort in the preparation of dissertations that they trusted would serve as enduring monuments to their subjects' outstanding and invaluable service, particularly in regard to their influence upon, and contributions to, the field of education.

Jesse Stuart's observation concerning the lack of subsequent use of research studies served to challenge this writer's effort to select a topic and, in turn, develop a study that would be useful, especially to future generations of educators. This writer is confident that the information contained within the study has potentiality for extensive utilization rather than relegation to a safe and secure nook of oblivion.

---

[3]Ibid.

The Purpose of the Study

This study consists of an effort to determine, analyze, and record the major contributions to education of Maycie Southall who, during her career, progressed from modest beginnings as a rural elementary school teacher of only twelve students to principal and then to county supervisor; a short time later she was advanced to the position of state supervisor of elementary education, and she subsequently became a prominent professor of education whose influence throughout many years on countless administrators, supervisors, and teachers is immeasurable. Maycie Southall's leadership is not confined to the educational institution setting but is also exemplified through contributions to educational literature; extensive affiliations with professional organizations; and participation in religious, civic, and legislative affairs.

The writer trusts that the completed study provides a cohesive, accurate, and permanent record of the life, accomplishments, and contributions of one whose career has been devoted to the service of education. Prior investigation ascertained that no adequate study of the life and achievements of Maycie Southall had been developed; thus, the premise of this study is that an orderly and permanent record of Maycie Southall's life and contributions is warranted because, as a leader in both supervision of instruction and childhood education, she has played a significant role in the history of education not only in her native southern region but across the nation.

Although an analysis of any one of Maycie Southall's numerous and varied contributions to education would suggest that the permanency of such a record is merited, one chapter is included in this study which directs attention specifically to the subject's participation in the activities of an educational organization, The Delta Kappa Gamma Society International. The largest honorary educational organization for women in the world, Delta Kappa Gamma's membership consists of approximately 150,000 educators. There is a paucity of written material available on the well-known leader, Maycie Southall, who as one of the sixteen Xi State founders helped to organize the Tennessee unit in 1935, became its first state president, and is widely recognized as the only Tennessean who has served as president at the national level. Thus, a secondary purpose of this study is to provide, especially for the Tennessee chapters of Delta Kappa Gamma, a source of reference concerning a distinguished and venerated leader of long-standing. It is anticipated that this source of material will be utilized extensively in program planning by the membership of Xi State which consists of approximately 3,500 educators across the state of Tennessee.

This study is worthy of the time, effort, and diligence requisite to its fruition because:

1. The study of Maycie Southall's achievements may motivate other educators to become even more effective contributors to the needs of education.

2. The study provides material pertaining to efforts expended during this century in the promotion of early childhood education.

3. The study contains some background information relative to the concept of role conflicts experienced by women educators.

4. The study affords some insight into recent legislative efforts that have resulted in the provision of public kindergartens in Tennessee.

5. The study makes available a source of historical data for Delta Kappa Gamma members.

Rationale

A study of the life and educational contributions of Maycie Southall is deemed feasible because:

1. As a pioneer educator, Maycie Southall played an important role in the intellectual growth and development of Nashville, Tennessee. Since the city is planning its bicentennial celebration at the same time that this study is being compiled, it is fitting that Maycie Southall's efforts be recognized and recorded for posterity.

2. During 1979, the year in which this study is being undertaken, the Delta Kappa Gamma Society International is celebrating its fiftieth anniversary. The theme for the golden anniversary is "Honor the Past; Celebrate the Future." Because of her outstanding contributions at all levels to the leadership of this large organization, it is particularly

appropriate that Maycie Southall's efforts and services to
The Delta Kappa Gamma Society International and to education
in general be recorded at this time.

3. There are few studies available at George Peabody
College for Teachers pertaining to women educators. The life
and educational contributions of Maycie Southall are of such
stature that a carefully researched record of them merits
inclusion among the institution's valuable collection of biographical dissertations.

4. Much publicity has been given to the designation of
the year 1979 as International Year of the Child. Because
of Maycie Southall's genuine interest in, and promotion of
efforts that would improve education for, the child, the
timing seems perfect for directing attention toward this
particular educator during this particular year.

Organization of the Study

The organization of the study provides for seven chapters. The first chapter consists of an introduction to the
study.

The second chapter is addressed to Maycie Southall's
heritage, her early years, and her initial educational experiences. The conclusion of this chapter marks the completion
of her formal education which culminated in conferment of the
Ph.D. degree in 1929 by George Peabody College for Teachers.

The third chapter encompasses a longer period of time,
thirty-five years, during which Maycie Southall taught at

George Peabody College for Teachers; she accepted a full-time position in 1929 and remained at the educational institution until her retirement in 1964. Emphasis is directed toward Maycie Southall's impact upon the development of supervision of instruction; her professional contributions as reflected by the prestige accorded the institution which she served; and her performance as a teacher of teachers, of supervisors, and of administrators.

The fourth chapter focuses attention upon the contributions of Maycie Southall to The Delta Kappa Gamma Society International. This chapter includes her efforts both as state and national president. During the same year that Maycie Southall began her career at George Peabody College for Teachers, a Texas educator, who had served as a state superintendent of public instruction, was cultivating an idea that was destined to have a monumental effect upon literally thousands of women educators during the ensuing decades. Annie Webb Blanton had conceived the idea of forming an organization that would unite women educators in their efforts toward improving education. Twelve educators are credited with having founded the organization on May 11, 1929. Then, in 1935, the originator came to Tennessee to assist a select group of women educators in establishing Xi State, the name of the Tennessee unit of Delta Kappa Gamma. Maycie Southall was one of the original sixteen organizers of Xi State and has played a vital role in its growth throughout succeeding years.

The fifth chapter is devoted to a presentation of additional endeavors, achievements, and honors that reflect some of Maycie Southall's contributions to education.

The sixth chapter calls attention to projects and accomplishments associated with the later years, the time following Maycie Southall's retirement in 1964 from her professorship at George Peabody College for Teachers.

The seventh chapter summarizes and presents major conclusions of the study.

Review of Related Research and Literature

A search for information pertaining to a history of women educators reveals a dearth of printed material. One writer penned: "Women's efforts have routinely been dismissed as inconsequential . . . by those who have compiled the record of the past."[4] Another author noted that ". . . virtually nothing at all gives an overview of the history of women in education."[5] A similar thought was expressed by still a third observer who offered: "Typically, current United States history textbooks devote one out of several hundred pages to women's lives and contributions."[6]

If the entire spectrum is narrowed to a specific historical period of time and geographical location, the scantiness

---

[4]Carol V. R. George, ed., "Remember the Ladies" (Syracuse: Syracuse University Press, 1975), pp. 1-2.

[5]Patricia Sexton, Women in Education (Bloomington, Ind.: Phi Delta Kappa Educational Foundation, 1976), p. 24.

[6]Anne Chapman, "Women in the History Curriculum," Social Studies 69 (May-June 1978):117.

of written records becomes even more obvious. The time frame
upon which this study rests encompasses primarily the early
years of this century, and the setting for the study is the
southern region of the United States. In direct reference to
this period of time, these comments were penned:

> A cursory examination of the card catalog of any
> large library and the indexes of major journals for
> books and articles on women discloses a striking de-
> crease in their number after the mid-1920s that curves
> up again only in the 1960s. The years 1927 and 1959
> appear to be the inflexion points.[7]

From still another vantage point, the dearth of material
about pioneer women educators in Tennessee becomes evident.
One organization undertook the task of compiling a book concerning outstanding women educators of the past in Tennessee.
The book was made available for purchase in 1961. Approximately two years later the organization decided to send a
copy of the publication to each state librarian as well as
to the librarian of Radcliffe College. A letter describing
the gift suggested that, as the book provided valuable information pertaining to education in Tennessee and emphasized
in particular the efforts of many women educators, the dona-
tion should be an asset to each library. Louise Oakley, who
wrote the letter to the librarians, reported to the members
of the organization:

> Letters of appreciation were received from thirty
> state librarians and the librarian of Radcliffe College.
> The recurring note in the letters was "The book fills a

---

[7] Jo Freeman, "Women on the Move: The Roots of Revolt,"
in _Academic Women on the Move_, ed. Alice S. Rossi and Ann
Calderwood (New York: Russell Sage Foundation, 1973), p. 1.

noticeable gap in our research facilities, as we have little material on pioneer women in education in Tennessee.[8]

The previous comments are strengthened by the fact that one can survey the shelves lined with innumerable dissertations in libraries only to find a very limited number of studies pertaining to women educators whose contributions to the teaching profession are associated with the early part of this century.

Perhaps the question should be raised: Of what import is the development of the history of women in education? In simplistic terms, a better understanding of the present should result from one's relating to his or her past: "Though we cannot say history holds the key to all life's problems, there is good reason for believing it holds the key for many problems pertaining to living together in societies."[9] Too, a study of the past can enhance an awareness of, and orientation toward, the future. One author offered: "What emerges from insightful discussions of women in the past is a sense not only of individual achievement, but more importantly, of commitment to social change."[10] The same author continued: "In other words, studying history--their own history, of course--

---

[8]Louise Oakley, "Some Facts about Light from Many Candles," report prepared for the membership of Xi State, August 1967, p. 4, Archives of Xi State, Tennessee Education Association (TEA) Building, Nashville.

[9]Clarice T. Campbell, "The Historian's Task," The Delta Kappa Gamma Bulletin 32 (Summer 1966):34.

[10]Florence Howe, "Sexism and the Aspirations of Women," Phi Delta Kappan 55 (October 1973):102.

can make women future-oriented and socially committed."[11] An awareness of the present, based on an understanding of the past, may promote thought about the future. The author concluded by stating: "The pattern is very simple. Until you have a history you have no future. For women, it is a new experience, partly because our history has been . . . obscure to us. . . ."[12]

A Delta Kappa Gamma member expressed her convictions regarding the value of historical research about women by noting that ". . . interest and energy expended on studies of pioneer activities will result . . . in added appreciation and understanding of earlier educational experiences."[13] The author noted that, in addition, such studies will lend themselves to ". . . a more vital awareness of present and future pioneering that is needed in educational things, pioneering, much of which can be done by women."[14]

When the review of related research and literature is narrowed to a specific subject such as, for example in this particular study, the life and contributions to education of Maycie Southall, the obtaining of germane documents becomes increasingly difficult. Although her teaching career has been amply filled with educational experiences sufficient for

---

[11]Ibid.

[12]Ibid.

[13]Ruth M. Jackson, "Values of Research on Pioneer Women Educators," The Delta Kappa Gamma Bulletin 23 (Spring 1957): 49.

[14]Ibid.

a number of studies, very little has been recorded concerning
Maycie Southall's life and contributions to education. As
stated earlier, one of the main purposes of this study is to
research, compile, and record in one document information concerning the significant educational experiences woven throughout the fabric of Maycie Southall's many years of involvement
with various facets of education.

A survey of related literature has revealed that a short
biographical presentation about Maycie Southall is available
in Light from Many Candles, a book by Lucille Rogers. Brief
sketches about her life and achievements are included in two
documents entitled Our Heritage, a history of the Delta Kappa
Gamma Society compiled by Eunah Temple Holden and published
in 1960 and 1970. Some information may be gleaned from such
sources as, for example, an article published in The Peabody
Reflector entitled "The First Lady of Childhood Education" by
Etha Green. Several articles in various volumes of The Delta
Kappa Gamma Bulletin also contain pertinent biographical data.

Maycie Southall's publications were not extensive. They
included primarily chapters in national yearbooks and similar
documents, bulletins, and articles pertaining to childhood
education that have been printed in a variety of journals and
periodicals.

The preliminary search did not produce an abundance of
relevant documents; however, any conclusions drawn at this
stage concerning ultimate scarcity of material would have
been premature. The material, found through other sources,

was voluminous; and its extrication became both fascinating and eventually rewarding. Thus, in spite of the apparent elusiveness of a loom upon which a researcher could hope to weave a historical fabric concerning the achievements of a woman educator in the early 1900s, it is easy, in retrospect, to concur readily with Patricia Sexton who provided at least faint encouragement when she penned: "The records are there, buried in the main body of history and literature, and some rather devoted digging may be required. . . . What is known may be intriguing enough to stimulate such excavations."[15] Therefore, with the encouragement of many former students, colleagues, and friends of Maycie Southall who upon hearing of the proposed dissertation waxed quite eloquent in their enthusiasm concerning such an endeavor, it behooved this writer to ". . . become a sleuth of the stacks, a veritable bibliographical bloodhound"[16] in order to ferret out, sift, and refine the bits and pieces pertinent to the study.

One author suggested: "Originality is the touchstone of all true research, for research means adding new knowledge to the field in which it is undertaken."[17] Thus, it is trusted that this study serves to add some measure to an area of research in which there is, at present, meager documentation.

---

[15]Sexton, Women in Education, p. 24.

[16]William W. Brickman, Research in Educational History (Norwood, Pa.: Norwood Editions, 1973), p. 214.

[17]Tyrus Hillway, Introduction to Research, 2d ed. (Boston: Houghton Mifflin Company, 1964), p. 292.

Method of Research and Sources of Data

The historical method of research is used in this study. In this sense, method refers to ". . . a reasonable plan for attacking and solving the problem under investigation, making use not of intuition or chance experience or pure logic, but of scientific principles based upon objectivity and common sense."[18] The historical method, also known as documentary research, can in all probability be regarded as the oldest form of genuine research.[19] Because of its stringent requirements, the responsibilities incumbent with utilization of the historical method weigh heavily upon the researcher:

> A good historical study is perhaps one of the most difficult to do. It demands rigor and objectivity and the evaluation of evidence to determine its validity that is far more difficult to achieve than in the descriptive or experimental approach.[20]

The methodology appropriate to historical research includes four overlapping steps: collecting materials; evaluating their trustworthiness and usefulness in regard to the research problem; synthesizing the information drawn from source materials; and finally both analyzing and synthesizing in order to accept or reject hypotheses, make final interpretations, and reach conclusions.[21] The prescribed procedure was followed in this study.

---

[18]Ibid., p. 140.

[19]Ibid., p. 141.

[20]George W. Smith, Quantitative Methods of Research in Education (Washington, D.C.: College and University Press, 1975), p. 79.

[21]William Wiersma, Research Methods in Education, 2d ed. (Itasca, Ill.: F. E. Peacock Publishers, 1975), p. 155.

Primary sources were utilized throughout the study where possible. When secondary sources were included, they were evaluated carefully regarding their trustworthiness from the standpoint of source as well as content.

Almost any object may be potentially useful as a source for gleaning information about the past; for instance, some of the sources used in this study were written documents, recordings of the spoken word, and keepsakes. Documents found helpful included handwritten letters, newspaper clippings, legal records, institutional files, periodicals, and yearbooks. Interviews taped previously by friends of Maycie Southall contained pertinent information. Also, keepsakes proved to be beneficial to the study; for example, a handmade Christmas card that had been mailed in 1938, seemingly insignificant at first glance, served as a source of information because it summarized through use of a clever design many facts about Maycie Southall's activities during that year. Still another example involved an exquisite gold bracelet, a treasured possession bequeathed to Maycie Southall by the originator of Delta Kappa Gamma; the engraved bracelet is significant because it was presented to Annie Webb Blanton by the membership as the organization's first national achievement award.

Major steps taken in search of pertinent data for this study are traced: The research efforts began by utilizing preliminary sources such as the Dissertation Abstracts and Dissertation Abstracts International (title changed in 1969). Also, both on-line and manual searches were made utilizing

Educational Resource Information Center (ERIC) facilities.
Next, a thorough manual search was made of all volumes of the
Education Index published since 1929 followed by a similar
search of Current Index to Journals in Education (CIJE) established in 1969.

As noted earlier, the preliminary search provided some
pertinent material; of particular benefit were biographical
sketches, Maycie Southall's publications, and background information relevant to the era under scrutiny. But, as one
author stated, "An exhaustive survey of the ground covered by
others is only the starting point for original work of one's
own."[22] Thus began a rewarding investigation.

One of the most productive avenues of search consisted
of a manual examination of all available volumes, from the
early 1920s to the present time, of The Peabody Reflector, a
publication filled with articles about the faculty, students,
and campus events at George Peabody College for Teachers. Although an index is available, a manual search was necessary
in order to find incidental reports of specific activities
in which Maycie Southall was engaged during her years at the
institution. Manual searches were also made of other campus
publications such as student newspapers, yearbooks, catalogs,
and bulletins; all were helpful in reconstruction of the past.

The records of Xi State, the Tennessee unit of The Delta
Kappa Gamma Society International, are housed in a vault at

---

[22]Hillway, Introduction to Research, p. 293.

the Tennessee Education Association Building in Nashville.
As the records are not indexed, they were reviewed manually.
Middle Tennessee State University provided access to several
volumes of <u>The Delta Kappa Gamma Bulletin</u>.

Another technique utilized to obtain pertinent information is described: Maycie Southall served as advisor to many
students at George Peabody College for Teachers. An effort
was made to identify all students who had completed programs
at the doctoral and specialist levels under her guidance.
All dissertations and independent studies prepared between
1929 and 1964, during her tenure, were examined in search of
acknowledgments by students for her assistance. Subsequently,
a list of the names of her advisees was compiled, addresses
were obtained in the Office of Development and Alumni Affairs,
and letters were mailed to former students requesting their
analyses of her contributions to education (see Appendix).
As requested in the inquiries, suggestions were provided in
the feedback concerning additional contacts to whom letters
were also sent; thus, information was sought and received
from many different sources. Among additional correspondents
were former colleagues, presidents and department heads during Maycie Southall's tenure; former co-workers in a variety
of national and international organizations; former students
at the master's and bachelor's levels; former student assist-
ants, relatives, and friends.

Letters of inquiry were sent to key personnel, including
current and past state and national/international presidents.

of The Delta Kappa Gamma Society International. Contacts
were made with many other national and international organizations in which Maycie Southall participated in various
capacities. Officers, leaders, and directors of archives
were consulted in search of pertinent information.

Contacts were made with Maycie Southall's relatives in
Hampshire, Tennessee, and Douglas, Georgia; they were helpful
in furnishing information and additional leads, especially in
regard to her heritage and early years. Attempts were made
to verify records of her formal training as well as early
employment through visits to, or correspondence with, appropriate educational institutions.

Maycie Southall gave permission for exploration of her
professional and private files which proved to be beneficial
to the fruition of this project. Pictures and memorabilia
were made available and discussed at length during many interesting and informative interviews held at her home while
this study was in progress. Several other interviews were
held which included Mary Hall, one of the sixteen founders
of Xi State, who resides in Murfreesboro, Tennessee; former
colleagues at George Peabody College for Teachers; and relatives and friends in Nashville and Columbia, Tennessee.

Tapes of recently recorded interviews by Maycie Southall
that are housed in the Oral History Department, University of
Texas at Austin, were obtained and reviewed. The tapes were
generously shared by O. L. Davis, Jr., a professor of education who conducted the interviews.

Background material was gleaned through an examination of the John Stevens Collection currently housed in the Education Library, George Peabody College for Teachers. Included among the papers are original and unpublished manuscripts and records of Lucy Gage, a pioneer educator, with whom Maycie Southall was closely associated during her early years at the educational institution.

In an attempt to procure authentic material from primary sources, more than two hundred persons were contacted during the development of this study. Their contributions were generous.

Limitations

Maycie Southall's services and contributions to education throughout her teaching career have been innumerable. Thus, the study was by necessity limited to an overview of many of her accomplishments with emphasis on her major contributions. The research revealed that many of her efforts were directed toward involvement in organizations which stressed educational goals and the advancement of women in education; consequently, one chapter is included which is designed to serve as a representative example of Maycie Southall's commitment to the improvement of education through organizational activities. The selection of Delta Kappa Gamma for the focus of the representative chapter was purposely made, not because it is the educational organization in which Maycie Southall has devoted the greatest amount of effort, but for still another reason; that is, a secondary purpose of this study is to provide a reference for Delta Kappa Gamma members who may desire a source of information for use in program planning. Therefore, although acknowledgment is granted that Maycie Southall has served as a leader in many major educational associations, this study devotes an entire chapter to one organization; however, some information is included in the study about additional endeavors in which she has played a principal role.

The setting for the study focuses primarily upon the current century; yet, limitations were encountered by the fact that few persons could be found who were able to share firsthand information about Maycie Southall's childhood experiences.

The study is somewhat limited by the fact that several of Maycie Southall's former advisees at the doctoral and specialist levels are deceased.

Difficulty was encountered in obtaining and verifying accounts of Maycie Southall's early formal education and teaching experiences due to lack of preservation of records in some schools and destruction of records by fire in two county systems.

To me, Dr. Southall epitomized graciousness,
dedication, optimism, and a great sense of fairness
and justice. She had a faith she could live by, a
self she could live with, and a cause she could live
for.

Mary Northcutt Powell
Personal letter
May 30, 1979

CHAPTER II

THE FORMATIVE YEARS

As She Grew

In 1979, a former student, later turned professor, reminisced: "I met Miss Southall in 1953, and she was never called
<u>Doctor</u> Southall."[1] He made the comment approximately fifty
years after the subject of this study had received her Doctor
of Philosophy degree. The statement reflects the consensus of
comments expressed by several former students who came under
the guidance of Dr. Maycie Katherine Southall during her professorship at George Peabody College for Teachers. A close
colleague of hers for a number of years at the same educational
institution recently observed: "I never heard of the Katherine
but suppose she had it tucked away somewhere, all along."[2]
Although she is frequently addressed in current educational
circles as Dr. Southall, the subject responds without reservation to informal salutations. In an attempt to communicate
readily the information contained in this study to potentially
diverse readers, the subject will hereinafter be referred to
as Maycie Southall.

[1]Robert S. Thurman, personal letter, June 29, 1979.

[2]Otis McBride, personal letter, July 15, 1979.

22

The ninth child in a family of ten, Maycie Southall was born in Maury County, Tennessee, on July 7, 1895.[3] Her father, William Albert Southall, Jr., and her mother, the former Mary Louise Delk, had been united in marriage in the same county on December 4, 1876.[4] William A. Southall, Maycie Southall's paternal grandfather, was born on January 17, 1808, and was joined in matrimony to the former Sarah A. N. Scott who was born on October 14, 1816; both had come to Tennessee from near Richmond, Virginia. William A. was the son of James Southall and the former Julia Flippin whereas Sarah A. N. was the daughter of Robert Scott and the former Lucy Hughes.[5]

The maternal lineage indicates that Mary Louise Delk's father, Jacob Benton Delk, was born in 1810; and her mother, the former Anne Crowell, was born during the same year. Jacob Benton was the son of Joseph Delk and the former Fannie Dawson whereas Anne was the daughter of Sam Crowell and the former Katherine Lentz.[6] Paul Delk, a cousin of Maycie Southall, who has made a considerable study of the family's ancestry noted that, according to tradition, the Delks are ". . . said to

---

[3]Maycie Southall, interview held in Nashville, April 23, 1979.

[4]Courthouse Records, "Marriage White, 1873-81; Marriage License Issued: No. 12259," 5:88, Maury County Court House, Columbia, Tennessee.

[5]D. P. Robbins, Century Review of Maury County, Tennessee, 1805-1905 (n.p.: published under the auspices of the Board of Mayor and Aldermen of Columbia, 1905; author later added 1906 Supplement and Corrections; reprinted by Maury County Historical Society, n.d.) p. 323 of Supplement.

[6]Paul Delk, personal letter, May 2, 1979.

have come from the Black Forest of Germany."[7] Maycie Southall
revealed further information about her genealogy by stating
that she is a descendant of German, English, Scot, and French
ancestry.[8]

The subject's childhood days were filled with the joy,
laughter, and fun typical when many children from large rural
families romped together at play. A friend since early childhood remembered with amusement that she and Maycie Southall,
along with siblings in the two families, thoroughly enjoyed
taking a dip in a swimming hole on the Southall family's farm.
In an attempt to alleviate undue concern for the safety of
the fledgling swimmers, Maycie Southall's older sister tied
ropes around the waists of the younger children, perched and
braced herself firmly on a nearby bank, and thus carefully
measured her consideration of a suitable depth by slackening
and alternately tightening the hand-held ropes. The swimming
hole frequently provided what might be more aptly described
as a mud bath than a refreshing dip, but frolicsomeness of
the Southall children and their friends was hampered neither
by ropes nor mud. The same raconteur told also of her rather
recent visits to the symphony where she maintains seats near
those reserved by her friend of many years, Maycie Southall.[9]

---

[7]Ibid.

[8]Maycie Southall, interview taped by O. L. Davis, Jr.,
held in Nashville, Tennessee, April 20, 1979.

[9]Virginia Parsons, telephone interview, Columbia,
Tennessee, May 20, 1979.

Such diversity of interests attests to the latter's genuine zest for life and enthusiasm for learning.

A former student, too, recently remarked that Maycie Southall's childhood must have been a carefree and happy time, one filled with many memorable experiences: "She told us in class of the fun she had playing in the hayloft as a child, especially in dressing up, playing stories on rainy days."[10]

During her early childhood, Maycie Southall's family resided in a very large and lovely home; known as Vine Hill, it is located in Maury County, Tennessee. Jean Jones said that her mother, the youngest of the Southall children, was born in the stately home.[11] One of the largest and oldest dwellings in Maury County, its classic beauty is enhanced by the landscape: "At Vine Hill, there is a panoramic view of rolling countryside and woodlands with Giles, Lawrence, Lewis, and Hickman counties visible on a clear day."[12] The home had been constructed with two sets of stairs leading to a ballroom on the second floor; one served as an entrance for the women and the other for the men. Dancing was forbidden, however, during the Southall family's occupancy of Vine Hill because of the parents' strict religious beliefs.[13]

---

[10] John Julia McMahan, personal letter, May 5, 1979.

[11] Jean Jones, interview held in Columbia, Tennessee, May 18, 1979.

[12] "Vine Hill One of Maury's Oldest, Largest Homes," Columbia (Tennessee) Daily Herald, July 1, 1971, p. 1.

[13] Southall, interview taped by Davis, April 20, 1979.

An icehouse had been built within a convenient distance
to the main building and has remained as one of the few relics
of its kind.[14] In this regard, Maycie Southall's adventurous
spirit, later to culminate in extensive travels, was to manifest itself at a very early age. Although she cannot remember
the incident, she has been told that she ran away from home at
the unlikely age of two years; while her family and neighbors
were becoming increasingly distraught after an entire night of
vigil accompanied by frantic searching, early the following
morning a cook employed by the family spied the tiny tot on
her way home, rubbing her eyes and asking for breakfast, from
an overnight stay in the icehouse.[15]

Of historic interest and value within its own right,
Vine Hill has recently been donated to a local historical
society by a descendant of Jonathan Webster, original owner
of the land on which his son, James Henry, built the imposing
house in 1841. "History records James Henry Webster as 'the
first white child' born in Maury County after it became a
county. . . . Maury became a county in 1807."[16] Apparently,
James Henry Webster had a penchant for quality both in con-
structing the family home and in educating his children:

> During the 1840's Webster conducted a school
> there for his children and those from the community.

---

[14]"Vine Hill One of Maury's Oldest, Largest Homes,"
p. 1.

[15]Southall, interview taped by Davis, April 20, 1979.

[16]"Vine Hill One of Maury's Oldest, Largest Homes,"
p. 1.

An advertisement in the Columbia Beacon in 1847 described the school as "second to none in the West." Webster announced that he had room for eight to ten students for the school, scheduled to commence April 1. Later the school was referred to as Goshen Seminary.[17]

Small schools, accommodating only a few families, were not uncommon during the ensuing decades. Maycie Southall recalled that, because of the large number of offspring, only four families were represented in the student body of one rural school attended for a time by the Southall children.[18]

Although the Southalls continued to reside in Maury County, they moved from Vine Hill shortly after their ninth child began to attend school.[19] The family moved on several occasions because the father, a farmer, also dealt in real estate; he would move his family into a home, improve the place, and subsequently trade it for another.[20] According to one source, Maycie Southall ". . . probably inherited her talent for speaking and her leadership ability from her father, who is reported to have possessed these qualities to a marked degree."[21] Pictures of William Albert Southall, Jr., in the possession of Jean Jones, his granddaughter, lend

---

[17]Ibid.

[18]Southall, interview taped by Davis, April 20, 1979.

[19]Southall, interview, April 23, 1979.

[20]Jean Jones, interview, May 18, 1979.

[21]Lucille Rogers, Light from Many Candles (Nashville: McQuiddy Printing Company for Xi State, Delta Kappa Gamma, 1960), p. 270.

credence to her description of him as a distinguished-looking
gentlemen with white mustache and gray hair.

Her mother should probably be recorded as the source
from whom Maycie Southall derived her deep, but not openly
demonstrative, religious convictions. An incident from the
latter's childhood, related by one of her close friends, suggests the mother's efforts to train her daughter in the right
precepts. In that era, girls were supposed to become adept
in the intricate art of needlework such as knitting, tatting,
and embroidery; thus, as Maycie Southall was learning to knit
and had little to do one Sunday afternoon, she decided to pur-
sue her new interest. Later, she reported to her mother an
account of the progress that she had made toward her project.
Upon hearing about the child's misguided use of her leisure
time, her mother marked with a knitting needle the place at
which the youngster had begun her Sunday afternoon work and
raveled the garment to that point. There was to be no knitting on Sunday in the Southall household, and her mother was
attempting to teach Maycie Southall that one does not progress by unfit or inappropriate use of time. The same friend
continued by relating that many years later an incident occurred which is indicative of Mary Louise Southall's lasting
influence: Maycie Southall had become very interested in
purchasing one particular automobile; and, after some discussion, the two friends looked at it while out driving on
Sunday afternoon. Although Maycie Southall decided to buy
the car, she rejected the idea of negotiating a transaction

for it on Sunday. Later, perhaps because of the conflict
between her concept of Sunday as a day of rest and the fact
that she had decided on Sunday to purchase the automobile,
Maycie Southall was never happy with the vehicle that had
earlier seemed so desirable.[22] Her religious conviction did
not, however, withstand the excessive pressures of her teaching responsibilities at George Peabody College for Teachers;
she frequently worked all or part of the day on Sunday in
her office or at home in order to maintain her heavy work
load.[23]

School Days

Before she was old enough to join the group, Maycie
Southall entertained herself in the afternoons by running
to the gate to meet the surrey in which her older brothers
and sisters would return each day from school.[24] Prior to
her own enrollment in school, the child had learned to read
from an older sister's books and remembers well one verse in
particular that served to influence her in later years; the
verse suggested that one's thoughts are, in part, expressed
in one's eyes. Thus, many years later during her teaching
career, Maycie Southall developed the habit of observing

---

[22]Billie Brannon, interview held in Nashville,
May 8, 1979.

[23]Maycie Southall, interview held in Nashville,
September 3, 1979.

[24]Etha Green, "The First Lady of Childhood Education,"
The Peabody Reflector 43 (Fall 1970):130.

carefully her students' expressions to determine when they
needed additional help from her.[25]

Even at a very early age, the ninth of the ten Southall
children was interested in school and wanted everyone else to
share her enthusiasm. While her brothers and sisters were
playing with neighboring children, Maycie Southall could often
be found devoting her time and attention to school concerns.[26]
One of her early memories consists of an incident in which the
director of a school permitted her, along with a few other
students, to view his private library of books. At that time,
the child had never seen so vast a collection and was utterly
fascinated by the notion that anyone could own such a prize
possession.[27] Her attraction to books and respect for education were becoming evident in her formative years.

Maycie Southall's special interest in mathematics can
also be traced to her early environment. Because there were
ten children in the family and each child's share of various
items was fairly and equally apportioned, learning fractions
in a practical way was very easy for her. Although she had
learned to read before entering school, the resourceful youngster soon found that she could depend upon an older sister
for help with mathematics. The assistance terminated rather
abruptly, however, for after a childhood squabble between the

[25]Southall, interview taped by Davis, April 20, 1979.

[26]Parsons, telephone interview, May 20, 1979.

[27]Southall, interview, April 23, 1979.

two, punishment meted out by the older sister consisted of refusing to help the younger child with her problems in arithmetic; thus, left to her own devices, Maycie Southall learned to work independently and subsequently developed a special interest in mathematics.[28] This interest continued into her collegiate years at which time she considered teaching advanced mathematics as a career. During that time, however, an incident occurred which directed her attention to young children. Her nephew was a student in a one-teacher school under the tutelage of a man who displayed his authority by frightening children with a whip. The child had become hampered in his efforts to learn because of his fear of the teacher. Thus, Maycie Southall's concern for her nephew and other young children in similar circumstances was a factor in influencing her decision and ultimately affecting the direction of her educational career.[29]

The school program in Maycie Southall's community consisted of eleven grades. Although her formal training had its beginning in a one-teacher school, her education was far from inadequate. By the time she was in the seventh grade, Maycie Southall was allowed to skip a grade; that is, the first part of the year was classified as the seventh grade, and the remainder was the eighth grade. Later, because she was one of the advanced students, Maycie Southall became

---

[28]Southall, interview taped by Davis, April 20, 1979.

[29]Southall, interview, April 23, 1979.

eligible to complete requirements for the tenth grade during a summer session; she was one of two students who successfully completed the work. Many years later, upon consideration of the effects of such educational practices, Maycie Southall reflected that skipping grades necessitated many adjustments by the student. In her case, for example, the period of time in school was shortened during which she could have explored more fully individual interests and refined one of her special talents, playing the piano; rapid advancement through two grades caused her to leave her peer group; and she was subsequently graduated from school at an extremely early age-- too young to know what she wanted to do with her life or to obtain a good job.[30]

Transportation to the secondary school in Columbia, approximately five miles from the Southall home, was by buggy. After the older Southall children were no longer in attendance, Maycie Southall drove to school in order that she and her younger sister, who was afraid of spirited horses, could complete their formal training. Upon arrival at the school during the winter, the driver's first activity, after removal of her gloves, was to warm her hands at the heater as her fingers would be stiff and swollen from the five-mile drive in intensely cold weather; then, Maycie Southall would go to her desk and begin her studies.[31] Such persistence was to

---

[30]Ibid.

[31]Southall, interview taped by Davis, April 20, 1979.

become a widely recognized trait in future years when she, as a professor, began to press for the cause of education.

Maycie Southall completed her formal schooling at the elementary and secondary levels in 1911 and was awarded her diploma from Columbia High School at fifteen years of age.[32] Her training had included attendance at both one-teacher and multi-teacher schools as well as both private and public schools. Reflecting about her early formal training, Maycie Southall recently expressed the opinion that she had encountered some very good teachers and some who were not so capable but that her early education was thorough and filled with valuable experiences which served her well during her own teaching career.[33] Although she did not know while still in school that she would become an educator, her early training in rural schools was to prepare her, in part, for future teaching and supervisory positions.

A Teen-age Schoolmarm

The Southalls, although not of great wealth, lived comfortably and were proud people.[34] Thus, in keeping with the times, the daughters were not encouraged to seek employment outside of the home; indeed, such action was hardly considered

---

[32]Maycie Southall, "Memorandum for the Appointment Committee," record in personnel file of Maycie Southall, Office of the College Archivist and Historian, George Peabody College for Teachers, [1920], p. 1.

[33]Southall, interview, April 23, 1979.

[34]Brannon, interview, May 8, 1979.

quite proper for the Southall girls. Thus, upon graduation from high school, Maycie Southall began making plans to enroll in college the following fall. In the meantime, however, her parents were successful in urging her to travel to Georgia for a visit with a sister who, although married, had become somewhat homesick for her family.[35] Maycie Southall did not go to Georgia, therefore, in search of a job; she intended, instead, to spend her vacation time during the summer with her relatives and then return to Tennessee. At that time, she had not the vaguest idea that her visit might initiate a set of circumstances which would culminate in launching a lifetime of service to education; but destiny and her teaching career were not to be kept in abeyance much longer.

While she was vacationing in Broxton, a trustee who had heard favorable reports about the Tennessean approached her brother-in-law and inquired about her credentials as a potential teacher. The trustee wanted to fill a position left vacant by a girl who had just notified him that, because of a conflict in plans, she would be unavailable. Because Maycie Southall was thoroughly enjoying her visit and her sister wanted her to remain there longer, the former discussed the job offer with family members; immediately undertook and completed satisfactorily within the same week the teacher examinations required in Georgia; and accepted the position which entailed teaching eight grades for a term of four months. The

---

[35]Southall, interview, April 23, 1979.

one-room schoolhouse to which she was assigned was located in a rural area a short distance from Broxton.[36]

Although Jack E. Willis, the current superintendent, was able to provide some information pertaining to the employment of Maycie Southall in Coffee County, Georgia, the beginning and termination dates of her work were unavailable.[37] Maycie Southall remembers, however, that her first term began on Monday and that her sixteenth birthday was celebrated within the week.[38] Accordingly, then, she began her teaching career on Monday, July 3, 1911, at the age of fifteen years; she became sixteen years old the following Friday.

Soon after she had agreed to assume her new duties, however, the would-be teacher began to react to her decision. The excitement of the new job was tempered with misgivings because of the teenager's inexperience. According to one source, Maycie Southall could hardly sleep for she knew very little about teaching and wondered what would be expected of her; however, her anxiety was somewhat alleviated when she subsequently realized that there were ". . . textbooks and that most of the pupils should already have learned to read."[39]

On the first Monday morning of the term, the teenager found herself in charge of twelve youngsters of various age

---

[36]Ibid.

[37]Jack E. Willis, personal letter, May 30, 1979.

[38]Southall, interview, April 23, 1979.

[39]Mildred Dawson, "A Living Pioneer in Tennessee," The Delta Kappa Gamma Bulletin 8 (March 1942):20.

levels. She was advised that three of her predecessors had been run off during the previous year; and the general disarray of the room, as well as obvious neglect of the surrounding grounds, attested to the fact. Thus, after she had expedited the preliminaries incumbent with a new school term, Maycie Southall turned to her first project as a beginning teacher which consisted of an effort to make the environment more conducive to learning; under her guidance and with her help, the students cleaned the building and cleared the adjoining grounds of the summer's growth of weeds.[40]

The role of a woman teacher was rather well defined in the early 1900s, and it extended to her wearing apparel. In order to look older, Maycie Southall pulled her hair into a style on the top of her head. Also, her relatively short dresses, although quite suitable for a teenage high school graduate, were not appropriate for her position as a woman teacher; therefore, the youngster borrowed her sister's shirtwaist blouses and longer skirts in an attempt to project more nearly the image expected of a woman in charge of a schoolroom.[41]

Maycie Southall boarded with a family whose son was her only eighth-grade student. Her days consisted of involvement with her teaching activities; and her evenings followed a pattern of dining with the family, hearing her eighth-grade

---

[40]Ibid.

[41]Southall, interview, April 23, 1979.

student recite his lessons because of insufficient time during the school day, and then retiring to her sparcely furnished room in order to grade papers and prepare for the next day's work.[42]

Although she was young, the fledgling teacher experienced very few problems with discipline. She recently attributed much of her success in getting along well with her students to the example set by her mother who, although lacking in formal training, had practiced psychology during the daily routine of family life; in fact, her mother had been so successful in her practical application of basic principles that Maycie Southall credited her with practicing more psychology than the daughter learned during her later completion of several college courses in this field. Thus, from the beginning, the teenage teacher knew how to treat her students; that is, she treated them as she, herself, would want to be treated. When disputes among the youngsters arose, she reasoned with, rather than punished, the participants.[43] Application of the simple, but effective, precept embodied in the Golden Rule served as the yardstick by which the new teacher and her students measured the worth of each other; her method of discipline required no other yardstick.

Maycie Southall made good use, too, of her own earlier experiences as a child in a rural school. She remembered, for

---

[42]Southall, interview taped by Davis, April 20, 1979.
[43]Ibid.

example, that she had already learned to read prior to entering the first grade and that, consequently, her own untrained
but quite intuitive teacher had permitted her, the youngest
student, to go outside and play briefly on occasion in order
to be able to come inside and settle down to her required
work. Maycie Southall, therefore, used the same technique
when she became a teacher; that is, she had an understanding
with all of her students that a young child who was hyper-
active could go outside and run around the school building a
specified number of times in order to be able to remain still
after he returned to work on his lessons.[44] Thus, both the
mental and physical needs of growing children were recognized
by the inexperienced but perceptive teacher. Almost seven
decades later, a former doctoral student under the guidance
of Maycie Southall while both were at George Peabody College
for Teachers expressed his opinion that the latter ". . . was
well aware that children were NOT adults LONG before educators generally recognized the fact."[45]

Although Maycie Southall realized that reading, writing,
and arithmetic were essential and consequently stressed them
daily along with other lessons, her imaginative mind soon began to explore ways through which education could be extended
beyond the classroom; for example, she developed a technique
through which the principles of nutrition could be taught by

[44]Ibid.

[45]George T. Guess, personal letter, May 31, 1979.

her, practiced by the students, and the results, or harvest, used to supplement the limited diets of those in her charge. As a wider variety of vegetables was needed, suggestions were sought from the students; the aid of the larger boys was then elicited whereby unsightly ground beyond the fence was converted into a garden plot; and the surplus vegetables, cultivated by the students, were later canned, with the help of the rural families, for school use. Because the new teacher wanted her students to develop an appreciation for the aesthetic as well as the practical, she encouraged them to work on beautifying the grounds by planting flowers along the fence inside the schoolyard and cultivating the vegetable garden in an adjoining plot beyond the fence.[46] Perhaps it was through such early efforts that the young teacher began to formulate her own philosophy of education which was to be exemplified during later years when she became a teacher of other teachers. One of her doctoral students during the 1950s at George Peabody College for Teachers recently shared his opinion ". . . that part of her philosophy can be stated as follows: Learning is best when it is done by doing."[47]

As the activities increased, the community became more involved, the reputation of the school improved, and the enrollment expanded. According to one researcher, more students began enrolling in school because there were many interesting

[46]Southall, interview, September 3, 1979.

[47]Paul P. Bryant, personal letter, May 15, 1979.

things going on such as lessons, gardening, and games. Before
the year ended, a total of $150 had been invested in a school
library that provided appropriate books for students at various reading levels. Playground equipment had also been purchased with funds raised through community-supported activities
such as, for example, ice-cream suppers. The popularity of the
school continued to expand, and Maycie Southall had enrolled by
the end of her first year of teaching a total of sixty-five
students.[48]

During ensuing decades, educators have become quite familiar with terms such as individualized instruction, creativity,
learning by doing, parent involvement, and school-community
relationships. Ahead of her time in many respects, Maycie
Southall, along with other pioneer educators, was helping to
pave the way for future generations.

Although filled with its share of hardships, her first
term of teaching had been truly rewarding; and, as a result
of this educational experience, Maycie Southall had found her
raison d'être. Her first term was to be followed by a succes-
sion of many years devoted to the cause of education.

Maycie Southall had met the requirements for employment
in her first teaching position simply by completing satisfactorily a set of examinations given to prospective teachers.[49]
After her first experience with helping students to learn,

---

[48]Mildred Dawson, "A Living Pioneer in Tennessee," p. 20.

[49]Ibid.

however, she realized that she also wanted to improve her own education. Upon completion of her first term in the Georgia school, Maycie Southall returned to Tennessee and enrolled in an educational institution at Murfreesboro in order to prepare herself for a career in teaching. Records currently housed at Middle Tennessee State University indicate that she began her work at its predecessor, Middle Tennessee Normal, in 1912 and attended intermittently between her terms of employment in the rural schools of Georgia and Tennessee.[50]

During her second successive term of teaching in Georgia, Maycie Southall was provided an assistant to help with the sizable number of students; the girl assigned to work with her, a daughter of the local trustee, possessed only an eighth-grade education. In spite of the youthfulness of both teacher and assistant, their concerted efforts met with success; but, at the close of her second school term, the Tennessean returned again to her native state in order to continue her work toward completion of a two-year diploma.[51] In those days, only two years of college work were available at the institution in Murfreesboro which had teacher training as its primary function. Then, Maycie Southall accepted a position as a fifth-grade teacher at Mt. Pleasant, Tennessee.[52] After completion

-----

[50]Sherian Huddleston, personal letter, May 28, 1979.

[51]Mildred Dawson, "A Living Pioneer in Tennessee," p. 20.

[52]Southall, "Memorandum for the Appointment Committee," p. 1.

of one term there, the school system in Columbia, her home
town, beckoned; and she responded to the opportunity. Although records of the subject's employment are unavailable
from the superintendent's office in Maury County, Mary Harris
Morgan remembers quite well when R. L. Harris, her father and
a former superintendent of schools in Columbia, employed her
friend, Maycie Southall, as a teacher.[53] According to one
account, Maycie Southall taught the sixth grade.[54] Another
source revealed that she taught there for an annual salary of
$585.[55]

Undaunted by rigorous schedules and very demanding work,
Maycie Southall enrolled in 1918 at George Peabody College
for Teachers, an educational institution which she attended
during ensuing summer vacation periods between teaching assignments.[56] She was informed through connections there of
a position available at Rover, Tennessee, and subsequently
was persuaded to accept as her patriotic duty a principalship;
the high school faculty was composed of four women teachers.[57]

---

[53]Mary Harris Morgan, telephone interview, Columbia,
Tennessee, May 18, 1979.

[54]Southall, "Memorandum for the Appointment Committee,"
p. 1.

[55]Maycie Southall, "Application Blank for Scholarship
in Peabody College," record in personnel file of Maycie
Southall, Office of the College Archivist and Historian,
George Peabody College for Teachers, [1927], p. 2.

[56]Southall, "Memorandum for the Appointment Committee,"
p. 1.

[57]Southall, interview taped by Davis, April 20, 1979.

Because of World War I, many men had enlisted in military service; and thus the educational responsibilities were relegated to women.

Although community schools did not become a familiar term among educational circles until several years later, Maycie Southall organized activities at Rover that involved the students, parents, and neighborhood in the cause of education. One such project consisted of an effort to beautify the school grounds, as well as prevent soil erosion, through planting trees. First, the students shared their ideas about the project; next, the boys identified suitable saplings in nearby woods; on a designated Saturday, the adults provided teams of mules to haul the trees while the girls prepared a dinner for the workers; and, as a result of plans initially developed by the students, the project found fruition.[58] The patrons, through participation in setting out a large number of trees, demonstrated their support for the leadership of an educator who became a pioneer in school-community living many years prior to the launching of the 1930-40 movement.[59]

According to the Office of Records, George Peabody College for Teachers conferred the Bachelor of Science degree upon Maycie Southall on June 8, 1920. She had worked diligently toward completion of her course work at that institution, as well as at Vanderbilt University, with a

---

[58]Ibid.

[59]Mildred Dawson, "A Living Pioneer in Tennessee," p. 20.

goal of becoming a mathematics teacher, possibly at the college level. A role conflict was, however, destined to guide in part her ultimate decision concerning the specific field of her future educational endeavors; that is, she was advised that men were expected to teach college mathematics and that women were more frequently associated with the role of working with small children. Thus, as Maycie Southall had also demonstrated exceptional ability to work with children and young people, she was encouraged to direct her future efforts along those lines.[60]

References from previous school administrators and college professors suggested potential success, especially in supervision and rural education; written in 1920, the letters are contained in Maycie Southall's personnel file and housed in the Office of the College Archivist and Historian, George Peabody College for Teachers. A former superintendent of schools in Columbia, who had known Maycie Southall as both a student and later as a member of his faculty, offered: "She is a fine executive, splendid instructor, a . . . disciplinarian unconscious of her powers to discipline."[61] Norman Frost, a highly respected professor of rural education at George Peabody College for Teachers, wrote concerning his student: "I should expect her to be successful as principal, as supervisor of elementary schools (especially rural schools)

---

[60]Southall, interview, April 23, 1979.

[61]R. L. Harris to J. J. Didcoct, May 10, 1920.

or as critic teacher."[62] Thomas Alexander, a widely known
professor of elementary education, shared: "Miss Maycie
Southall has . . . shown excellent ability . . . in supervision of instruction. Miss Southall is an A number one
student."[63] He continued by describing her as ". . . a
young lady of fine personality, very pleasing in her rela-
tions with her fellow students and teachers and [a] most
interested worker."[64] In conclusion, he added: "I would
recommend Miss Southall without hesitation for supervision
of elementary schools or for critic teaching in a normal
school."[65] Her instructor in home economics observed:

> Miss Maycie Southall impresses me as a woman of
> unusual capabilities. She is a good student, ener-
> getic, interested, and bright. She is thorough in
> anything she undertakes to do.
>
> Her personality draws people to her. She is dig-
> nified, yet very approachable.
>
> I believe she will make a teacher far above the
> average.[66]

Stepping Up

During the same year of her graduation, 1920, Maycie
Southall moved to Greenville, North Carolina, where she accepted a position as one of the early supervisors because

---

[62]Norman Frost to J. J. Didcoct, May 14, 1920.

[63]Thomas Alexander to J. J. Didcoct, May 8, 1920.

[64]Ibid.

[65]Ibid.

[66]Bernice C. Reaney to J. J. Didcoct, May 14, 1920.

she wanted very much ". . . to insure better teaching for rural children and was told it could be done by rural supervision."[67] From an annual salary of $1,000 at Rover Consolidated School, her pay increased substantially. Arthur S. Alford, the current superintendent in Pitt County, provided a copy of an undated record extracted from the Board of Education's files of the early 1920s which certified that Maycie Southall's annual salary at one time during her stay there was $1,800.[68] In spite of her youthfulness and the fact that she was a woman, her capabilities effected rapid advancement. Thus, another record on file in the same office showed that, after only four years of employment as a county supervisor, the native Tennessean tendered her resignation effective as of the end of May 1924.[69] She then accepted a position as a state supervisor of elementary instruction.[70] Raleigh, North Carolina, where her office with the State Department of Education was located, became her address for the next four years. During that time, her annual salary increased to $3,000.[71] In summary, Maycie Southall served as a supervisor of elementary education in

---

[67]Sam[uel C.] Nigh, "Dr. Maycie K. Southall," term paper prepared for course in Educational Leadership, George Peabody College for Teachers, [1953], p. 1, Private Files of Maycie Southall.

[68]Arthur S. Alford, personal letter, July 18, 1979.

[69]Ibid.

[70]Southall, "Application Blank for Scholarship in Peabody College," p. 2.

[71]Ibid.

North Carolina for a total of eight years, from 1920 through 1928; she was employed at the county level for the first four years and at the state level for the remainder of the time.[72]

Her years of service as a supervisor were filled with many adventurous and memorable experiences. At both county and state levels, Maycie Southall's enthusiasm was not to be quelled by hardships and frustrations encountered on the job. Made more difficult at times because she was a woman, each situation was resolved as it arose; and her sense of humor served well as the leavening agent requisite to her positive approach to her work.

Money was scarce, and paved roads were not much more plentiful. On her first day of travel from her office in a new Ford car, Maycie Southall found herself driving over dirt roads; she reached her destination but not without mishap. The tracks were so deep that the floor boards and lights of the new car were jarred loose; and, as a result, her lunch was last seen disappearing through a hole left gaping by an earlier loss of the floor boards. Work, however, must go on; and it did until early evening. Then, homeward bound, the relatively new supervisor had to drive several miles amidst the frustrations encountered by hunger because of lack of lunch, no lights while darkness was fast approaching, and on-coming traffic that was heavier than usual because of a county fair.[73]

---

[72]Southall, interview, April 23, 1979.

[73]Southall, interview taped by Davis, April 20, 1979.

Women were not expected to travel alone in the 1920s; and, consequently, hotels were not designed to accommodate single women. When she served as one of four state supervisors, however, Maycie Southall's work required that she travel throughout North Carolina. She remembers well staying in hotel rooms that had no locks on the doors; in such cases, she pushed furniture against the doors beneath the knobs in order to derive at least a minimal measure of security.[74]

Her position as a supervisor placed Maycie Southall in a prime position to become an avant-garde in the early testing movement which was to become popular in the 1920s. According to her transcript, in 1922 Maycie Southall completed a course in Improvement of Instruction Through Tests during her summer work at George Peabody College for Teachers. Utilizing information gleaned from the course, she became instrumental in giving some of the first group tests that were used in her jurisdiction.[75]

Maycie Southall did not think of her position as being that of an inspector. Again, earlier training at George Peabody College for Teachers had influenced her approach; for she is convinced, in retrospect, that her professor in Supervision of Elementary Instruction had not characterized the role of a supervisor as inspectorial.[76] Her attitude is

---

[74]Southall, interview, September 3, 1979.

[75]Southall, interview taped by Davis, April 20, 1979.

[76]Ibid.

exemplified by the fact that she wanted teachers to know when
she was planning to visit them; thus, she would notify the
proper personnel of her itinerary.[77] As funds were quite
limited and library facilities virtually nonexistent in the
smaller schools, the supervisor transported books to the children during her travels to work with the staff members; and
she wanted the news of her visits, associated with anticipation of a delivery of reading materials, to serve as a moti-
vational device for the students in their reading programs.[78]
She had found during her early teaching experiences in Georgia
that small children enjoy learning to read; and, in spite of
meager funds, Maycie Southall had at that time improvised a
way to obtain books through a process of having the students
seek permission to bring eggs from their farm homes after
which she sold the eggs and then purchased suitable reading
materials for her classroom.[79] Because she had learned while
still a young teacher in Georgia the importance of early development of reading skills, Maycie Southall continued as a
supervisor in North Carolina to stress cultivation of students' interest in learning to read and voluntarily used her
car as a traveling library. Children soon began to associate
her arrival with the acquisition of a new supply of books,
and they frequently plied their teachers with questions about

[77]Ibid.

[78]Maycie Southall, interview held in Nashville,
August 29, 1979.

[79]Southall, interview, April 23, 1979.

any news of impending visits by the supervisor. One child,
for example, asked when he could expect another visit from
Miss Santa Claus.[80]

Another of Maycie Southall's responsibilities as a supervisor consisted of working closely with the principals in
order to assist them in helping their faculty members. When
she worked directly with the teachers, the supervisor often
used demonstrations; although this technique was adapted to
the particular subject area in which the teacher needed her
assistance, much of Maycie Southall's effort was directed
toward reading improvement. Working with staff members on
curriculum problems, especially during in-service days prior
to the beginning of each regular school term as well as on
two designated Saturdays during each term, constituted still
another facet of the supervisor's responsibilities.[81]

Research efforts also played a part in the work of the
state supervisor; for example, because money was scarce and
supervision considered expensive during a time when consoli-
dation was becoming popular, the value of supervision became
increasingly questionable. Maycie Southall, through a con-
trolled study of two county systems, investigated the value
of supervision; her conclusions, which favored the employment
of supervisors of instruction in consolidated schools, were
printed in bulletin form and distributed throughout the state.
Entitled Value of Supervision in Consolidated Schools, a copy

---

[80]Southall, interview, August 29, 1979.

[81]Ibid.

of the 1926 publication has been retained by the North Carolina
Department of Public Instruction in its archival collection.[82]

While employed as a supervisor, Maycie Southall became
interested in attending educational meetings and conventions;
through such activities she began to develop an acquaintanceship with educational leaders at the national level that was
to expand significantly during ensuing years. Early in her
career, she started joining educational organizations; and
because her talent as a speaker was easily recognized, program planners soon began to seek her out as a platform guest.
Also, she continued her course work at George Peabody College
for Teachers during the summers; and, as a result of her efforts there combined with cognate work taken at Teachers
College, Columbia University, and the University of Chicago,
Maycie Southall found herself in a prime position to assimi-
late the ideas of the foremost educational leaders of the day.
A brief description of the educational climate at George
Peabody College for Teachers during the summer of 1929 provides some perspective concerning Maycie Southall's opportunities, as a student, for professional growth; one campus
publication offered:

> At the close of the second day's registration at
> Peabody College, when her doors opened for summer school,
> approximately 2,500 students had registered and many
> others were expected . . . before the close of the week.
>
> The outlook as we go to press indicates that all
> previous records for summer attendance will be exceeded.

---

[82]Vergie F. Cos, personal letter, July 6, 1979.

In anticipation of this heavy enrollment the faculty has been increased from 75 to 195 members, and drawn from the leading institutions of learning throughout the world.[83]

Maycie Southall has possessed, since early childhood, a strong desire for learning. The source of such a yearning, such as undue pressure or unusual encouragement by a member of her family or a schoolteacher, is nebulous. One of her nieces recently observed: "I suppose her family, as so many families do, did not really appreciate fully the potential that was embodied in one M. K. Southall."[84] Thus, even while working toward completion of advanced educational programs, Maycie Southall was more interested in study for the sake of learning than for the attainment of degrees; for example, she obtained special permission from officials at George Peabody College for Teachers which permitted her to study at Teachers College, Columbia University, and the University of Chicago; she did so because the former institution had gained a wide reputation for its courses in the philosophy of education whereas the latter ". . . then had an edge on research in education."[85]

Maycie Southall elected a career in education in preference to marriage, but the decision was of her own choice rather than from the lack of proposals for marriage. According to one of her close friends, there have been many suitors

---

[83]"Summer School Registration," The Peabody Reflector and Alumni News 2 (June 1929):18.

[84]Frances S. Whelchel, personal letter, July 10, 1979.

[85]Southall, interview, September 3, 1979.

along the way.[86] During the early 1900s, however, those women who wanted to teach were expected to sacrifice alternative opportunities for home and family in order to devote their time and undivided attention to education. Although she had seriously considered marriage during World War I, Maycie Southall refused her suitor's proposal upon his return from military service and continued her teaching career.[87] While preparing for her doctoral examinations several years later, another admirer tried to discourage her from pursuing requirements for completion of the degree because he realized that her success would dispel his hope for their marriage.[88] Then, in the 1940s when rumors were afloat concerning Maycie Southall's consideration of matrimony, the president of George Peabody College for Teachers stated in her presence that the reason he had not rehired one teacher was that he would not have a married woman on his staff.[89] Although her decision to refuse the marriage proposal was not based on fear of losing her teaching position, the role expectations of a woman teacher did, indeed, play a vital part in Maycie Southall's life.

The Terminal Degree

Maycie Southall completed the requirements for her Master of Arts degree at George Peabody College for Teachers in 1926;

---

[86]Brannon, interview, May 8, 1979.

[87]Southall, interview taped by Davis, April 20, 1979.

[88]Southall, interview, April 23, 1979.

[89]Southall, interview, September 3, 1979.

and, in recognition of further endeavor, the same educational institution awarded her the Doctor of Philosophy degree on August 24, 1929. She was one of two women among eight doctoral candidates who marched in the summer academic procession on the lawn of George Peabody College for Teachers.[90]

The educational institution had begun granting doctoral degrees only a decade prior to the year in which the name of Maycie Southall was added to the list of recipients. According to a June 1919 article, Joseph Roemer and Sidney Garrison had ". . . the honor of being the first students in the history of the college to have the degree of Ph.D. conferred upon them."[91] During the same year, Marie Hackl ". . . became the first woman to receive a Ph.D. from Peabody. . . ."[92] According to the Office of Records, she was awarded her degree on August 29, 1919. Five years were to elapse before another woman was to be so honored; then, in 1924, Nellie Angel Smith received the terminal degree.[93] The Office of Records verified the fact that, in 1928, Elizabeth Whitmore Baker became the third woman upon which the doctoral degree was conferred. The following year, two women, Maycie Southall and Katherine Vickery, joined the exclusive group. Upon completion of the

---

[90]"Geographical List of August Graduates," The Peabody Reflector and Alumni News 2 (August 1929):18. (Group picture on p. 7 and copy of Commencement Program on p. 10.)

[91]"Many Receive Their Diplomas at Peabody," Nashville Tennessean, June 11, 1919, p. 2.

[92]"178th Commencement," The Peabody Reflector 34 (May-June 1961):71.

[93]Ibid.

graduation exercises held in August 1929, a total of eighty-
six doctoral degrees had been awarded by George Peabody College for Teachers; five of the degrees had been conferred upon
women.[94] Additional perspective concerning the selectivity
of the group has been provided by one historian who wrote that
George Peabody College for Teachers ". . . awarded the first
Ph.D. in education to be given by a southern institution."[95]

In retrospect, the year 1929 becomes significant from
many vantage points. In a large sense, economic conditions
that ultimately were to affect the future of education culminated in 1929 in the Great Depression. In a narrower sense,
events were also falling into place that, although at first
glance appearing significant only from a personal standpoint,
were destined to play a role in shaping the future of education not only in the South but, indeed, even beyond its borders. It was the year in which Maycie Southall was awarded
her doctoral degree; it was the year in which she became employed as a full-time educator at George Peabody College for
Teachers, a position that she was to maintain for thirty-five
years until her retirement in the summer of 1964; and, although not known to her at the time, it was the year in which
an educational organization was born that was later destined
both to influence and to be influenced by her endeavors.

---

[94]"Degrees Conferred by George Peabody College for
Teachers, 1915-1967," The Peabody Reflector 40 (November-
December 1967):292-93.

[95]A. L. Crabb, "Statelier Mansions," The Peabody
Reflector and Alumni News 5 (August 1932):326.

In January, at the beginning of a year that can lay claim
to its share of influence upon the history of education, an
editorial simply entitled "1929" appeared in a campus publication, The Peabody Reflector and Alumni News, at George Peabody College for Teachers; poignantly presented was a message
concerning the inestimable value of an individual's contribution within the larger panorama of civilization's march.
Maycie Southall played her part; of such is comprised the
substance of the history of education and, in a still larger
sense, of history itself:

> A year is, but a small figure in the parade of time.
> It is an amazingly long parade and the marchers are many.
> But the metaphor is not a good one since it suggests that
> a year is complete in itself, a figure marching in a line
> of other figures but independent of them. Years are not
> like that. The calendar is wrong, 1929 did not begin on
> New Year's day. It began at the beginning. It lasts un-
> til the End.

> Students who do not very well comprehend History are
> likely to be plagued by "dates." If a date is a detached
> and unrelated thing their complaint is warranted for such
> a date would be both valueless and irksome. 1215 is one
> of History's important dates, and yet it marks but a step
> in a series of steps which has been under way certainly
> more than a thousand years--a step whose imprint is dis-
> cernible in the civic path we tread today. 1492 is one
> of history's best known dates, and yet it merely marks
> a time when forces long repressed broke through their
> bounds, profoundly altering the world's subsequent his-
> tory. The red fire which blazed in 1861 had been long
> smouldering.

> A year has no spiritual boundaries. At the best it
> but affords a vantage spot from which to survey the expe-
> riences of past years and to organize those experiences
> into the programme of years yet to be. At the worst it
> is 365 days and nights through which one pursues an un-
> seeing routine.

> This is to wish that 1929 may bring to all of us a
> clearer comprehension of the Unity which runs through
> all, which began at the First which lasts until the End.

From such a comprehension there will emerge a serener, more vital estimate of the parts we are to play.[96]

Because the commencement exercises held on August 24, 1929, served as a milestone--a point of departure from which many new ventures were to emerge--Bruce R. Payne, president of George Peabody College for Teachers, must have been addressing Maycie Southall's potentiality for service to education in his farewell message to the graduating class:

> In bidding you farewell may I say . . . that . . . it has fallen to the teacher to dream the dreams of man and lift up before him visions of his future. . . .
>
> It is your function not only to have dreams but to tell them; not only to be a prophet but to prophesy. "The prophet that hath a dream, let him tell his dream, and he that hath my word, let him speak my word <u>faithfully</u>" has always been the divine injunction. This word is heralded to you today. . . . Have a vision, tell the vision, but above all help these citizens of tomorrow to realize the vision that is yours.
>
> Socrates was eternally right; we must make real in the present the vision of the future. Your preceptors do not ask that you acquire great wealth. Financial success does not await one in your chosen profession. You are not required to become heroes or to sway empires. No ambition for glory or gain is expected. But I do solemnly charge you to bring vision to the youth of our land--dreams of justice to all men, of obedience to law, of untiring industry, of devotion to truth and honesty always and everywhere; dreams of universal peace, of human betterment, of friendliness and friendship, of patient good will to all mankind, and of consecration to an eternal ideal. . . .
>
> To . . . children you are a prophet and often the only prophet. Don't fail them. No man can receive such pure confidence and uplifted look of childish faith which is given to you and not be moved thereby, unless his pulse is dull and his feeling is poor. To them you are a seer, and as their only <u>seer</u> you must peer into the future for them that you may both warn them and prepare them for distant events. . . .

---

[96]"1929," <u>The Peabody Reflector and Alumni News</u> 2 (January 1929):17.

And I am asking you . . . clearly to conceive your dreams, preach them, fight for them, even until and unto death.

To this end you were born. As prophets and seers we send you forth. If you fail in this task, this institution has so far failed. For the endowment of learning is the equipment for vision. Upon this sacred threshold, then, and beneath these silent witnesses of the sky we consecrate you to awaken the dreams of the youth of our fair land, and may the gentle mercies of God go with you.[97]

Prior to the August graduation, President Payne had paid an unannounced visit to Maycie Southall and the faculty members who were conducting her doctoral examinations; although she was not advised until later of his reason for attending the meeting, President Payne wanted an opportunity to observe her because he was interested in offering her a position on his faculty; he needed someone to teach courses pertaining to elementary education. Thus, the message to the graduating class hardly served as one of farewell to Maycie Southall because she had decided to accept President Payne's offer of full-time employment for the ensuing year.[98]

The doctoral candidate must have listened carefully, however, to the farewell message and accepted the challenge because A. L. Crabb, her former minor professor at George Peabody College for Teachers, stated more than forty years later that among his broad acquaintanceship with the institution's alumni he could think of no person who had climbed as high or served as widely in her chosen profession as

[97]Bruce R. Payne, "Dreams," The Peabody Reflector and Alumni News 2 (August 1929):[4].

[98]Southall, interview, April 23, 1979.

Maycie Southall.[99] Although she had aspirations in 1929, the
graduate student could hardly have dared to dream that in 1965
Felix C. Robb, president of the educational institution from
which she had retired in 1964, would write to her: "I know no
one who has more genuine interest in Peabody at heart and who
has contributed more than you in your service and leadership
in this institution."[100] Neither could she have anticipated,
while marching in the August 1929 graduation line, that some
fifty years later a professor who had followed her teaching
career with interest would describe her as ". . . the most
underrated educator in Elementary Education";[101] nor would her
modesty have allowed her to imagine that a later co-worker in
educational associations would reflect in 1979: "Dr. Southall
is one of the 'greats' in elementary education in this century."[102] Perhaps what she did realize as early as 1929,
however, was that, as a later fellow worker in the Association
for Childhood Education International wrote recently, one of
Maycie Southall's ". . . strong goals . . . [is] reaching out
for new horizons."[103] During the years that followed the completion of her own formal training, Maycie Southall did reach
out to many new horizons.

---

[99]Green, "The First Lady of Childhood Education," p. 134.

[100]Felix C. Robb to Maycie Southall, January 25, 1965,
Private Files of Maycie Southall.

[101]Robert S. Thurman, personal letter, May 29, 1979.

[102]Eugenia Hunter, personal letter, June 3, 1979.

[103]Mamie Heinz, personal letter, May 29, 1979.

A Tribute to Dr. Maycie Southall

A womanly woman
Of social grace;
A professional person,
We now embrace!

In a college class
She could hold down a chair
To proclaim a message
Beyond compare.

She garnered respect
In lecturing or teaching;
Consulting, advising
She was ever outreaching.

Her words, pearls of wisdom
Acclaimed by all,
Who came under her influence
In Peabody's hall.

When problems confronted
Students out in the field,
She came to their rescue
And left them well healed.

Her forceful life style
Inspired all not to shirk;
Not to quit, or give up,
But to keep on--at work.

Just to know her was a blessing
In the way that she shared;
A disciplined soul--
Who proved that she cared.

Mary Browning
Personal letter
May 15, 1979

60

CHAPTER III

THE PEABODY YEARS

The Setting

Maycie Southall began teaching on a full-time basis at
George Peabody College for Teachers in 1929. She was to spend
thirty-five consecutive years at the educational institution
where, through her work in the Department of Elementary Education, she came in contact with thousands of graduate and
undergraduate students who were seeking preparation as administrators, supervisors, and classroom teachers. Her appointment to the faculty of George Peabody College for Teachers
placed Maycie Southall in a prime position to become associated with the great and near-great in educational circles
because the campus was reputed at that time to be a mecca for
the nation's educational leaders. Thus, some of the keenest
minds in education, including both colleagues and students,
belonged to those persons with whom Maycie Southall worked
daily during her many years at George Peabody College for
Teachers; for example, one of her colleagues was the widely
acclaimed authority on curriculum, Hollis Caswell, who is
currently president emeritus of Teachers College, Columbia
University. Too, pictures retained in Maycie Southall's
personnel file located in the Office of the College Archivist

61

and Historian, George Peabody College for Teachers, show
her seated as a platform guest with such notable visitors as
William Heard Kilpatrick, renowned interpreter of John Dewey
and advocate of the "whole child" concept, and James Bryant
Conant, nationally known author and educational leader.

As a student, Maycie Southall had carefully chosen repu-
table universities where she could learn directly from some
of the most brilliant educational thinkers of the era. At
Teachers College, Columbia University, for example, she was
exposed to the teachings of William Heard Kilpatrick as well
as to those of Edward L. Thorndike, a proponent of the "readiness" approach to learning; at the University of Chicago, she
was instructed by Alice Temple, a staunch advocate of early
childhood education; at George Peabody College for Teachers,
she came under the tutelage of Thomas Alexander who later became noted for his experimentation in teacher education at
Teachers College, Columbia University; and at George Peabody
College for Teachers, she was also influenced by the instruction of Charles McMurry, an advocate of Herbartian theories,
who was widely recognized for his work in elementary education methodology.[1]

During the early decades of the century, some major movements were gaining a stronghold that were to loom large upon
the educational horizon in later years while Maycie Southall
was associated with George Peabody College for Teachers; for

---

[1]Maycie Southall, interview held in Nashville,
June 5, 1979.

example, tests and measurements were being introduced into the
realm of education with much zeal by proponents and were subsequently falling into disfavor by critics of quantification.

Another educational movement that caught the interest
and imagination of Maycie Southall was the rapid development
of kindergartens in the United States around the turn of the
century. Briefly, Elizabeth Peabody is credited with having
opened in 1860 at Boston a small school that resembled a
kindergarten; then, ten years later, she was instrumental in
establishing in the same city the first public kindergarten
in this country.[2] During the next few decades, many earnest
educational pioneers, mostly women, advocated establishing
kindergartens. Several proponents used their teaching positions at the college level to espouse their cause; Patty Smith
Hill, for example, who was a prominent leader in the kindergarten movement was employed at Teachers College, Columbia
University. Patty Smith Hill taught Maycie Southall in the
late 1920s; she also taught Lucy Gage who had enrolled there
earlier because of her strong interest in the training of
young children.[3] Lucy Gage became a full-time faculty member
of George Peabody College for Teachers in 1920 and continued
in the same capacity until her retirement in 1942.[4] Along

---

[2] Encyclopaedia Britannica, 11th ed., s.v. "Peabody, Elizabeth Palmer."

[3] Maycie Southall, interview held in Nashville, December 15, 1979.

[4] Carrie Bailey, "Life and Work of Lucy Gage, Pioneer Teacher and Leader" (M.Ed. thesis, George Peabody College for Teachers, 1960), p. 96.

with many other prominent supporters of the kindergarten movement, Lucy Gage was concerned with fundamental educational
principles of unity, continuity, and self-activity. During
her years on the Nashville campus, she worked diligently to
combine nursery school, kindergarten, and the first six grades
of elementary school into one continuous eight-year unit.[5]
Although Lucy Gage worked mainly in early childhood education
and Maycie Southall's efforts were focused chiefly on elementary education, their interests were mutual in many respects;
and the same educational responsibilities were often shared
by the two women. Thus, Maycie Southall, the younger of the
two, partly through her association with Lucy Gage soon developed an appreciation for nationally recognized leaders of
early childhood education as well as their methods.

Lucy Gage had studied in Chicago under several prominent
figures, one of whom was John Dewey, a proponent of a movement termed Progressive Education.[6] The 1920s and 1930s are
frequently associated with the major thrust of this educational movement. Maycie Southall's training as a student
during the years when Progressive Education was in its hey-
day, as well as her later association with colleagues such as
Lucy Gage, resulted in her utilizing with her students various
principles of the movement when she became a teacher; however,
according to one source, Maycie Southall ". . . was never

[5]Ibid., p. 40.
[6]Ibid., p. 27.

labeled a kind of progressivist as was Lucy Gage."[7] In a
recent interview, Maycie Southall stated that she joined the
Progressive Education Association when it had only two hundred members and remained active until its dissolution during the 1940s; she was on the list of speakers and promoted
the organization by giving many free addresses in various
cities while en route to other meetings and conventions.[8]

Her Philosophy

Although difficulty is encountered in determining the
philosophy of another person, several of Maycie Southall's
former students, colleagues, and friends have shared their
opinions of her views. A former colleague who worked with
Maycie Southall during her entire tenure as a regular staff
member provided insight:

> Maycie Southall's major concern was the education,
> growth, and development of children. She always assumed
> that Peabody's major purpose was gathered around the
> little child. Early childhood education and elementary
> education constituted her major concern throughout her
> career. She and Lucy Gage had similar philosophies al-
> though they disagreed on ways of achieving their goals.

> Maycie believed in citizenship training, character
> building, skill development, and personality growth.
> She had a philosophy about skills. Children should be
> taught to read, write, speak, spell, listen, and ob-
> serve. Listening was a skill. Her basic belief in the
> education of the child was important to her. The Pea-
> body Demonstration School was a technique that she used
> to realize her goals. Maycie always had large classes.
> She would send her students to the Demonstration School
> to observe; she went with them; then they would come

---

[7]John E. Windrow, interview held in Nashville, May 8,
1979.

[8]Southall, interview, December 15, 1979.

back, and all of them would discuss what they had observed. Many of the teachers at the Demonstration
School were her own students and close friends. She
had a close relationship with the teachers there. She
stayed close to the students, too. She recognized that
the Demonstration School had limitations, so she would
send her students out into the public schools to observe actual situations there. Also, case studies were
important to her.

Maycie had an interaction with her environment.
She had a tremendous influence on people. She was a
great and powerful influence verbally. She prepared
her speeches carefully, she had a message in each one,
and she delivered them well. Frequently she spoke on
administration, organization, and finance of public
education especially in the elementary grades. Curriculum was also a matter of importance to her. She would
state her basic philosophy and then point out that the
purpose of the curriculum is to make that philosophy
come true. The curriculum is to help achieve the growth
of the child.

Maycie was genuinely sincere. She would fight for
her students; they always knew that they would have her
support. She had large classes and many advisees.

Educating the parents to help improve the schools
was of great importance to Maycie. She was, therefore,
active in the PTA.[9]

Rubie E. Smith, retired chairman of the Department of

Elementary Education, Murray State University, described

some of her experiences during the late 1930s while complet-

ing an M.A. degree at George Peabody College for Teachers:

I am grateful I did my graduate work at Peabody
during what I consider "golden years" both there and
especially in the South. Those were the years of
John Dewey, William Kilpatrick, Laura Zirbes, Agnes
Snyder, other Columbia University leaders, Dr. Southall,
Lucy Gage, and others. Then we spent our time and
energy on working with children and teachers in the
true belief that all learners are different, that all
children have needs and are gifted, and that we can
build teachers who can work with these differences.
We believed the science of the subject tells us how
to teach it.

[9]Windrow, interview, May 8, 1979.

I attribute much of my own creative approach to teaching and my deep life values to Dr. Southall and other great souls with whom I have worked. . . .

My classes in 1937-39 were a joy, both in philosophy and her gracious charm. . . . One statement has particularly guided my life: "Don't scatter your fire; if you do, you won't have any."[10]

Another former student directed attention to Maycie Southall's philosophy:

Here are some of the ideas she held as to the manner in which children grow and how they should be taught if their greatest potential was to be developed:

Children grow best in an atmosphere that is child-like. Their world is close to nature. Therefore, take them outside to explore, to see, feel, and touch. Bring some of that outside world into the classroom for further experimentation and enjoyment. Encourage them to question, to make mistakes, and to use their imagination. She helped us to understand that we as teachers will not be guides in this wonderful process of learning unless we understand their nature and needs and ways in which they grow and develop. . . .

I am glad to report that Dr. Southall's influence continued to be an inspiration to me to seek to improve my teaching through continued study, observation, and experimentation.[11]

Dell C. Kjer, one of Maycie Southall's former doctoral candidates, analyzed his professor's educational philosophy:

Her philosophy was a mixture of Pestalozzi, Dewey, Kilpatrick, Bode, and others with a lot of practical common sense; it was generally "progressive." One (veteran) student (male) said, "Dr. Brearley is like a cannoneer--he fires one round and if it hits you, you're knocked out; but Dr. Southall fires a shotgun, and her wisdom spatters all over--everyone will get a shot." (Quotation is paraphrased.) This is perhaps not a very genteel expression but quite descriptive of her teaching (lecture) style.

---

[10]Rubie E. Smith, personal letter, June 2, 1979.

[11]Nona Sparks, personal letter, July 23, 1979.

She knew her history of education including all
the leaders, both men and women, of the distant past
and recent past as well as the current leaders.

The first day of class (Summer School 1946), she
walked in carrying a picture of Lucy Gage, hung it up,
and said, "I think you should know that the last of the
Big Three in Childhood Education just slipped away--
Patty Smith Hill is also gone [May 25]." (Lucy Gage
had died the year before [October 30, 1945] and Alice
Temple a short time later [January 6, 1946]). So I
became acquainted with three educators in one day--
much more to come, as I discovered through the years.
(Quotation is paraphrased.)

Her philosophy was expansive, emphasizing all aspects of life. She believed in flexibility and a wide
range of knowledge and experience--an interdisciplinary
approach long before it became popular in the 1960s.[12]

After almost fifty years of teaching, Mary Louise
Anderson retired; she recently reported that she and a friend
went to George Peabody College for Teachers because of Maycie
Southall:

Dr. Southall's philosophy stemmed from Dr. Dewey's
philosophy of Experimentalism as he meant it to be:
liberty for children without license, freedom with
responsibility, and exploration and discovery in learning. In the years since Dewey and Kilpatrick, we have
moved along toward smaller groups, child-centered
classrooms, more study of individual children, and
the value of teachers' listening to children in order
to provide more meaningful learning experiences for
them. . . . She kept an open mind--never closed to
worthy new ideas.[13]

Anne Grove recalled that Maycie Southall served as her
major professor during the early 1940s, and she summarized the
latter's philosophy:

Dr. Southall's philosophy might be summed up in
"the whole child's" being the major goal of education.

_____

[12]Dell C. Kjer, personal letter, August 8, 1979.

[13]Mary Louise Anderson, personal letter, May 30, 1979.

"Readiness" and "activity" were two major factors to be considered.

Dr. Southall stressed the importance of providing a meaningful background setting through which basic learning would rise if carefully planned for. Intrinsic motivation was to be derived from interest, centered with real-life problems.

Unit teaching with primary and secondary objectives, along with appropriate supporting activities, was encouraged. Concomitant learnings in terms of appreciations, insights, etc., were major outcomes to be expected in addition to actual content. . . .

Much observation in the Demonstration School was required. This was guided with sheets organized to show time, setting, and observed behavior with space for parallel comment from the experts met in reading and intended to interpret this behavior. . . .

Dr. Southall was admired, respected, and followed by most of her students and communicated well; for she was well-organized, steeped in her material, and zealous to make converts to "progressive education." She exuded a "love" for teaching but, more importantly, exemplified a love for learning. . . .

With her majors Dr. Southall did careful planning of courses to be taken with emphasis on training the "whole" teacher to deal with the "whole" child. Thus, we were prepared to do art, music, physical education, nature study, health, etc. . . . The child-centered, interest-centered approach. . . characterized the methods promoted by Dr. Southall.[14]

George T. Guess, retired from a professorship in elementary education at Central State University, Edmond, Oklahoma, stated that he enrolled at George Peabody College for Teachers in order to study with Maycie Southall, a member of his doctoral committee:

Elementary Education was a "sorry stepchild" in educational circles until Dr. Southall (and two other female specialists in childhood education) came on the scene. Her (their) influence at national, regional,

---

[14]Anne Grove, personal letter, July 30, 1979.

and local levels lifted the education of children from baby-sitting to profitable experiences for the child.

> . . . Miss Southall was an early advocate of the now common knowledge that both personal and scientific influences are an element of child development.[15]

Regarding Maycie Southall's propensity for the scientific is a communication that she composed in 1942 as a tribute of appreciation to Lucy Gage upon the latter's retirement:

> As teacher, colleague, and friend, you have greatly influenced my teaching. When I was certain, you caused me to doubt. When I wavered, you bolstered my courage. When I attempted the scientific, you helped me to be more philosophical. May many teachers know you as the great teacher you are.[16]

Clemit O. Humphreys, whose educational career encompassed thirty-seven years of employment in West Virginia, recalled the views of Maycie Southall, his major professor during 1946-47:

> Dr. Southall's thesis was the "whole child." She subscribed to Dewey's "you learn to do by doing." The thing that I remember is that she felt every room in the building should be equipped with every audio-visual available and that other equipment should include cots or mats, cooking stoves, refrigerators--anything that could be used in teaching. As I remember, she put more emphasis on this than on textbooks.
>
> She was actually in the lead as a "modern" educator.[17]

Maycie Southall's attitude toward excessive use of textbooks has changed very little since the 1940s. She still

---

[15]Guess, personal letter, May 31, 1979.

[16]Maycie Southall, "An Appreciation of Lucy Gage," Gage Book of Memoirs, 1942, John Stevens Collection (unpublished papers of Lucy Gage), Education Library, George Peabody College for Teachers, Nashville. (Handwritten.)

[17]Clemit O. Humphreys, personal letter, July 14, 1979.

believes very strongly in the importance of emphasizing reading skills when one is working with young children. In her
opinion, textbooks, workbooks, and phonics are frequently
emphasized too much in the teaching of reading skills. She
advocates the developmental approach to learning the language arts, beginning with listening and continuing through
the stages of speaking, reading, writing, and spelling.[18]

Maycie Southall participated as a member of Mary Northcutt
Powell's doctoral committee during the early 1960s; the latter,
who has more recently served as chairman of the Department of
Elementary and Early Childhood Education, Moorehead State
University, reminisced:

> Dr. Southall was totally devoted to training strong
> leaders in the field of education. As I recall, this
> could be accomplished only through mastery of theory and
> practical application. Most important was a knowledge
> of children--how they learn, why they don't learn, etc.
> She had great faith in young people and their ability to
> achieve--if that is what we expect--nothing is gained,
> indeed, a great deal is lost by consistently lowering
> standards. This also permeated her college classes.[19]

John Julia McMahan, who taught for forty years, addressed
various aspects of Maycie Southall's philosophy:

> Her philosophy of "get the job done regardless of
> who gets the credit" should help us move forward as a
> true profession and thus re-establish the esteem teach-
> ing once held among the parents and lay people of our
> nation. . . .

> Her philosophy of a professional person's need for
> continuous study and growth so as to serve better his
> profession and mankind, if held to a greater degree today

---

[18]Southall, interview, December 15, 1979.

[19]Mary Northcutt Powell, personal letter, May 30, 1979.

and in the future, would . . . help teaching regain its high esteem in American society. . . .

"Seek ye to better things for children, and things will be bettered for teachers," she reasoned and quoted to us in classes. We sensed this was a basic philosophy of hers, and many of us caught it from her! How true it is!

Her lifetime actions have come of her caring; this has been her philosophy of life.[20]

Haidee L. Smith, a retired teacher who contributed more than forty-six years to elementary education in Missouri, described the views of the professor who guided her through an Ed.S. degree: "Dr. Southall's philosophy was one of a truly dedicated teacher who was interested in the potentiality of each student."[21] The same contributor suggested implications for education to be derived from such a philosophy:

We need teachers who are willing to study, to learn all that they can in methods, materials, etc., in order to develop the full potentiality of each child. We need teachers who are not afraid to be a decent human being character wise. How can you be an example if you don't have integrity or good moral values?[22]

A Role Model

In spite of a lapse of several years since some of her former students, colleagues, and friends have been associated with Maycie Southall, many remember quite vividly her role as an educator. Maycie Southall's retirement prevented her from serving as an advisor, a position to which she had earlier

---

[20]John Julia McMahan, personal letter, May 21, 1979.

[21]Haidee L. Smith, personal letter, May 17, 1979.

[22]Ibid.

been appointed, for Carol L. Schlichter's doctoral study. The
latter, currently in charge of the Program for Gifted and
Talented at the University of Alabama had, however, completed
several courses earlier with Maycie Southall. She recalled:

> . . . I draw up very strong images when I remember
> her; I feel that her forceful but charming and persuasive
> personality served as one of the few positive, female
> role models in my graduate work. I feel she represented
> a minimum of compromise and maximum success in the inte-
> gration of significant personal and professional charac-
> teristics--a synthesis I am committed to for myself.[23]

Another woman described Maycie Southall as a role model
for potential educators:

> Much of Dr. Southall's leadership was behind the
> scenes and low key; however, when she believed in some-
> one or a "cause," you were <u>aware</u> of that strength and
> support. As a woman in a leadership role, she was far
> ahead of most others. . . . She was a model of scholar-
> ship and professionalism. . . . Students, young people
> need effective role models.[24]

Anne Grove, who has taught in both the United States
and abroad, remembered the example her professor set for students:

> Dr. Southall disciplined herself and held up for
> her students high standards of professional behavior.
> She often stated that teachers communicate their own
> behavior to students as part of the educative process.
>
> Dr. Southall has certainly served as a model of
> dedication to teaching, and her ideas have served as
> a constant challenge to be developed in the classroom.
> Through her influence and that of others, I have made
> a career of teaching, having taught more than twenty-
> five years.[25]

---

[23]Carol L. Schlichter, personal letter, June 22, 1979.

[24]Marjorie E. Ramsey, personal letter, May 9, 1979.

[25]Grove, personal letter, July 30, 1979.

Dell C. Kjer, who has known Maycie Southall quite well for many years because of his varied professional and educational associations with her, respected the exemplary role portrayed by his friend:

> My wife and I met at the old Peabody Kindergarten—both influenced by Dr. Southall. She is one of the best friends and most influential persons in our lives. What remains is love, respect, and wonder, almost awe at the tremendous level of everything good that Dr. Southall represents. Perhaps I didn't even write the word "intelligence" which should have been first. What a modern day feminist she would have made, but I am sure it would have been tempered with justice and respect for all masculine colleagues; and her own moral sense was too strong to become militant as it is defined today. By the way, Dr. Southall attended church regularly but never wore her religion on her sleeve. . . . Catholics, Jews, Protestants, all loved her.[26]

The same contributor described the image Maycie Southall projected to others. He noted that her personality was ". . . electric; charismatic; you could feel her presence. It reached out and touched everyone. I imagine you could say she projected the image of an educator of the highest category."[27] He added that his former professor ". . . was a southern gentlewoman (lady), but she didn't wear white gloves or carry a white linen purse all the time, if ever. She dressed beautifully (she was—is—beautiful), and her beautiful inner self caused her to glow."[28] He provided further insight:

---

[26]Kjer, personal letter, August 8, 1979.

[27]Ibid.

[28]Ibid.

She was polite, courteous, warm to individuals, and willing to talk with students and parents. She knew their family backgrounds, always remembered names (I don't know how she did it), and kept track of them even after they left Peabody. She drew hordes of her students everywhere she appeared as a speaker or guest.

She was kind. There was no end to her kindnesses.

She loved beauty--art and music. She encouraged students to participate by attending concerts, etc. She gave things freely--tickets, books, materials-- to many students; she was generous to a fault; for example, she had students to her apartment--an open house for every graduating class, but other students were included if she knew they were around. She was especially kind to foreign students, and there were many. Refreshments appeared as if by magic, always in the best of taste and in a comfortable but beautiful style. She held many conferences with students over meals that she had prepared. She was a popular guest for students to take to one of the many wonderful restaurants in Nashville. She had "charisma" although thirty years ago we didn't call it that. She accepted everyone and seemed to treat everyone alike.

She could get angry or irritated. . . . She dictated a letter to the dean one day, expressing her disagreement and noting that "Peabody was founded to blaze trails, not to pack them!" (I typed it for her, so I know.)

Another day (commencement, early in the morning), I met her crossing from her office to the Administration Building. I said, "You look upset; is something wrong?" She answered by naming a student, an older woman from a very rural area of Tennessee who had sacrificed a great deal to work on an M.A. degree, and then adding, "I just found out she was notified this morning she cannot graduate today because she lacks a B average. I am going to the registrar's office to change one of my grades to an A so she can graduate. It would be morally wrong to disappoint her so. Think of the effect this would have on the children she teaches for the whole year. It's better for me to change the grade so the student will not suffer the disappointment and the children will not suffer because of the lack of her success." This experience has stayed with me to this day. I learned a great life's lesson in humaneness and have profited from this lesson several times in my career. The student counted first--her self-concept and self-respect--but the effect on the children is also not to be ignored. Such lessons I learned only because I

worked closely with Dr. Southall; they were not generally known--she made no public displays of her professional and personal "humanism."[29]

Marjorie S. Snyder, who was awarded a doctoral degree
by George Peabody College for Teachers, perceived her former
professor as a role model:

> Dr. Maycie K. Southall epitomizes the professional
> educator. She obviously has had many invaluable experi-
> ences which she has willingly shared with others. Her
> knowledge of research, her skills and understandings,
> and her dedication to her students make it impossible
> to enumerate her most valuable contributions to the pro-
> fession. She is the rare scholar with humane concerns--
> a model for all whose lives she touched.[30]

Mary Louise Anderson's observations typified the general
impressions conveyed by several former students: "Dr. Southall
was innately a lady. Her dynamic and forceful personality
never seemed to make her too pushy. She was accepted in all
circles and contributed to many, many organizations. She has
friends wherever she goes."[31] Maycie Southall, according to
one observer, did not stoop to unkind or disparaging remarks.[32]
The fact that she was viewed by others as a role model was
expressed by a former student and advisee:

> Her personality was charming--dynamic. She always
> looked attractive. Her advice was sought by students
> and co-workers. She could hardly cross the campus with-
> out being stopped by students and co-workers. She was
> a delightful hostess and entertained students often.[33]

---

[29]Ibid.

[30]Marjorie S. Snyder, personal letter, January 15, 1980.

[31]Anderson, personal letter, May 30, 1979.

[32]Ethel B. Miller, personal letter, October 18, 1979.

[33]Emma L. Farrell, personal letter, May 17, 1979.

A former colleague shared some of his memories concerning the role portrayed by Maycie Southall:

> My . . . general impression was of her great "civility"--if that is the right word: a graciousness, a gentleness, a quietness in personal relationships. I do not mean in the least to suggest any retiring quality as I write these words. Although at this date I cannot remember specific instances, the general impression stays clear that Dr. Southall was a fighter--obviously on the national scene for the kind of education in which she believed, but also on the campus, within the faculty, for causes about which she cared.
>
> One other memory: She was such a hard worker. She demanded a great deal of her students in the way of reports, etc., and this in turn put a great load on her: reading, correcting, reacting, etc. I certainly retain a memory of her still hard at work in her office many, many times as I left my desk for my home.[34]

Maycie Southall's assiduous work in behalf of education was not short-lived; comments made recently by fellow members in an educational organization attest to her continuing influence as a model of professionalism. One member noted: "In my opinion, Dr. Southall is one of the giants of women in education in Tennessee. She has a great capacity for work, and equally important, a great capacity for inspiring others to work diligently for the good of children. . . ."[35] Another member remarked: "No matter where Dr. Southall was or is or with whom she was or is, she always speaks out for the issues she feels important."[36] A third member expressed: "In education, Dr. Southall has achieved much . . . in helping shape

---

[34]James L. Hymes, Jr., personal letter, June 10, 1979.

[35]Willene Paxton, personal letter, February 21, 1980.

[36]Geraldine B. Dement, personal letter, February 24, 1980.

lives of students so as to mold good teachers who are concerned, dedicated, and ready to carry on the cause."[37]

The Classroom

Glimpses of the classroom setting between 1929 and 1964
at George Peabody College for Teachers, shared through impressions recalled by students, colleagues, and friends, indicate
Maycie Southall's prominence as a staff member and her effectiveness as a teacher of administrators, supervisors, and
teachers. In the everyday incidents, perhaps seemingly insignificant at first glance, are mirrored a portion of the history of elementary education, insight into the thoughts and
actions of one whose life has been filled with vision comple-
mented by enterprise, and a view of the influence effected by
an individual committed to educational endeavors.

High Expectations

The fact that Maycie Southall's classes were large and
her advisees numerous was not due to a reputation as a teacher
who required very little work; quite the contrary seemed to
be true for many of her former students recently referred to
rigorous requirements and assignments. According to a former
student, Maycie Southall's ". . . classes were always crammed.
She required many papers, and she would absolutely drown us in
assignments; but, for some reason, we would just gasp and come
up for more!"[38] Another former student stated: "I thought

---

[37]Barbara J. Hinson, personal letter, February 24, 1980.

[38]Brannon, interview, May 8, 1979.

Dr. Southall very demanding at the time, but afterwards I
realized how much I learned from her."[39]   A former student
and assistant described his professor as ". . . a relentless
worker who never knew when a student had done enough."[40]   Re-
inforcement of the same trend of thought came from another
statement: "There was no doubt of her love for teaching.
Her expectations were high, and most of us tried to reach
that level."[41] The consensus was further strengthened: "She
demanded much and usually got it from the serious student."[42]
Maycie Southall's high expectations seemed to be generally
recognized and accepted by diligent workers:

> Undergraduate students generally were a little
> afraid. She tolerated no nonsense and spoke honestly
> and firmly to many who showed irresponsibility, tardi-
> ness, etc. She was always sympathetic with real prob-
> lems. Graduate students who might not want . . . to
> do the work she required just stayed away.
>
> Always her analysis of a student's work or pro-
> gram was in terms of the effect one would have on
> children being taught.[43]

From Texas came the reflections of Vernon Eady, a retired associate professor of education, who has known Maycie
Southall for more than forty years. He described four of
her classes:

---

[39]Virginia S. Turner, personal letter, October 15, 1979.

[40]Humphreys, personal letter, July 14, 1979.

[41]Ramsey, personal letter, May 9, 1979.

[42]Ethel B. Miller, personal letter, October 18, 1979.

[43]Kjer, personal letter, August 8, 1979.

The classes were very thorough. They were <u>hard</u>.
They were interesting. They were meaningful. These
classes have been my major assignment for thirty years
of college and university teaching. Only the people
who were interested and enjoyed reading appreciated
the classes. These classes made me have recognition
as a student when I attended Columbia, Southern
California, and U.C.L.A.[44]

Nona Sparks remembered assignments that addressed the

role of a teacher in training children:

I had several classes with Dr. Southall prior to
and including the year I received my M.A. degree in
1940.

Her assignments were unforgettable! They were
lengthy, though understandable, exhaustive, and exhaust-
ing, requiring work and more work.

I went to work in earnest; and before long I was
able to respond mentally and verbally, understand, and
enjoy her class lectures. They were never dull for she
interspersed them with suitable illustrations gleaned
from her wide range of knowledge and from her personal
experiences.

She invited class discussion and was able to obtain
responses from us that let her know whether we were keeping up with current assignments and appropriating them
to the best advantage.

If any class members had been halfhearted about
any of her courses, after the first test they either
went to work in earnest or left the class of their own
accord. . . .

Many of our assignments sent us to the library to
read what had been written about . . . what the teacher's
role should be as the leader in helping to develop young
minds intellectually and emotionally.[45]

Souci Hall reminisced about her major professor's

rigorous classroom requirements:

During the time I was at Peabody, Dr. Southall
was in great demand as a guest speaker in other states

---

[44]Vernon Eady, personal letter, January 11, 1980.

[45]Sparks, personal letter, July 23, 1979.

representing various organizations, especially Delta Kappa Gamma and the Association for Childhood Education International. Being absent from her classroom was not a time for us to have leisure time; she gave us so much work to do while she was away that we welcomed her return in order to have a breather.[46]

A retired educator analyzed Maycie Southall's expectations of her students: "Few considered her a driver; most considered her an inspirer whose philosophy and spirit were . . . significant . . . because she was helping us in our self-growth toward more effective teaching."[47] The professor was very desirous that her students become effective educators; thus, she developed and maintained a high level of expectations for both her students and herself. An observer recalled:

Dr. Southall expected much from her students, but she gave much to them. Few college professors gave such complete professional bibliographies for student use. Few college professors used the techniques advocated for teachers-in-training to use in their classrooms more frequently in college classes than did she. She had a thorough grasp of the development of public education in Tennessee. She had had personal contact with most of the greats and near-greats in the country. She kept on the cutting edge of educational philosophy and issues by her attendance at national conventions. All of this became a part of that which she used to motivate effectively her students to acquire interest in becoming good teachers.[48]

Emphasis on Educational Research

Maycie Southall thought that students should become familier with educational research in order to serve more

---

[46]Souci Hall, personal letter, July 31, 1979.

[47]McMahan, personal letter, May 21, 1979.

[48]Ruth McDonald, personal letter, May 9, 1979.

effectively as teachers, supervisors, and administrators.
According to a former student, "Her classroom instruction--
in spite of a usual too heavy load--was a demonstration of
her philosophy of instruction: personal, warm, individualized, with a reliance upon research."[49]

A former student recalled extensive use of the library:
"Dr. Southall has ever been a forceful leader and extremely
busy. I amassed hundreds of note cards and 'lived' in
Peabody library's stacks! How grateful I have always been
for those wide, wide readings."[50] Another former student
remembered the emphasis placed upon knowledge of available
research:

> While taking one of Dr. Southall's classes, I
> found it necessary to spend much time in the library
> doing research which incidentally has been invaluable
> through the years. One of my friends asked how much
> it cost to rent a room in the library to which I ex-
> pressed some degree of surprise. He went on to say
> that since I was practically living in the library,
> he was sure I had rented a room there.[51]

A doctoral recipient, whose college contacts with Maycie
Southall spanned the years 1928 through 1951, learned to appreciate the library and, in turn, tried to teach her students to realize its worth:

> I am not sure, but I have always thought that her
> class put in my hands the first "real" bibliography for
> a class that I have ever had; and I certainly used it.
> It led me to good use of the library which I have tried

[49]Guess, personal letter, May 31, 1979.

[50]Rubie E. Smith, personal letter, June 2, 1979.

[51]Euleta Murdoch, personal letter, October 19, 1979.

to pass on to my students. Her classes were important
to me. . . . She led us to have high standards for our
work. I studied hard during the year, and she answered
letters giving advice. She communicated effectively in
conference and in letters. One looked forward to having
a conference with her.

The time she gave to her work was evidence of her
love for teaching. . . . Dr. Southall gave me what I
needed in my work; thus I always returned for her
guidance. . . . Her methods in teaching and guidance
have been so effective with me that I tended to use
them in my teaching. . . .

Her classes were almost always large. I remember
hearing one of her students say he had to come back to
her to get "caught up" in Education.[52]

Maycie Southall was interested in staying abreast of
contemporary happenings in education and was conscientious
in her efforts to share knowledge with her students. According to one observer, the professor ". . . kept up-to-date
with books and journals and revised bibliographies at least
once a year."[53] The same observer noted:

Dr. Southall always had carefully planned course
syllabi and bibliographies. She handed out many almost
perpetually useful materials. Most were years ahead of
the time, so I was up-to-date until the pendulum swung
to the extreme right. Now I go by my rural school
training for skills and find that even what I learned
in 1931 was too far out for today's narrow approach to
reading and mathematics.[54]

The research efforts were designed to be meaningful,
and the students accumulated materials to be used in later
years; for example, from New Mexico came the comments:

[52]Farrell, personal letter, May 17, 1979.

[53]Kjer, personal letter, August 8, 1979.

[54]Ibid.

One was quite aware that one's annotations and term
papers were read and checked by her, not by a graduate
assistant. What interest and industry this revealed!
The many hours she spent on this! One realized even then
the value she placed on better understanding and guiding
each individual in her classes. . . .

Assignments made in her classes were very meaningful. The annotations we made were referred to often in
later years. How far-reaching were their use and influence. They helped us convince co-workers and administrators in our innovative efforts![55]

Leadership

Memories of bygone days recently shared by many former
students serve to depict a scenario of Maycie Southall's classroom leadership during her thirty-five years at George Peabody
College for Teachers. Selected descriptions of incidents provide insight from a variety of vantage points into the effectiveness of the leader.

A former participant as a graduate student in six of
Maycie Southall's courses described his professor's leadership
ability: "Her's was not a demanding type but rather one of
quiet expectancy. She assumed (expected) things would be done
after the original initiation."[56]

Leadership meant to Maycie Southall guidance, motivation,
and support for the student's self-development through his
educational endeavors. An observer recalled:

Dr. Southall emphasized the indirect approach in
teaching and guidance--leading the student to discover
the truth for himself. She was able to motivate and to
teach others to motivate in teaching. I kept notes of

[55]McMahan, personal letter, May 21, 1979.

[56]Bryant, personal letter, May 15, 1979.

classes, reading cards, and bibliographies until I retired. I treasured them.[57]

Louise Oakley, a retired assistant professor of education

who sought Maycie Southall as her advisor and major professor

in 1937, recalled demonstrations of leadership:

> Dr. Southall was effective as an educator. Not only
> was she good in her lectures, but she was wonderful in
> her evaluation of the work of her students. She read our
> note cards and wrote suggestions on them. She read our
> papers and told us how to improve. She advised us of
> courses we needed to take in other fields. She always
> gave other educators credit for the work they had done or
> were doing.[58]

An observer stated that she put into practice Maycie

Southall's example of leadership during her own teaching ca-

reer:

> She had the knack of silencing the "blabby" people
> who talked too much. She encouraged free discussion;
> but she could pleasantly say, "We've heard from you now.
> Thank you for your ideas. Now let's hear from someone
> else." I worked hard to emulate her in this respect.[59]

A current principal of an elementary school in Nashville

shared: "Having attended very formal . . . schools, I found

Dr. Southall's ideas very new and refreshing. . . . I could

relate the theory learned to my teaching experience."[60]

A former student assistant described Maycie Southall's

emphasis on objectivity in the classroom:

> Dr. Southall has a photographic memory. She could
> read a thing once and remember it. . . .

---

[57]Farrell, personal letter, May 17, 1979.

[58]Louise Oakley, personal letter, May 23, 1979.

[59]Anderson, personal letter, May 30, 1979.

[60]Margaret Millspaugh, personal letter, January 18, 1980.

I can still see Dr. Southall in Research class, jabbing her finger for emphasis on data, even when a student was giving a report. It was as if she were pinning that fact to some mental picture. She never forgot any of it either. . . .

Dr. Southall was a gracious hostess and frequently entertained her students and former students. In the classroom she was very objective and interested primarily in the subject matter, but out of the classroom she showed a good sense of humor and a more subjective interest in people.[61]

A former student provided an example of the congeniality

displayed by Maycie Southall in the classroom:

I remember in the 1940s, when the GI's were on campus, we were in class in the old Psychology Building. It was a warm summer day, and all the windows were open. Outside one window was a big tree. As Dr. Southall was talking to the class, a bird in the tree began to sing very loudly. It became difficult for us on the back row to hear. As Dr. Southall paused for a moment, a young GI sitting near the window halfway hung his head out the window and commanded, "At ease, out there!" Silence-- then the class really laughed--Dr. Southall included.[62]

From Illinois came comments pertaining to the leadership

displayed by Maycie Southall:

My first encounter with Dr. Southall was as Illinois Chairman for UNESCO, for ACEI. She, as you know, was on the President's Committee for UNESCO. I say encounter advisedly for want of a better word. Meeting Dr. Southall is much more than an introduction--one is confronted with so much charm, ability, knowledge, and leadership that she is almost unbelievable. I went to Peabody because of Dr. Southall.

. . . Dr. Southall did expect serious study and participation from her students. . . . What did I learn from Dr. Southall? Much--but most of all, self-confidence and a more gracious way to meet many situations.[63]

---

[61]Ethel B. Miller, personal letter, October 18, 1979.

[62]Haidee L. Smith, personal letter, May 17, 1979

[63]Irene Duckworth, personal letter, July 8, 1979.

The same observer, Irene Duckworth, who is retired from
a teaching career that spanned forty-five years in elementary
grades, related a specific classroom experience:

> The class had just broken up into small discussion
> groups (Dr. Southall was not present) when a gentleman
> from the Near East, a foreign student, turned to me
> and said, "You write--I'll think." My reply went some-
> thing like this, "Yes, I'll write, but I'll also think.
> Dr. Southall expects both of all of us. We'll also
> need to read." My "friend" looked around the group,
> received affirmative nods and replies, and then said
> with quite a bow, "It's done here." I learned later
> that he was, I believe, head of the educational depart-
> ment of his country. I assure you this was a serious
> and polite conversation. (These are exact "quotes" of
> the gentleman.)[64]

Dell C. Kjer worked closely with Maycie Southall while
he was enrolled as a doctoral student and employed as her
assistant; pertinent insights are extracted from his generous contributions:

> I had many courses with Dr. Southall over the
> years. . . . I can say definitely there was little or
> no overlapping, and the content was clearly differen-
> tiated for each course. Dr. Southall was even pretty
> good about not using the same illustrations, telling
> the same stories, or using the same assignments for
> the different courses. . .

> Supervision of Student Teaching was one of the
> best courses I have ever encountered. I learned more
> about teacher education in that course than any other.
> Everything was far ahead of its time. It was in this
> course that I learned about Towson State University's
> excellent laboratory experience program in Elementary
> Education. That is one reason I changed positions--to
> participate in the best at TSU. . . . I have taught
> thirty-nine years . . . [including] . . . to date four-
> teen years as professor at Towson State University
> . . . [and am also] . . . presently coordinator of
> Graduate Early Childhood Education.

[64]Ibid.

Dr. Southall used lecture, discussion, student oral reports, much group work and teamwork, and encouraged the use of audio-visual aids.[65]

The same contributor recalled that although democratic leadership and student participation on faculty and college committees were encouraged, there was respect for the privacy of those who participated in classes and groups. He added that enrollees in Maycie Southall's large classes numbered ". . . up to 125 or so. . . . She gave objective examinations and required term papers even in large classes."[66] He continued by describing Maycie Southall's leadership:

As a leader, she was forceful. Each idea she had for herself (as a proposed project) was planned, organized, and carried to completion, including an evaluation. She was successful in obtaining the help and/or cooperation of students both graduates and undergraduates, former students, and off-campus educators. Helpers worked many hours and diligently, as much out of loyalty to Dr. Southall as for any other reason, except they were usually aware that the project (conference, workshop, meeting) would result in a new and valuable experience to those who participated.[67]

Perhaps the most succinct description of Maycie Southall's leadership in the classroom was contributed by one of her former doctoral students, Marjorie E. Ramsey, who is currently serving as dean for Student Personnel Services and professor of Early Childhood Education at Kent State University. She averred: "In Dr. Southall's class, you became a scholar."[68]

---

[65]Kjer, personal letter, August 8, 1979.

[66]Ibid.

[67]Ibid.

[68]Ramsey, personal letter, May 9, 1979.

Concern for the Individual

Maycie Southall was genuinely interested in the welfare of her students. Not only was she sincere in her concern for the student as an individual but she communicated that personal interest to the student. Many contributors of information to this study referred to Maycie Southall as both teacher and friend. One retired teacher penned:

> From my first contact with her, I admired and respected her. She was a person you soon vowed you would never let down.
>
> Her statement, "There is no test, and likely will never be one, to measure the influence of someone's belief in you, making you keep on doing your best, not letting down the person with this belief in you," made in class in summer 1936 remains true.
>
> Her faith in me remains a prime influence even in my retirement years.[69]

Maycie Southall worked diligently in an attempt to know not only her subject but the individuals in her classes. A current principal in Nashville recalled:

> One class must have had at least 125 enrolled. Dr. Southall would give us an overview and challenge, divide us into smaller (10-15) working groups and get us involved in research, literature review, and interpretation. She would ask us questions to help us remain practical, call us by name, show interest in our employment success and production, and then regroup and reassign.[70]

From another vantage point, an observer described Maycie Southall's interest in her students that extended beyond the classroom doors and beyond the scheduled classroom hours:

[69]McMahan, personal letter, May 21, 1979.

[70]R. C. Henderson, personal letter, May 13, 1979.

Dr. Southall seemed to know a lot about her students. She was friendly, pleasant, and would stop for a chat if she met a student on the campus. Once she said she had to have a good breakfast to prepare herself for the day. I am sure she needed extra energy for all of her daily activities. . . .

She had her classes come to her home in groups. That was an unusual experience for me. To be in her home was a delight. She is a wonderful hostess, conversationalist, and has the knack of making her guests feel comfortable.[71]

Comments pertaining to Maycie Southall's tireless efforts with individual students came from a recipient of an Ed.S. degree, Bertha M. Gammell, who lives in Coral Gables:

Dr. Southall was my beloved advisor and instructor. She was _interested_ in each student, was _thorough_, and if one didn't know how to do something—for example, write a short résumé of a book on a card—she worked with the student until he or she knew how; it made no difference how long it took. Sometimes, she would even say, "Come to my apartment tonight so we can work uninterrupted."

She considered each student as a special person under her supervision and was very thorough in getting students to do work required. She was also a _friend_.[72]

Maycie Southall believed in educating the whole person and in extending learning experiences beyond the classroom; thus, she provided opportunities by using her home as the setting for her students to develop an appreciation for the aesthetic and social aspects of life. A former student recalled: "She often had groups of students to her apartment; it was a pleasant as well as a learning experience."[73]

---

[71]Haidee L. Smith, personal letter, May 17, 1979.

[72]Bertha M. Gammell, personal letter, October 23, 1979.

[73]Eady, personal letter, January 11, 1980.

A former student was impressed by Maycie Southall's faith
in the individual: "She was the same all the time and never
seemed to be too tired to help; she thought everyone has talent and everyone should use his talents in some way."[74] The
same contributor stated that one of the outstanding things she
learned from Maycie Southall was a ". . . love and respect for
all people as she thought everyone was capable of doing something if he would make the effort and give the time."[75]

Several enrollees in Maycie Southall's classes expressed
amazement at her ability to remember them in later years. One
observer stated that her former professor ". . . had a phenome-
nal memory for students. You could meet her, as I did, some
years later at a convention, and she instantly recalled your
name, where you were teaching, and was sincerely interested in
your work."[76] Another observer described her as being ". . .
sincerely interested in each individual."[77] He added: "She
showed a sincere interest in me when I was her student and
since."[78] From a friend in an educational organization came
remarks about Maycie Southall's reputation among students: "I
have known many who had work under her at Peabody. They always
used superlatives in describing her. It has been interesting

---

[74]Turner, personal letter, October 15, 1979.

[75]Ibid.

[76]Powell, personal letter, May 30, 1979.

[77]Henderson, personal letter, May 13, 1979.

[78]Ibid.

to know of her <u>continued interest</u> in those whom she taught.
<u>She does not forget students</u>."[79] Comments from another friend
of many years, Anna Belle Darden, included:

> I first met Dr. Maycie K. Southall in Nashville
> during a Childhood Education meeting in 1949. My
> major professor, Dr. Laura Zirbes, from Ohio State
> University was in Nashville for the ACEI meeting.
> She introduced me to Dr. Southall.
>
> Dr. Southall brought students from Peabody College
> to visit and observe in the Austin Peay State Demon-
> stration School where I taught. (It is now Byrnes L.
> Darden Elementary School.)
>
> She is the type leader who never forgets and
> always through her gracious manner makes everyone feel
> that she really cares. . . .[80]

Jess R. Beard, head of the Department of Elementary
Education at Iowa State University, recalled his professor's
interest in his family:

> I always appreciated Dr. Southall's interest in me
> as an individual. She knew that my wife and I had never
> been south of the Mason-Dixon line before, and she was
> very gracious in pointing out things that we might want
> to see and do in the region. She also frequently in-
> cluded our four-year-old son when she had teas or other
> social affairs at her apartment. He still remembers her
> with a great deal of affection.[81]

Strengths/Weaknesses

Many former students and associates of Maycie Southall
recently provided their analyses of her strengths and/or weaknesses in her role as professor at George Peabody College for
Teachers. Selected for inclusion was a list of her strengths,

---

[79]Zora Ellis, personal letter, April 26, 1979.

[80]Anna Belle Darden, personal letter, May 4, 1980.

[81]Jess R. Beard, personal letter, November 1, 1979.

prepared by Dell C. Kjer, which provides not only a summary
but which typifies the impressions shared by many contributors:

1. Established purposes and objectives (talk about
current management by objectives--Dr. Southall was doing
this in the 1940s and 1950s; in fact, Peabody College
seemed to be administered in this fashion).

2. Developed major ideas for overall as well as
details.

3. Had high standards for accomplishment for herself and students; high expectations for everyone with
whom she worked.

4. Displayed flexibility; allowed students to plan
for themselves in many instances.

5. Had an extremely broad or wide knowledge of education in the United States and other countries.

6. Shared all new knowledge with her students.

7. Was an inveterate worker herself; spent long
hours on the job; always carried work home; seemed never
to sleep.

8. Was extremely loyal to associates; never criti-
cized colleagues nor students severely.

9. Was extremely loyal to Peabody and its purposes.

10. Helped with everything at the College.[82]

Information gleaned from numerous contributions to this
study concerning Maycie Southall's weaknesses as a professor
of education seemed to focus attention on one item: her handwriting. One observer wrote: "Since all who knew Dr. Southall
admired her, it is interesting to record that she, like the
rest of us, had a human failing, though a minor one. Hers lay
in the fact that her handwriting was not always legible."[83]

---

[82]Kjer, personal letter, August 8, 1979.

[83]Flora Rawls, personal letter, May 11, 1979.

Another observer remembered: "She had a practice of writing short notes when she returned our assignments; our trouble was reading them. We had difficulty knowing if the comment was favorable or unfavorable, but we enjoyed trying to decipher them."[84] A third observer recalled: "Now we look back and smile over our frustrations because we could not read her writing. She sometimes couldn't read it after it got cold!"[85] A fourth observer exclaimed: "Her handwriting was atrocious! For several days I once tried to decipher her comments on my dissertation copy and finally realized she was complimenting me on my writing!"[86] William Van Til, Coffman distinguished professor emeritus of education, Indiana State University, reinforced the above statements by calling attention to the same trait:

> Dr. Maycie Southall was one of the best known and effective members of the Division of Curriculum and Teaching which I chaired at Peabody from 1951 to 1957. She had charm and insight and was a genuine influence in the organization I was to serve as 1961-62 president, the ASCD.
>
> . . . I shall add [to the information gathered for this study] a campus legend, probably apocryphal:
>
> Dr. Southall's handwriting was notoriously bad, possibly as bad as mine. One day a student went to her secretary for help in deciphering the comments Dr. Southall had written on the student's paper. The student said apologetically, "I want to profit from Dr. Southall's comments, but unfortunately I can't read them." The secretary looked at the paper and responded,

---

[84]Souci Hall, personal letter, July 31, 1979.

[85]Rubie E. Smith, personal letter, June 2, 1979.

[86]Ramsey, personal letter, May 9, 1979.

"Dr. Southall says here, 'This is a very good paper, but you should improve your handwriting.'"[87]

Major Interests

The educational interests of Maycie Southall have been many, and they convey a general impression of balance among a variety of endeavors. All of her educational efforts emanated from a central source: her commitment to teaching. The major interests in which Maycie Southall invested extensive time and effort encompass these specific areas: availability of kindergarten programs for all children; educational opportunities for foreign students (the enhancement of international understanding through the educative process); improvement of education through participation in educational organizations; and a commitment to the mission of George Peabody College for Teachers.

Kindergarten Programs
for All Children

Early in her teaching career, Maycie Southall developed an appreciation for kindergarten programs. As the years passed, her interest deepened; and her efforts increased. Because her many years of work found at least partial fruition during the 1970s, after she had retired from the teaching profession, some highlights of Maycie Southall's efforts in behalf of kindergartens are presented in Chapter VI of this study which is entitled "The Retirement Years."

[87]William Van Til, personal letter, January 18, 1980.

Educational Opportunities
for Foreign Students

Maycie Southall's exceptional interest in the welfare
of foreign students was well known among her associates at
George Peabody College for Teachers. Her belief in the importance of developing effective teachers for all children
recognized no geographic boundaries.

Maycie Southall delivered a speech in 1961 in which she
stated:

> The nature of Peabody's program has been such that
> it has drawn many persons in positions of educational
> leadership from many . . . countries of the world. In
> fact, few, even on this campus, recognize the great im-
> pact this institution has had on education abroad.
>
> A quick review of the foreign students who have
> graduated reveals that we have a large and a very in-
> fluential group of graduates in most of the major coun-
> tries of the world. . . . The countries having the
> largest number of our graduates are: China, Korea,[88]
> Germany, India, Brazil, Japan, and the Philippines.

An examination of records retained in the private files
of Maycie Southall revealed that more than four hundred foreign students had enrolled in her classes. An excerpt from
a speech given by Maycie Southall in 1973 indicated that her
students had ". . . come from every state in the Union and
fifty-two foreign countries."[89] She purposely provided many

---

[88]Maycie Southall, "These Our Founders," speech delivered at Founders Day meeting, George Peabody College for
Teachers, February 15, 1961, Private Files of Maycie Southall.

[89]Maycie Southall, "Response to Award as Outstanding
Alumna of Middle Tennessee State University," speech given
during Alumni Meeting, Middle Tennessee State University,
May 5, 1973, Private Files of Maycie Southall.

opportunities both during and outside of classes for ample
association with international students. According to one
source, she was keenly interested in all of her students and
was ". . . especially considerate of the foreign students who
studied with her. She often invited these students to her
home for tea. . . ."[90] Rodney Tillman, professor of education at George Washington University, recalled: "It always
interested me that she made sure the international students
got into her home."[91] He, a former colleague, elaborated:
"She found time for working with the whole person; that is,
she was concerned with those aspects which extend beyond
schooling."[92] From a co-worker in an educational organization came the statement: "Dr. Southall has a broad love for
people throughout the world and saw the great possibilities
in the UNESCO program. She has always worked hard in the
interests of students from other lands."[93]

Although numerous examples could be presented concerning
Maycie Southall's interest in improving educational opportunities, quantification of data is not the purpose of this
study; instead, the attempt is made to interpret her many
contributions to education through her influence upon individuals. Thus, three selections are presented that provide

[90]Sue White, personal letter, January 5, 1980.

[91]Rodney Tillman, personal letter, July 11, 1979.

[92]Ibid.

[93]Alida W. Parker, personal letter, May 17, 1979.

insight into the manifold ways in which Maycie Southall has touched the lives of foreign students and educators.

The first example was instigated by correspondence from Ola B. Hiller, a past international president of Delta Kappa Gamma: "I have known several persons who have studied with Dr. Southall at Peabody. They have had high praise for her both as a person and as a professional educator."[94] She added: "Some of her students from other countries have been most grateful for her contributions to their training. One of them was Senorita Hilda Martin. She was for a long time in the Ministry of Education in Lima, Peru."[95] Subsequent correspondence with Hilda Martin provided:

> In the spring term of 1958 and fall quarter of 1959 I had the privilege to attend Dr. Southall's sessions. . . . It is exactly twenty years ago; and I always remember when Dr. Southall with enthusiasm, love, and a good sense of humor encouraged us to become more perceptive and more interested about children's needs, resources, and strategies on teaching that could meet developmental needs. She used to ask us a description of a child we knew more, and also to select an anecdote, a play, a song, and story of a specific age, in order to present in class for analysis and discussion, then to put in practice and again to report the result. After we experimented and developed . . . criteria, we had to prepare our portfolio of learning resources.
>
> My studies at Peabody and especially Dr. Southall's guidance helped me to become more sensitive and to develop a scientific attitude toward children, which means continuity in learning and full enjoyment in my professional work.
>
> I think because of Dr. Southall's influence, my life is devoted to Education. I realize the great need for learning materials in this country; therefore, I decided to write three books for children. . . .

---

[94]Ola B. Hiller, personal letter, May 2, 1979.

[95]Ibid.

Dr. Southall was always warm and friendly with foreign students. She invited us to her home several times.
Also, as sponsor she invited me to become a member of the
Elementary Council, student branch of the Association for
Childhood Education International. The Council worked
to foster a better understanding of childhood education
among all its members. I enjoyed participating in several programs. . . .

Later on, I have seen Dr. Southall on two occasions:
in New York in 1969 at the Delta Kappa Gamma annual convention and in 1970 at the ACEI annual convention in
Atlanta. During plenary sessions she was always forceful in her suggestions and recommendations, especially
in behalf of deprived children. I think because of all
these facts I could describe Dr. Southall as a person
with extraordinary sensitivity, great intelligence, concern, and many effective actions in behalf of children
not only in the U.S.A. but in the world.

Among professional positions I could say that dur-
ing more than fifteen years I worked at the Ministry of
Education as specialist in Teacher Education. In 1970,
I became the first president of ACEI Branch in Lima. I
worked in that organization four years (1970-1974). I
have organized seminars and workshops for teachers. . .
In 1975 I worked with UNESCO as a curriculum consultant.
This year I was assigned as director of Educational
Extension at CENFOTUR. It is an Educative Center of
Industry and Tourism. Until April I worked out there a
project to help children to know more about our cultural
heritage and attractiveness of Peru.[96]

The second example came from Sun Hi Lee Ro, president of

a junior college in Korea:

I have known Dr. Southall since I was a graduate
student from 1958-1961. I had some classes with her.
Dr. Southall is a generous, kind, and thoughtful person.
She is full of love and understanding for others.

As a foreign student, my English often needed cor-
rection. Dr. Southall spent many painstaking hours to
correct my grammar and sentence construction.

I can vividly remember one day when I needed help
with my thesis. Dr. Southall, although very busy, agreed
to look over my draft and return the paper the next day.
When I received the corrected paper the following day, to

---

[96]Hilda Martin, personal letter, June 19, 1979.

my surprise, she had not only returned the paper but had
also included a box of homemade cookies and some fresh
strawberries. What a delightful way to have my paper
corrected! I have often related this incident to my
Korean students who have remarked that I was very fortunate to have had such a thoughtful person.

I am presently president of Pai Chai Junior College
for training mainly kindergarten teachers and Christian
workers.

In 1972, eleven years after I was graduated from
Peabody, I returned to the U.S. to attend the United
Methodist General Conference in Atlanta, Georgia. I
passed through Tennessee to visit Dr. Southall who had
arranged a luncheon for me with some other Korean students. She also presented me with a book, <u>Dauntless
Women in Childhood Education: 1856-1931</u>, in which she
had inscribed, "May these American pioneer leaders, most
of whom I have known and loved, prove inspirational to a
Korean leader in childhood education whom I have known
and loved! May 4, 1972."

I was deeply impressed by her continued kindness,
especially since I had left the school eleven years before.[97]

The last of three selected examples was extracted from a

Christmas letter in which Maycie Southall related to friends

some of her travel experiences during 1970:

For years I had promised myself and my international
students that I would visit them as soon as my time and
money permitted. This spring I rather impulsively decided to join a . . . group for a world tour. . . .

We visited thirteen countries on four continents and
the forty-ninth and fiftieth states of the U.S.A. . . .
The three-day boat trip down the beautiful inner waterway
from Juneau to Seattle was a fitting climax. . . .

Time did not permit a get-together with former students except in Bangkok. When I arrived there, I was
greeted by the smiling faces of three who were preparing
elementary teachers in three different colleges in Bangkok; one who was teaching English in the University; two
who were principals of large secondary schools; one who
was broadcasting a lecture series on child development

[97]Sun Hi Lee Ro, personal letter, July 23, 1979.

from the King's Palace every Sunday morning; and one who
is the private secretary to the King and writes all his
speeches. No one could possibly measure the influence
and impact of these Peabody graduates and others like
them upon the education of their country.[98]

Although Maycie Southall suggested in her letter that
the influence of the graduates of George Peabody College for
Teachers is immeasurable, of equal interest is the fact that
her earlier influence upon those same graduates, as well as
many others, is likewise immeasurable.

Participation in Organizations

Maycie Southall's contributions to education rode, to a
large extent, on the spoken, not written, word. Her reputation as a powerful speaker has been widely recognized.

Her published materials are not voluminous. Her major
contributions include chapters in national yearbooks, bulletins at both state and national levels, and articles published
in professional journals. She served for many years on the
editorial boards of two campus publications, The Peabody
Reflector and the Peabody Journal of Education. Her most
significant writings are noted in her Personal Data Sheet
which appears in Chapter V of this study. Although her published materials are not extensive, Maycie Southall's private
files include numerous unpublished speeches, both typed and
handwritten, that she used throughout years of frequent speaking engagements. She eagerly accepted an astounding number
of invitations to speak to groups whereby she could espouse

---

[98]Maycie Southall, "Christmas Letter," correspondence to
friends, 1970, Private Files of Maycie Southall. (Duplicated.)

the cause of childhood education. On many occasions, Maycie
Southall's itinerary was recorded in The Peabody Reflector;
the frequency of her travels and both the number and variety
of groups to whom she spoke are almost beyond belief. John E.
Windrow noted that his former colleague's presentations were
well received because of her reliance upon, and inclusion of,
carefully studied research.[99]

A former student addressed her professor's efforts by
stating: "While Dr. Southall did not do the writing, quantity-
wise, that some educators have, her total contributions to education are most significant. We know that our Master Teacher
did not write except in the heart and actions of others."[100]
The same observer added:

> She used research findings very effectively in her
> teaching, in her speeches and writings, and in her com-
> mittee work. She never neglected her teaching to do
> research as research or to write. . . . Although her
> number of publications might be more limited than is
> acceptable by many colleges or universities today, her
> comprehension of the role of research is very signifi-
> cant.[101]

Maycie Southall's first and foremost commitment was to
her students. One observer pointed out that the professor,
". . . as well as others on the faculty, could devote time to
the students, for she was not so subject at that time to the
'publish or perish' syndrome."[102] Maycie Southall believed

---

[99]Windrow, interview, May 8, 1979.

[100]McMahan, personal letter, May 21, 1979.

[101]Ibid.

[102]Grove, personal letter, July 30, 1979.

in providing for her students educational experiences that
extended beyond the classroom. Too, she thought that the
betterment of education could be realized through dedicated
participation in professional organizations. She envisioned
such groups as media through which members could communicate
with others and, in so doing, develop understandings, solve
problems, and reach goals common to all. The professor was
gifted with an unusual ability to speak eloquently and per-
suasively; and many educational groups felt the impact of her
presence as a dynamic leader, candid speaker, and enthusiastic
participant. One organization in which Maycie Southall has
displayed exceptional leadership is The Delta Kappa Gamma
Society International. Chapter IV of this study emphasizes
her efforts in behalf of that organization. Because of the
extraordinary amount of time and energy that she has devoted
to a sizable number of organizations, Chapter V of this study
addresses her outstanding efforts and subsequent influence on
education through such media.

Commitment to the Mission of George Peabody College for Teachers

The mission of George Peabody College for Teachers has
traditionally been the training of administrators, supervisors, and teachers to educate others effectively. During
her affiliation with the educational institution, Maycie
Southall became extremely dedicated to its mission. According to one observer, "Dr. Southall had a strong belief in

education, a strong commitment to Peabody, and a way of impressing everyone with the importance of professionalism."[103]

An example of Maycie Southall's strong belief in education was shared by one of her nieces, Frances Whelchel:

> . . . She was always interested in the education of her kin as well as those she taught. She encouraged every niece and nephew to pursue either a college degree or career training and promised them (us) that she would see us through the first year. Consequently, four of her nieces and one great-nephew carried through on this promise, using that year to get us started. Thank goodness, she stood by us and also that we were able to repay her later for her help. On a teacher's salary, that was really stretching her budget.
>
> . . . She really has Peabody College, education, and teaching at the core of her being; and I am sure that will be one of her last thoughts on this earth: Long live Peabody.[104]

A vignette of Maycie Southall's loyalty to George Peabody College for Teachers was shared by Sam Wiggins, a former colleague, who is currently associated with Cleveland (Ohio) State University:

> Years ago there was a minor cheating scandal involving a few Peabody students, and a small blurb about it appeared in _Time_ magazine. At about that time, Maycie happened to be on a plane returning to Peabody from a speaking engagement and spotted this blurb "maligning" Peabody, as she expressed it. She confided to me that she had never torn anything out of a magazine before, except her own copies, but was overcome by the thought that dozens of other passengers would be reading this; so she tore the article out and destroyed it. "I know there were millions of copies of the thing printed," she explained, "but at least I could reduce the damage done to Peabody's reputation a little bit. I felt guilty, but I felt it was my duty to uphold Peabody's good name against smirching of its reputation this way."[105]

---

[103]Ramsey, personal letter, May 9, 1979.

[104]Whelchel, personal letter, July 10, 1979.

[105]Sam [P.] Wiggins, personal letter, October 15, 1979.

Campus Involvement

In addition to her regular teaching responsibilities, Maycie Southall accepted positions of leadership in a variety of campus concerns. She was in charge of several conferences and workshops held during many summer sessions, she served as a member of influential faculty committees, and she devoted considerable time to student activities.

Leadership in Conferences and Workshops

A brief description of a conference that Maycie Southall directed in 1950 is presented as an example of her efforts. According to an article in a campus publication, groundwork was being laid during the spring quarter for about a dozen workshops and conferences that would ". . . comprise an integral part of the 1950 summer session."[106] Such meetings had become popular attractions:

> Requiring enormous amounts of faculty time and planning, these conferences have for a great number of years been a significant phase of Peabody summer schools, attracting thousands of professional men and women, as well as hundreds of laymen, to the campus.

> Generally speaking, this summer's conferences are being designed for specific groups, with an emphasis on the question, "What direct bearing will the program of this meeting have upon the professional lives of southern administrators and teachers, and subsequently on the lives of the children of the South?"[107]

Maycie Southall directed the conference entitled "Southern Leaders in Childhood Education." Emphasis was placed on the

---

[106]Ruth Lee, "Summer Conferences and Workshops," *The Peabody Reflector* 23 (April 1950):105.

[107]Ibid.

improvement of educational opportunities for children in the

South:

> Initial conference of the summer quarter will be
> the second annual conference of southern leaders in
> childhood education slated for June 21-23. . . .

> "Working Together for Children" will be the general
> theme of the meeting which is being planned to bring to-
> gether the educational leaders of the southern region to
> unify and coordinate their efforts into a program of
> action directed toward improving the educational oppor-
> tunities of the children of the South.

> Conference membership will consist of a group of
> educational leaders who have been recommended by one
> or more of several national organizations, vitally con-
> cerned for the welfare of children. Each person is to
> be selected because of the position of professional
> leadership or influence held in the organization and
> state represented at the conference.

> Participating in the activities of this year's
> conference will be representatives from 17 state and
> national organizations. . . .

> Dr. Southall has announced that the nation's top
> persons in the field of elementary education will be
> brought to the campus as consultants for the three-day
> meeting. . . .[108]

An evaluation of the June conference was printed in the

July issue of The Peabody Reflector:

> One of the outstanding conferences on Peabody cam-
> pus this summer was the second Conference of Southern
> Leaders in Childhood Education. Its purpose was to find
> ways of improving the education of children in the south-
> ern region by unifying and coordinating the efforts of
> the lay and educational leaders in this region with those
> of the state and national agencies. It brought together
> representatives from more than 17 cooperating organiza-
> tions, all of which are vitally interested in the welfare
> of children. Under the capable leadership of Dr. Maycie
> Southall, who directed the conference, study groups at-
> tacked the following ten major problems affecting the wel-
> fare of children: Indecent Living Conditions in School;

---

[108]Ibid.

Indifference to Children's Welfare; Teachers Poorly Pre-
pared for What They Are Doing; Lack of Inspired Leader-
ship; Unwholesome Pressure on Children; Three Isolates:
Home--School--Community; Meager and Unbalanced School
Living; Little or No Guidance Services for Children;
School Living Which Miseducates; Ill-Defined Goals.

The conference closed with carefully laid plans
for continued study and the distribution of its pro-
ceedings.[109]

A conference participant recalled that the study groups
". . . brought their findings, conclusions, and implications
together for the joint closing session."[110] She evaluated:
"From this, significant influences toward improving opportunities for children resulted; and waves from it continue today.
We left with deeper commitment and renewed enthusiasm."[111]

Membership on Faculty Committees

Maycie Southall served as a member of various committees
that were instrumental in directing the course of George Peabody College for Teachers. Two committees, to which she devoted extensive time and effort, were the Committee of Eleven
and the Ruml Plan Committee.

The Committee of Eleven was formed in 1945 by Henry H.
Hill soon after his induction as president of George Peabody
College for Teachers. President Hill selected the members
from faculty nominations. The committee was charged with
the responsibility of inquiring into the unique function or

---

[109]"Editorial Comment," The Peabody Reflector 23
(July 1950):202.

[110]McMahan, personal letter, May 21, 1979.

[111]Ibid.

functions of the educational institution. The members studied
carefully the issues during regularly scheduled weekly, as
well as called, meetings throughout the academic year. The
committee formed twenty-two subcommittees and reviewed their
reports. The members sought counsel from educational consultants at the national level, from alumni, and from interested
organizations. After they had studied the role of George Peabody College for Teachers, the members made recommendations
and summarized their efforts in a report to President Hill.[112]
The work of the committee did not go unheeded according to a
statement made by President Felix Robb in 1961: "Our last
. . . study with wide faculty participation was conducted
about 15 or 16 years ago by the Committee of Eleven. At that
time approximately 150 separate recommendations were produced,
the majority of which were eventually put into effect."[113]

President Hill solicited nominations from his faculty in
1959 and subsequently appointed Maycie Southall to membership
on the Ruml Plan Committee, so designated because its members
were directed to study the ideas presented by Beardsley Ruml,
assisted by Donald Morrison, in a publication entitled Memo to
a College Trustee (New York: McGraw Hill Book Company, 1959).
The committee members were charged with appraising the sound-
ness of the ideas and determining their usefulness in regard

[112]"The Unique Role of Peabody College," including letter
from F. Lynwood Wren to Henry H. Hill, The Peabody Reflector
19 (November 1946):363-64.

[113]Felix [C.] Robb, "President Looks at Peabody's Problems, Needs, Aims, Hopes," The Peabody Reflector 34 (September-
October 1961):133.

to the educational institution's future. They studied carefully both the instructional program and fiscal problems after
which they prepared a publication entitled A Report to the
Board of Trustees of George Peabody College for Teachers.[114]

Support of Student Activities

Maycie Southall contributed her support to student activities that were oriented toward education. A campus organization to which she gave an exceptional amount of time and effort
was the Elementary Council, a branch of the Association for
Childhood Education International. Lucy Gage had earlier organized the local group.[115] She and Maycie Southall shared
responsibilities as faculty advisors for several years. Both
educators continued to support the organization in an advisory
capacity until near their retirement from the educational institution in the 1940s and 1960s, respectively. The Elementary
Council was a very active campus group; according to a 1960
article, the unit was thought to be the only one in the country
that met during the summer.[116] Additional details concerning
Maycie Southall's work with the Elementary Council are included
in Chapter V under the subheading "Association for Childhood
Education International."

---

[114]Sam P. Wiggins, chairman, and others on the Ruml Plan
Committee, A Report to the Board of Trustees of George Peabody
College for Teachers (Nashville: The College, 1960), p. ii.

[115]Betty Friedrich, "Student Organizations," The Peabody
Reflector 18 (November 1945):360.

[116]"Summer Officers of Elementary Council with Dr. Hunter,
National ACEI Head," The Peabody Reflector, Summer Supplement
11 (July 28, 1960):[4].

Influence

During the 1920s, Maycie Southall became the recipient of three degrees conferred by George Peabody College for Teachers. During the same decade, she also attended classes at Teachers College of Columbia University and the University of Chicago because she wanted to learn directly from the renowned educational leaders of the era. Then, in 1929, Maycie Southall accepted a position on the teaching staff of George Peabody College for Teachers which was to span a period of thirty-five years. She had apparently selected wisely the educational institutions for in 1934 Lester M. Wilson and I. L. Kandel wrote:

> If four institutions of higher education were to be named which are exerting the greatest influence upon public school practice in the elementary and secondary fields, these might well be: Teachers College of Columbia University; School of Education of the University of Chicago; Stanford University; and George Peabody College.[117]

An article written in 1965 addressed the leadership contributed to education by the women graduates of George Peabody College for Teachers. Extractions include:

> In its long history, it is not known just how many women have attended Peabody but the number would be impressive. We do know 1,958 were graduated from the old South campus, and from its present campus Peabody has graduated 17,369: 8,533 bachelor's, 8,564 master's, 173 specialists in education, 24 doctors of education, and 75 doctors of philosophy. 2,696 different women attended Peabody in one of its big years. Of these, 1,496 were graduate students. In that same year, 227 were awarded the M.A. degree.

---

[117]Lester M. Wilson and I. L. Kandel, Introduction to the Study of American Education (New York: Thomas Nelson and Sons, 1934), p. 296.

> The quality of teaching done by these and their
> fellow teachers throughout the country and the leader-
> ship they have provided constitutes one of Peabody's
> great services. The 99 women doctoral graduates have
> contributed their creative influence to all the major
> areas of the nation, from New England to California;
> from Florida to Washington. Some of the College's
> choice doctoral daughters have remained at Peabody, as
> instances: Susan Riley, Susan Gray, Maycie Southall,
> and others. Some on leave have returned to their
> positions where they have established themselves in
> their college's highest tradition. . . . These have
> taught well a prodigious number of students, who in
> turn have taught well a prodigious number of others.[118]

Maycie Southall had an opportunity to influence a large

number of women who attended the educational institution for

she was a professor of elementary education and traditionally

elementary education majors have been women; however, many

men also came under her influence, especially through enroll-

ment in her courses that pertained to supervision and cur-

riculum. In spite of her reputation as a professor of high

expectations, her classes were extremely large. Many former

students have recently referred to the size of their classes

in which more than one hundred enrollees was not unusual.

Especially large classes were experienced during the

1950s because of the enrollment of World War II veterans.

Too, the summer sessions traditionally increased the size

of the student body because of the nature of the educational

institution; that is, administrators and teachers employed

during the academic year sought professional improvement

during their vacation. Maycie Southall's recent analysis of

---

[118] "Peabody Women . . . An Editorial," The Peabody
Reflector 38 (March-April 1965):inside front cover.

class records kept in her private files revealed that during
the summer of 1950, for example, she taught three courses in
which a total of more than 325 students had enrolled.[119]

Maycie Southall's educational efforts included an unusual
amount of correspondence pertaining to projects, educational
organizations, and students. A former student assistant was
impressed with the volume of her correspondence: "Her desk
was never cleared. She was slow in answering mail, but she
answered it all conscientiously over a period of time. She
wrote more letters than any other professor on campus (her
secretaries kept track as did the mailing room)."[120] Her far-
reaching influence upon the careers of her students can be
realized, in part, through an analysis of the time and energy
she spent in preparing recommendations on their behalf for
potential positions in education. Maycie Southall retained
copies of many of her letters of recommendation; they are
filed alphabetically according to each student's surname.
For the purpose of this study, records filed under one alpha-
betic letter, the "B," were selected for enumeration; more
than 230 letters of recommendation were counted in this portion alone. A former student provided insight into Maycie
Southall's influence upon educational careers through letters
of recommendation by sharing her personal experience:

> I have thought of her fondly through the years. I
> had taught in Oxford [Mississippi] for 18 years before

---

[119]Southall, interview, June 5, 1979.

[120]Kjer, personal letter, August 8, 1979.

I went to Peabody in 1948. She will probably remember our conversations about William Faulkner's mother with whom I lived for 16 years. . . . I took a year away from teaching in 1948 to get my Master's degree. Miss Southall was my major professor. . . .

She always took a special interest in each of her students whom she had as majors and gave them much of her time. I remember the special conferences that she had. Her days were filled with teaching and conferences. . . .

When I left Peabody, I was offered several jobs through Miss Southall's recommendation, not my application. I chose to go to Delta State College in Mississippi as first grade teacher in the Demonstration School and assistant professor of education. I stayed there for six years and was then offered a job as kindergarten teacher and assistant professor of education at Mississippi State College for Women. I had charge of the kindergarten program which included the teaching of a course in kindergarten education to college seniors. I stayed there for 16 years and retired in 1971. . . .[121]

Maycie Southall's influence upon education has been felt in a variety of ways. From a recipient of a Ph.D. degree, the requirements of which were completed under the guidance of Maycie Southall, came the analysis: "Dr. Southall's service to education would be difficult to measure, it is so great."[122]

During the initial stages of this study, a letter of inquiry was sent to selected persons in order to obtain information from primary sources concerning the life and contributions to education of Maycie Southall. The letter suggested inclusion of anecdotes or incidents that would tend to reflect the real Maycie Southall within the context of her service to education. The letter included a request that the respondents be objective in their replies; that is, the letter admonished:

---

[121] Frances Ward, personal letter, January 8, 1980.

[122] Maude Myrtice Pledger, personal letter, May 4, 1979.

"Although 'sweetness and light' are flattering, the quality of Dr. Southall's efforts will be reflected most clearly through substance." (See Appendix.) Attached to a response from a former student to the letter of inquiry was an informal, but thought-provoking, aside:

> Sorry this treatise is "sugar and light." However, this is why Maycie Southall is who she is in the field of education. I appreciate the fact that specific anecdotes may lend themselves to sigmas and square roots, thence to a fine, fine dissertation. Such treatment of the life of Dr. Southall in education offers a very poor commentary.[123]

Excerpts from the same respondent's letter have been interspersed throughout various portions of this study; in regard to Maycie Southall's influence on his life, he shared:

> . . . She was a member of my doctoral committee-- for which I shall forever be grateful. When times got rough with the committee, Dr. Southall held my hand. Her counseling, advice, and guidance were most beneficial. . . .

> Prior to studying with Dr. Southall I had served as secondary instructor of mathematics, athletic coach, and administrator. Through her influence I have since been an elementary school principal and for the past twenty years professor of elementary education.[124]

Many, many testimonies to Maycie Southall's influence have been contributed by students, colleagues, and friends. The attempt is made in this study to interpret her influence not through tabulated data, although the number of responses has been impressive, but through reflections shared by a representative few of the many whose lives have been touched by her efforts.

---

[123]Guess, personal letter, May 31, 1979.

[124]Ibid.

Regarding his former colleague's influence, Rodney Tillman
commented: "I know of few who have contributed as much as
Dr. Southall and none who have done more for furthering elementary education."[125] Another observer shared:

> Dr. Southall was, and is, one of the most sincere,
> capable, dedicated educators of her day. She did not seem
> to me at any time to be promoting Maycie K. Southall, but
> she was continually promoting education. Her aim seemed
> to be to raise the standard of all education. She wanted
> all children to have an education, or a better education,
> as the case might be--and what better way to do this than
> to educate teachers![126]

Several contributors addressed Maycie Southall's role as
a dedicated teacher. According to one source, "Her most significant influence has been as a teacher herself working
through her students, so many of whom have been outstanding
teachers who went on to supervise or to teach other teachers
within a school system or college."[127] Another source provided: "I suspect that her great influence was through the
people who came under her guidance at Peabody."[128] Many students came to the educational institution because of Maycie
Southall: "There is no doubt she was a great influence in
the South; and through her work and that of her students, she
influenced many to come to Peabody."[129] Students returned
to the campus because of her presence there: "She inspired

---

[125]Tillman, personal letter, July 11, 1979.

[126]Duckworth, personal letter, July 8, 1979.

[127]Grove, personal letter, July 30, 1979.

[128]Humphreys, personal letter, July 14, 1979.

[129]Ibid.

scores and scores of students to keep coming back to Peabody
to continue their study with such a dynamic and forceful
instructor."[130] Her reputation spread:

> She has been a real advocate in attracting students
> to Peabody, not only personally but through her students.
> My county supervisor . . . had been a major of hers and
> had contributed greatly to my appreciation of what Pea-
> body afforded in terms of professional preparation. (My
> mother had always referred to Peabody as the Columbia of
> the South.)[131]

Maycie Southall's efforts became known to students in
other teacher training institutions. Elizabeth Whorley, who
attended Middle Tennessee State University, remarked:

> To those of us who were educated at schools that
> were, at that time, primarily teacher training institu-
> tions, the name Maycie Southall became synonymous with
> Peabody and with education. Middle Tennessee State
> University had its Mary Hall--Peabody had its Maycie
> Southall. It was realized these two had common objec-
> tives.
>
> As a beginning teacher, it was not uncommon to
> read an article or hear an in-service program with the
> Southall name attached. Her knowledge in depth and
> scope in all educational concerns, methods, and issues
> was recognized.[132]

Maycie Southall's attractiveness as an educator was not
confined to her home state; a co-worker in an educational
organization stated: "North Carolinians have always felt a
special affection . . . for she served in our state . . . as
a consultant. . . . Quite a number of teachers sought their
Masters' degrees from Peabody because of her example and

---

[130]Sparks, personal letter, July 23, 1979.

[131]Grove, personal letter, July 30, 1979.

[132]Elizabeth Whorley, personal letter, February 21, 1980.

influence."[133] Another co-worker in an educational organization noted that the professor's reputation had begun to
spread early during her teaching career: "Many years ago
(1935-39 during my undergraduate years and 1939-40 when I
began my graduate work) and many states away (Pennsylvania),
I heard of Dr. Southall and her work for public kindergartens
and primary education."[134]

A professor emeritus of California State University
described Maycie Southall's influence at the national level:

> She has been influential nationwide in encourag-
> ing her students and fellow workers to implement the
> child-centered educational practices that Teachers
> College faculty set up (largely in theory, not so much
> actual practice). Dr. Southall kept her feet on the
> ground and thus taught her students to go out and set
> up child-centered programs that worked.[135]

Maycie Southall's influence reached beyond the nation's
borders. Mary Jo Husk, a retired elementary school supervisor,
recently described her professor of the 1940s: "Dr. Southall
is known throughout our country and in foreign lands. She has
former students all over the world. . . . She was a very dynamic teacher and is still a woman of great influence in many
circles."[136] Dorothy Morton, 1979-81 president of Xi State,
The Delta Kappa Gamma Society International, remarked that
Maycie Southall's ". . . recognition extends beyond the borders

---

[133]Phebe H. Emmons, personal letter, June 6, 1979.

[134]June Wilcox, personal letter, April 8, 1980.

[135]Mildred Dawson, personal letter, May 23, 1979.

[136]Mary Jo Husk, personal letter, February 14, 1980.

of the United States into many lands where outstanding former students honor her as they serve in their own country."[137] John Julia McMahan addressed Maycie Southall's reputation in this country and internationally:

> Dr. Southall was my major professor. My under-
> graduate major professor at East Texas State Teachers
> College, Commerce, Texas, had taught in Peabody Demon-
> stration School; many others were Peabody graduates.
> She and many others urged me to select Dr. Southall as
> my major professor. How fortunate I have felt through-
> out these 43 years that I did! She has been a true,
> abiding friend. Her influence is immeasurable. . . .

> Few educators have the knowledge of the educational
> field that Dr. Southall has. Her depth and breadth of
> each area--early elementary, elementary, curriculum,
> supervision, teacher education--have been recognized
> and respected by her colleagues both in this country
> and abroad. She is one of the outstanding thinkers and
> leaders of this century.[138]

Numerous former students readily acknowledged the influ-ence of Maycie Southall on their educational careers. One, for example, wrote: "Dr. Southall helped me greatly to en-vision and build a beautiful forty-one years with children and teachers."[139] From another former student came the com-ments: "Dr. Maycie Southall is one of the peaks of my gradu-ate work. She has initiated more programs and motivated more people in behalf of children than anyone else I know."[140] Currently employed as a coordinator of federal programs with the Hughes (Arkansas) Public Schools, Euleta Murdoch wrote:

---

[137] Dorothy Morton, personal letter, April 29, 1980.

[138] McMahan, personal letter, May 5, 1979.

[139] Rubie E. Smith, personal letter, June 2, 1979.

[140] Harold C. Cauthen, personal letter, January 12, 1980.

In my opinion, Dr. Southall is elementary education personified for doubtless her influence has touched more teachers than anyone else in the South or perhaps the nation. Had it not been for Dr. Southall, I would never have gone on to complete my Ed.S. degree; so I am very grateful for her influence.[141]

Two letters that addressed various facets of Maycie Southall's influence are included; the first was contributed by Robert Gilstrap, professor of education at George Mason University, Fairfax, Virginia:

There are many teachers who pass through our lives as students. From kindergarten through doctoral studies, the number probably comes close to one hundred adult members of our society with whom I had direct contact as a learner. Although each of those teachers probably influenced my life in ways that I do not even fully realize, only a few of them stand out in my mind as memorable teachers. Maycie Southall is one of those teachers.

When I arrived at Peabody College for Teachers in the summer of 1961 to begin my doctoral studies as a National Defense Education Act Fellow, I felt quite a bit of apprehension. I had never studied there before and knew no one on the faculty or student body. I was told, however, by my mentor, Dr. Dell Kjer of North Texas State College in Denton, to be certain to make an early visit by the office of Dr. Southall, his former advisor on his doctoral program. Anxious to make contact with someone who at least knew someone whom I knew, I took Dell's advice and went to meet Dr. Southall.

Although the details of this first meeting are not as clear as I would like due to the passage of time, my initial impressions of Dr. Southall are still vivid. Surrounded by stacks of correspondence and professional journals and student papers, Dr. Southall was conferring with her student secretary on a high priority item that appeared to be of importance beyond the small Peabody campus. She was talking quickly and excitedly about the topic at hand and truly radiated with enthusiasm.

I introduced myself . . . and explained that Dr. Kjer had suggested that I come by to meet her. She interrupted what she was doing and chatted with me for several minutes indicating what I felt was a genuine interest in me as a

[141]Murdoch, personal letter, October 19, 1979.

new student at Peabody. I left my first meeting very
impressed with her warmth and beauty as a person. It
was a first impression that never changed.

In the fall of that year, I registered for my first
course with Dr. Southall. As I recall, the course was
entitled "Research in Elementary Education." The first
day of class stands out in my memory because she arrived
holding, along with her materials, a small bud vase with
a pink rose in it. She placed the vase on the table and
began talking enthusiastically about what we were to do
during our term together.

Perhaps there was a day when Dr. Southall failed
to bring a flower to class in an attempt to make the
environment of our drab classroom more beautiful, but I
don't remember. Later when I became a teacher educator
as well, I remembered how much Dr. Southall's vase and
flower had meant to me as a symbol of her philosophy of
teaching; and I made special efforts as well to make my
classrooms places where my students would want to be.

I had many opportunities to work with Dr. Southall
throughout my two years at Peabody. Although she was
not my major professor and advisor, I had frequent contact with her as a member of the Elementary Council, a
student branch of the Association for Childhood Education International. Dr. Southall also involved me in
some of the state and national activities of ACEI as
well. Through her example, she helped me better understand the significant role that professional organizations can and should play in the education of teachers
after they have received their initial training. Because of these experiences, I have continued my active
involvement in professional organizations that are
primarily concerned with the continuing education of
teachers.

I could give many more examples supporting why she
is one of those few memorable teachers in my life as a
student and how she has inspired me as a teacher educator. . . . If I were to put into one statement, however,
what I learned from Dr. Southall, I would have to focus
on the ways in which she revealed her concern for her
students and the children whom they were to teach. She
showed me by her example that it was possible to be a
successful teacher educator and leader by putting one's
major emphasis on people rather than the subject matter
being taught. I shall always be thankful for the experience of knowing and working with her and appreciate
being able to put into writing some of my thoughts.[142]

---

[142]Robert Gilstrap, personal letter, January 22, 1980.

The second letter selected for inclusion because of its relevance to the subject of Maycie Southall's influence was written by Elizabeth Sutton Dawson, retired from her position as educational specialist, Education for Disadvantaged Children, U.S. Office of Education, Washington, D.C.:

We received your letter of May 12 [1979] regarding Dr. Maycie K. Southall of whom we are tremendously fond and to whom we feel greatly indebted.

My husband who was a doctoral student with her at Peabody was quite ill and suggested that I try to comply with your request; but he was so ill I just did not find the time, and since his death on September 15 I have been involved in a number of necessary responsibilities.

Dr. Dawson placed Dr. Southall at the top of his list of educators. His professional associations with her spanned more than fifty-five years. In fact, it was she who introduced me to Dr. Dawson on Peabody College campus in 1941 (I am his second wife). He was speaking at the Curriculum Conference. I was a graduate student of hers, and she had excused the class session to hear Dr. Dawson. (She was my major professor for my Master's degree in 1941.)

I think Dr. Southall has been and continues to be one of the very great educators of our time. She always had advanced ideas about education; and, in my book, she has done more to improve instruction in the schools of the southern region than any other one person. Truly, she is a friend of the child, any child and all children regardless of creed, color, age, sex, or ability. She is an ardent student of child growth and development, and no one has a deeper understanding of children than does Maycie K. Southall. Indeed, she has had a brilliant career filled with noteworthy activities and crusades for the welfare of the nation's children and youth. . . .

One little story: When Howard A. Dawson was a student at Peabody, he had his wife and little son, age 3-5, with him. Little Howard knew his way around the campus and was frequently seen riding his tricycle on the walks; but one day his mother missed the tricycle, and no one could find it. Bright and early one morning after it had been missing three or four days, Maycie Southall appeared at the apartment door with the tricycle. She was en route to the library very early and strolled among the flowers and shrubs while waiting for the library to open. Suddenly, she came upon the tricycle hidden under some shrubbery; and, even with her busy schedule, she took time to deliver it to Howard, Jr. This is typical; Maycie Southall always found time to do kind deeds for others.

. . . You can see I am an admirer of Dr. Southall; I love her and am grateful that I was privileged to have had her as a professor.[143]

As Others Saw Her

From the numerous communications contributed to this research project, seven letters were selected as the closure for Chapter III. They were chosen on the basis of pertinence to the history of elementary education during the time frame under review, to the significant role played by George Peabody College for Teachers in the training of teachers and educational leaders, and to the diversity of aspects from which can be viewed Maycie Southall's life and contributions to education. Presented chronologically, the letters were purposely selected to represent various periods of time during her teaching career.

Maude Myrtice Pledger's letter was prefaced with a personal note which included: "The enclosed is my 1928 story. I am not at all sure it is well told. I only know that life took a new turn for me then."[144] The writer continued: "In fairness, I should say that I had wonderful years at what is now University of Central Arkansas. Otherwise, I could not

---

[143]Elizabeth Sutton Dawson, personal letter, October 20, 1979.

[144]Maude Myrtice Pledger, personal letter, May 20, 1979.

have done the Peabody work as I did. I have warm places in
my heart for both schools."[145] Then, she related:

> In August 1928, I went to Peabody for the first
> time. In some way I got registered for a course in
> which I was the only classroom teacher. The other stu-
> dents were principals, supervisors, and candidates for
> higher degrees. Dr. Southall was one of the latter
> group. In the last half of the term, there were oral
> reports. I worked hard on mine, but I was paralyzed
> with fright at the thought of getting up before that
> group. When my day came, I got up with my charts; and
> Miss Southall came from the back row to help me hold
> them. She really came to help hold _me_ up! When the
> class was dismissed, she followed me out of the build-
> ing to tell me the report was good and I did well.

> When the summer was over (I went), I left Peabody
> planning never to return. I did not go back in 1929.
> In the meantime, Miss Southall became Dr. Southall and
> a faculty member; so I returned in 1930 and 1931 when
> I got the Master's degree. I went because she was there.

> In the mid-thirties, I began spending more summers
> at Peabody with nothing special in mind. I loved school
> and learning. One evening I was driving with her when
> she brought up the subject of a higher degree. She
> thought that I had done too much to throw it away. I
> stated rather emphatically that I could not do it. I
> had no notion of trying to do it. Suddenly she drove
> into a parking space and said, "We are going to settle
> this thing right now." Of course, you know who won; but
> I was sure in my own mind through the exams that I could
> not do it. When the last chapter of the dissertation
> was in, I walked down Eighteenth Avenue alone and laughed
> aloud at how far a little town girl had come.

> Both of these situations tell of one of her strong-
> est traits--the capacity to support without allowing one
> to become dependent. She supplied that kind of support
> to many who needed it.

> At one time, I taught in a demonstration school in
> a state university where all the teachers in the elemen-
> tary school were her majors. It is one person's opinion,
> of course, but I think it was one of the best elementary
> schools I ever saw in action.

> Dr. Southall is a unique person--the only one of her
> kind. There are strong convictions of the objectives of

----

[145]Ibid.

Peabody and its work. That and integrity, personal belief in good work, and fairness make the unique person.

P.S.: Dr. Southall worked alongside male professors
all the way. That was not always easy. A few may have
tried to make it less easy. This, I believe, did influence her no matter how hard she tried. It took a courageous woman in those days. There are some changes since
then. I know because I spent my last two decades teaching university classes where I was the only woman in my
department. They were happy years.[146]

D. L. Mumpower met Maycie Southall in 1935 when he

entered George Peabody College for Teachers. Employed as

her aide, he learned to respect her as a model for his pro-

fessional behavior. He addressed particularly her efforts

during the 1930s:

First, may I compliment you on your choice of subject for a doctoral dissertation. Dr. Southall has,
indeed, contributed much to the field of education; and
it is fitting that her contributions be recognized in
this way.

Second, let me clarify my relationship with her.
I was never a student, graduate or undergraduate, of
hers. My major at Peabody was English, so I never was
fortunate enough to take any of Dr. Southall's classes.
But I was her student aide during my four years as an
undergraduate student, and I saw a side of her that
perhaps her students didn't see.

Incidentally, I never called her Dr. Southall. To
me, she was always Miss Southall. She was such a feminine person and so ladylike that I didn't feel right
calling her by such a defeminizing term as "Doctor." I
guess you'd say it was a compliment to her femininity.
At any rate, that's the way I felt it; and I hope that's
the way she took it. (I shall call her Dr. Southall in
this communication to make my comments consistent with
your study.)

When I entered Peabody in 1935, I secured some . . .
financial help through the National Youth Administration.
This paid my tuition, requiring in turn that I put in so
many hours each week working in an assigned place. My
assigned place was the office of Dr. Southall. It was
the first of many lucky breaks I had while at Peabody.

---

[146]Ibid.

My duties were mainly secretarial. Dr. Southall carried on a voluminous correspondence; and it was my job to take the letters she would dictate to me (I had studied a little shorthand), type them, and prepare them for mailing. There were other duties, such as running errands, but typing correspondence was my principal activity. Though her office was in the Social-Religious Building, my desk and typewriter were in the Administration Building; so I spent considerable time shuttling back and forth from one to the other.

We must have both been satisfied--she with me as an aide and I with her as a boss--for each year the assignment was renewed. I even worked through the summers. When I graduated in 1939, I left Peabody and went off to teach. (During the next 40 years, I taught high school English for 7 years, was a high school assistant principal for 3 years, taught 22 years at the college level, spent 2 years in graduate school, served 5 years in the Army, and have been retired for 1 year.) After my first year of teaching, I returned to Peabody for the next two summers for graduate study. Someone else was in my place in Dr. Southall's office, so I was assigned elsewhere-- this time in the Placement Bureau working for Dr. Otis McBride. (I called him "Otis" but never felt free enough to call Dr. Southall "Maycie," any more than I could have called my mother by her first name.) After World War II, I returned for one more summer's work to receive my M.A. degree; but then I was on the G.I. Bill and no longer had to type letters to pay for my tuition. Even though I did not work for Dr. Southall during my graduate summers, I maintained contact with her for I always had great respect and admiration for her.

As everyone knows, Dr. Southall was a very hard worker and was thoroughly dedicated to her work and to Peabody College. She exacted this same dedication from me, though she didn't do it through the use of force. Somehow (I have never fully understood how) she made me _want_ to work. Perhaps she did it by example, for she certainly did set an excellent work example for students and workers like me. One had to go at a fast pace just to keep up with her, but it wasn't that one felt driven to keep up--rather, it was that she made one _want_ to do it. In spite of her long hours, she was careful never to demand more of my time than the exact hours per week I was required to put in. And when there was personal correspondence for me to type, she did not let the Government pay for it as many would have done; instead, she counted it as extra work and paid me out of her own pocket.

Sometimes instead of dictating a letter, she would write it out in longhand. I don't need to tell you what this meant, for anyone who has ever read (or tried to read) Dr. Southall's handwriting knows what I'm talking about. She has such a quick mind that her hand, in trying to keep pace with her thoughts, has to abbreviate words in order to get them all down in time to start on the next thought. This abbreviation was accomplished not by consciously omitting letters but by turning letters and even whole syllables or words into long squiggly lines. I achieved a fair amount of success at reading her handwriting; but it was never easy, even for her. I distinctly recall one morning she showed me something she had written the night before and asked me, "What does that say?"

As I had great respect for her as a person, so also did I have great respect for her as a professional worker. When I was an undergraduate student, I always thought that if I ever got a doctor's degree I would want to be as learned and as dedicated as Dr. Southall. I did finally get a Ph.D. in 1957--in psychology at the University of Missouri. Though I had other professors as models for my professional behavior, none ever inspired me to standards higher than Dr. Southall's.

As an English major, I knew little about elementary education. But after four years of working with Dr. Southall, I became a convert to the importance of that field. It was not that she purposely indoctrinated; rather, it was that she brought so much enthusiasm to her work that it was infectious. One could hardly be around her without feeling the tremendous importance of elementary education in the lives of boys and girls. The experience gave me a better balanced picture of the whole educational process, and today I think I am a better psychologist because of it.

Even in those days (the 1930s), when I was majoring in English, I had strong leanings toward psychology. I think it was this that caused me to reject one aspect of educational philosophy that Dr. Southall espoused. She was dead set in those days against ability grouping. But I thought it was something that would benefit students and teachers alike. Dr. Southall and I never talked about this, and she would probably be surprised today to learn that my feelings about ability grouping had been so diametrically opposed to hers. She, of course, had good reasons for opposing ability grouping, mainly on social grounds; but I felt there were equally good reasons for using it. Whether her views have mellowed over the years, I don't know. There seems to be much more ability grouping in schools now than there was in the 1930s, and my own feelings on the subject have not changed. But if Dr. Southall and I had ever discussed our differences on this subject, I am certain

she would have presented her side forcefully and eloquently. Though I have now formally retired from education (after spending the past 21 years on the faculty
at the University of Southwestern Louisiana), I still
work part time in the field of psychology, mainly doing
psychological testing of exceptional children. In this
capacity I have occasion to recommend various forms of
ability grouping, and I often wonder what Dr. Southall
would say about that.

In the previous paragraph, I said that Dr. Southall
would have presented her side "forcefully." Well, she
was a forceful person but in a quiet way. She knew the
field of education so well that anything she said had
the force of solid scholarship behind it. That was the
kind of forcefulness she displayed.

Since I spent many hours in Dr. Southall's office,
I came in frequent contact with her graduate students.
I even typed master's theses for some of them (for a
fee, of course). What impressed me most in her relationship with these students was her seemingly inexhaustible
patience. The word "unflappable" had not been invented
then, but whoever invented it must have had Dr. Southall
in mind. She answered some of the dumbest questions
without even losing her "cool" (another addition to the
language) and without causing the student to feel the
least embarrassment. Occasionally in my presence she
would give vent to some feelings of disgust or anger,
but she was always too much of a lady to express these
feelings in front of the students themselves.

When I received my B.S. degree . . ., Dr. Southall
gave me a graduation gift. It was a most appropriate
one--a Peabody plate. I say it was appropriate because
it symbolized two of the loves of her life--Peabody
College and the field of education. The plate serves as
a constant reminder to me of those two forces--forces
for good, not only in my own life but in the lives of
many, many others. It is also a reminder to me of
Dr. Southall and my association with her. I may dis-
card other souvenirs, but I could never part with that
Peabody plate. . . .[147]

William M. Alexander, professor emeritus of the College

of Education, University of Florida, chaired the Department

of Education at George Peabody College for Teachers from

1958 until his resignation in 1963. His acquaintance with

---

[147]D. L. Mumpower, personal letter, June 9, 1979.

Maycie Southall dates back, however, to the early 1940s. He reminisced about her contributions to education:

> I am pleased to have the opportunity offered by your letter . . . to contribute to your dissertation on Dr. Maycie Southall. I first became acquainted with Dr. Southall in the early 1940s and worked closely with her during my faculty days at Peabody, 1958-63, so that I have followed her career with interest and admiration for many years!
>
> My acquaintance with Dr. Southall started with a Tennessee Supervisors Meeting we both attended some time during the period I was on the faculty of the University of Tennessee, 1941-43 (before I went into military service, World War II). I remember very clearly how attractive she appeared, what fine contributions she made to the meeting, and her personal interest in me as a colleague in the same state also much interested in supervision and curriculum development. Our acquaintance was interrupted by World War II but resumed through the Association for Supervision and Curriculum Development in which we both worked as members, committee members, contributors, and officers throughout the life of the organization.
>
> When I was appointed to the Peabody faculty in the fall, 1957, one of my first notes of good wishes and help came from Maycie. It may have been hard to read, but it was very heartening! That summer, when I was first offered the appointment and was giving lectures at Peabody, she entertained me with a group of students and faculty in her apartment. I am sure that no member of the Peabody faculty has welcomed and entertained as many new faculty members and students as Dr. Southall! When I became chairman of the Department of Education, later in 1958, I had special reason to observe her indefatigable energies in behalf of students and the College. No faculty member went to greater effort to work out student programs, to find schedules that fitted, and to resolve conflicts of many kinds. When I resigned the chairmanship in 1963, it was Maycie who kindly gave me a tribute (she wrote it out, having it typed, for me, and I keep it in my "Pepper-Upper" file!) for the Department.
>
> During 1969-71, I was president of the Peabody Alumni Association; and therefore during 1969-73 I was a member of the Peabody Board of Trustees. In these capacities, I further observed Dr. Southall's contributions (as an alumni officer also) to the Association and her invaluable counsel to trustees who sought it.

Dr. Maycie K. Southall has made great contributions to education through her students, her influence on Peabody College and its program, and her leadership in professional organizations. I have told her too seldom and too little of my great respect for her. I am pleased to tell you and others who may read my statement or portions thereof in your dissertation. It will have to be a great dissertation to do justice to its subject![148]

Harold D. Drummond, recently retired from his position as associate dean of the College of Education, University of New Mexico, joined the staff of George Peabody College for Teachers in 1947. He was impressed with Maycie Southall's dedication to the mission of George Peabody College for Teachers and with her work in the Association for Childhood Education which he observed during the thirteen years he was associated with her:

. . . As you may know, I was at Peabody from 1947-60 in Elementary Education. For several years, Maycie and I were the only persons on the staff with specific responsibilities in that area. We were joined by Grace Champion from Lexington, Kentucky; Mildred Hoyt (director of Child Study Center); and James L. Hymes (now of Berkeley, California). Maycie outlasted most of us!

My memories of Maycie are many and varied. She was perhaps the most dedicated single person I have known to the perception of the Peabody mission. She had almost the zeal of a missionary in actual performance and effort. She was, undoubtedly, the single best-known leader in early childhood education in the whole region known as the South.

And, even eclipsing her dedication to Peabody, there were times when I thought Maycie was even more committed to the Association for Childhood Education International. I remember when she returned from the national meeting and enthusiastically announced that "International" had been added to ACE. Maycie was a mover in that organization for years. It was the

---

[148]William M. Alexander, personal letter, May 23, 1979.

precursor of NAEYC and has, in recent years, rather
been eclipsed by the latter organization. No group
was working as hard in the 1950s to meet the needs of
young learners, to help parents understand what those
needs were, and to help teachers work with children in
humane and stimulating ways as ACE. Partly because of
her very effective work in that organization, I tended
to move into working with ASCD (where Maycie was also
very active, especially with supervisors) and with the
DESP (now NAESP).

Maycie has astounded me ever since we left Peabody
in 1960 to come here. She remained very active and
very involved for years, according to mutual friends
from Nashville. Our contacts have been primarily
through Christmas cards since 1960, so it is hard to
comment much about the last decade.

Maycie was not always easy to work with closely.
Neither was I! We were both busy as one-armed paper
hangers. Enrollment in the Peabody summer school just
after World War II was usually somewhere between four
and five thousand. I routinely taught classes with
125 students in them--at the graduate level! We would
not think of permitting that to happen here--but I
rather expect that students working at the master's
level there at that time, especially in the '50s,
probably got a higher level of effective instruction
than anywhere else in the nation. Those were the days
of Goslin, Benjamin, Hobbs, Van Til, Alexander, Stanley,
Whitaker, Allen, Cooper, Wirth, Hymes, Wiggins, Hall,
Riley, and Southall at Peabody. It was a fascinating
place to be--an intellectually stimulating place to be.
Of course, Henry Hill dominated the place--and to some
extent ran the College like a southern plantation.

Maycie was a substantial cog in the operation. Her
standing with alumni was always great. She knew more
former students on a first-name basis, I suspect, than
any Peabodian except, perhaps, John Windrow, who worked
at that constantly because of his assignment. Maycie
worked at it through her classes, through ACE (she was
always going somewhere to speak to ACE groups), through
ASCD, and through an enormous correspondence that she
attempted to carry on with inadequate secretarial help.

. . . She was one of the kindest, most gracious
persons I have known. She was so busy that she had
little patience with students who did not work hard and
effectively. Some of them brought their problems to
me. I would be very surprised if the reverse were not
also true!

I suspect that Maycie never really forgave me for leaving Peabody. I'm sure I was regarded as a "back-slider." From a "missionary's" point of view, I suppose that interpretation might be accurate. We have never regretted, however, going there from Stanford or coming to the University of New Mexico. We have warm feelings about Peabody and the many friends we made there, and always will have. Among those friends, of course, was Maycie K. Southall--a real southern lady![149]

Robert S. Thurman became acquainted with Maycie Southall when he enrolled in her class as a graduate student in 1953. According to him, the professor was not called "Dr." Southall on campus:

> . . . There probably are a number of reasons for this. One, there was a tradition at George Peabody College at that time to call all of the professors "Miss," "Mrs.," or "Mr." In fact, as I recall, only one professor on campus was referred to as "Dr." There is a deeper reason. One time when I was her assistant, I opened a box and found a very ornately carved desk plate engraved with "Dr. Maycie K. Southall." I commented on how attractive it was and asked why she did not put it on her desk. She smiled and said, "I'm a little bit like the Texan who said that if people didn't know he was from Texas, he didn't tell them because there was no need to embarrass them. If they did know, there was no need to say anything." That little incident really described Miss Southall--she never made any attempt to impress anyone. She was the same kind of individual whether she was dealing with an incoming freshman, a doctoral student, or another one of the top educators in the United States.

> I entered George Peabody College as a beginning graduate student in the summer of 1953 and was a student in her course on Supervision. She said something to the effect that we needed to have a broad base of knowledge as well as considerable depth. She required that we do considerable reading in the library and that we keep annotated reading cards. I was greatly impressed with her lectures. She was not a well-organized lecturer in the sense that she developed ideas in a very sequential manner, but in almost a conversational tone she would explain her ideas and quote people and writings. I was most impressed and decided I had to know what these

---

[149] Harold D. Drummond, personal letter, June 22, 1979.

people said, too. As a result, I spent more time in the library reading for her course than I did for the other three courses put together. In all, I took four classes with her and was amazed to find that each one was quite different although the philosophy that she had permeated each one.

I returned to be a full-time student in the summer of 1954 and asked Miss Southall to be my major professor. She agreed and asked if I would be her assistant for the next year. This meant that I spent about two hours a day working with her in the office, gathering materials, doing library research, and assisting in classes as needed. That was quite an experience. At times after we had worked very hard or when she would receive a letter, Miss Southall would begin to reminisce about people whom she had known or events that she had taken part in. She told, for example, of her work with UNESCO in setting up a charter and other kinds of activities. She told of working with Mrs. Eleanor Roosevelt and what a gracious lady Mrs. Roosevelt was. She was on a first-name basis with many of the outstanding educators in the United States, people I had read or heard about; and she made them come alive to me through personal incidents. After completing the Master's degree, I decided to work toward the doctorate with Dr. William Van Til. After he left, I asked Miss Southall to chair my doctoral committee; and she graciously agreed.

Because of Miss Southall's influence, I became quite active in the Association for Childhood Education International at the national level and in the Elementary Council on campus. She attended each meeting and encouraged all of her undergraduate and graduate students to take part. She set a model for us to follow, and many of us did--I am still active in the Association for Childhood Education International. Through these organizations, she introduced me and other students to educators around the country. I always enjoyed going to the ACEI study conference with her because she would take time to help me get acquainted with so many people and to make sure that I got involved in many of the activities in the conference.

What is her educational philosophy? It's difficult to describe another person's philosophy because you let your own enter in; but I do know the influence she has had on my educational philosophy because of her comments, suggestions, and her own activities. Miss Southall believes deeply that the school belongs to parents, not to teachers. In this sense, then, parents should assist in developing the curriculum through advisory groups and through working closely with the teachers in setting goals for the school. She also believes that the curriculum includes everything that happens to the child in and out of the school because the influences outside of the school definitely influence what the child does in school. Not only that, but what happens to the child in the school should have a direct bearing on how the child thinks and behaves outside of school. She stressed that we should have a broad concept of education, not a narrowly defined, highly specialized view. We should be as concerned about what is happening to children at all levels of the school program as we are with what is happening at our particular level.

Miss Southall is deeply committed to the concept of democracy both in and out of school. Because of her southern upbringing, I believe that sometimes this created some difficulties for her especially in racial matters; but I was at Peabody when the student body was integrated and found her to be very accepting of all students regardless of race. As I understood her concept of democracy, she believed that people should have an active role in the decision making process--parents, teachers, and children. This meant, among other things, that children should have an active part in planning the curriculum and in carrying out the plans. She implemented this in her own teaching. I remember helping her with an undergraduate class and was amazed to watch her work with these students in planning what would be studied during the quarter and the approaches to be used.

Another aspect of her philosophy is that a person has to have considerable knowledge of what has gone on before in order to plan the present and the future. She would say something about education being like a person standing on the shoulders of another person in order to reach higher--we should be better today because of yesterday. Because of this, she insisted that we spend considerable time in the library finding out what other people have taught and insisted that we do thinking for ourselves. . . .

Several things stand out as I reminisce. She was a very, very busy woman. Many of my colleagues today complain because they teach two classes with twenty-five students each and they may have two or three doctoral students and one or two committees. Miss Southall, along with others at Peabody, taught four courses of four quarter hours each which met four days a week. In addition, she had a very heavy doctoral load both as a chairman and committee member, served on numerous committees for the College, and was active in a number of national professional organizations. I recall one summer her telling me that she got about three hours of sleep a night because she was so busy reading dissertations, writing reports, and working on class papers. At the same time, I never had any difficulty in getting in to see her in the office; and I never recall a time when she indicated to me that she was too busy to talk with me. Because of this load, she sometimes was rather absent-minded. She would call me Bob, Rob, and Robert-- and I think sometimes she couldn't remember which was my real name. Each quarter she would invite a group of us to come over to her home for an afternoon snack. I especially looked forward to the times when she would have country ham served with beaten biscuits. She had a maid (I can't remember her name now) who would have everything in order when we would come in, and the food would be delicious. We would just sit around and visit as we snacked. You must remember Miss Southall did not receive very much salary at that time, and she paid for all of it out of her own pocket. She had a very special affection for my family; and I recall one Christmas when I had almost no money at all, she called to tell me that she had just come back from Georgia and for some reason had brought two Christmas trees. "Bob, I don't have any need for two Christmas trees. Why don't you come over and take one of them off of my hand?" You see, she would never have embarrassed me by indicating she knew I probably couldn't afford to buy one that year; she tried to make me feel as if I were doing her a favor. I went after the tree. We had her over one evening for dinner, and my wife fixed meringues with fresh strawberries and ice cream. Years later Miss Maycie commented about those meringues and how delicious they were. She had a very fond feeling for young children and families. As I described the things that she did for me, keep in mind she was the same with many other students. She had no favorite, to my knowledge. Now, having said all of this, there's another aspect to her personality. She was a very outspoken person who believed in saying what she believed. When she believed in something, she spoke up even to the point of disagreeing with you. This took some getting used to on my part.

Now, it is rather difficult to pinpoint the kinds of influence she has had on me as a person and as a teacher. I do know that she got me interested in professional organizations and that she helped me to consider the role of the professor to undergraduate and graduate students (both by the way she worked with me and through our many conversations), to have a deep concern for what happens to children and to speak up, and to have a high standard for one's self. She also influenced my thinking by showing that a person can be gracious, caring, and human. That may sound strange to say it that way, but I have known many professors who never let the human aspect of their lives show through to students. As a result, they were aloof and removed. Miss Southall was neither.

Related to her influence on me is her influence on Elementary Education. I am appalled that a person who has contributed so very much to the education of children in the United States could receive so little national recognition. She has served as president of so many organizations, she was such a mover in the Association for Childhood Education and the Association for Supervision and Curriculum Development, she had such an influence on the Education Policies Commission and especially the statement on education for all American children back in the mid-1940s, and on and on and on. Yet, so few people today know of the contributions she has made. There are two reasons for this. Number one, she is a woman. Women educators have never received the recognition they deserve in our national history. The other, Miss Southall is a very modest person who did not attempt to push herself forward in a manner to call attention to herself. She was more concerned about the influences she had than for recognition. There's probably a third reason why she has not received this recognition. She did not jump on bandwagons just to be popular. I remember several years ago at a conference when people were speaking up favorably for the child development associate (CDA) and the role of the Association for Childhood Education in this movement. Miss Maycie stood up at the business meeting to raise some very serious questions about the movement and what it would mean to the profession of teachers. This was a very unpopular thing for her to do, and she was not well received. Yet, the points that she made were valid; and her concerns were borne out later. . . .

Now, you asked about my own personal background. I received the doctorate in 1959. At that time I was an associate professor at the Kansas State Teachers College at Emporia; from 1961 to 1964 I was assistant director of the National Council for Accreditation of Teacher Education; and in 1964 I joined the Department of Curriculum and Instruction at the University of Tennessee. I am a professor and teach in the area of Early Childhood Education.

Oh, yes, one more thing: You cannot talk about Miss Southall with any of her students without someone making a comment about her handwriting. Her handwriting required someone who knew her quite well in order to interpret it. One year I was assistant to another professor to whom she wrote a number of notes, and I became

an indispensable person for him because I was the only
one in the office who could read them. . . .[150]

O. L. Davis, Jr., currently serving as a professor in
the College of Education, The University of Texas at Austin,
met Maycie Southall in the mid-1950s when he attended George
Peabody College for Teachers as a graduate student. He was
especially impressed by her loyalty to the educational institution where she taught, to her students, and to children:

> My recollections of Dr. Maycie K. Southall are
> quite vivid but are not extensive. We knew one another
> throughout my three years on the Peabody campus, but I
> had only one course with her. She did serve as a member
> of my doctoral committee.
>
> First off and always, Miss Southall--then, we never
> used "Dr." for any of the Peabody professors--is a
> gracious lady. I mean nothing sexist. I mean to honor
> her charm, her bearing, and her impeccable demeanor.
> Other words might suffice, but "lady" has persisted in
> my mind over the years as I remember her. Never coarse,
> absolutely tough, uncompromising in her values about
> teaching and scholarship, tender and sensitive, she
> exemplified the qualities I associate with the tradi-
> tional South. Miss Southall would appear, even on the
> hottest of Nashville summer days, tastefully dressed,
> if not (in our graduate student-peasant terms) elegantly
> dressed. I think I never saw her on the campus, and I
> saw her only there, in casual attire.
>
> Miss Southall always was interested in me and my
> plans, while on the campus and years after I graduated
> when we would meet at Peabody breakfasts at ASCD. She
> knew my wife's name and my sons'; and their welfare
> was not a cosmetic, but rather a genuine interest--
> especially after my wife's quite serious health problems.
> True, Miss Southall always called me "Bill" for some
> unexplained reason; but she was consistent, never "Bill"
> and something else, even my name. I was "Bill" only in
> oral communication; I was "O. L." in writing. After I
> graduated, I became "O. L." in both circumstances. I
> remember being amused by this "slip" at the time and
> never felt she was abusing me. Quite the opposite, she
> remembered me well enough, or some "Bill" well enough

---

[150]Thurman, personal letter, June 29, 1979.

to use the name with me. Really, I believe I felt I
was special. Another incident indicates how seriously
interested she was in me as a person. I told her of it
recently; and, characteristically, she doesn't remember
it.

Joan, my wife, and I were among a small group she
invited to her apartment across from the campus. During the light conversation, Miss Southall asked me what
my dissertation was to be about. I responded something
like, "Mr. Drummond and I are interested...". She looked
at me very seriously and noted, "Students write dissertations. Mr. Drummond has completed his. I want to know
what you are going to do." Never again did I use "we"
in referring to "my" dissertation. Further, how I talked
about it was a serious matter. I know I have thought of
that incident over each of the nearly 60 dissertations I
have supervised and have related the story untold times.
Miss Southall taught us, helped us become professionals,
Peabody professionals, whenever and wherever she decided.

I really credit Miss Southall for introducing me
to educational research. Others taught me techniques.
Still others encouraged my research production. Her
course on Research Affecting Elementary Education in-
ducted me quite unceremoniously into the research literature of our field. I read and read in the Peabody stacks
that summer of 1955. I know I breathed dusts of generations of graduate students as I pulled down bound volumes
and read and abstracted. I had no idea, I recall, that
anyone had ever been interested _for_ _research_ in the size
of pencil for young children, in experienced teachers'
ability to assess reading readiness, or in the effects
of direct instruction on children's development of chro-
nology. I soon learned. Abstracting according to quite
rigid standards, I then thought--and each abstract was
checked! Her poor assistant. The first weeks passed
and I was reading more; and, surprisingly, I had passed
over the threshold and I was enjoying the reading more.
I was on the research hunt--a fox chasing a rabbit. I
not only still remember some of the studies I read and
discussed that summer, I know many more now for I have
continued to build on the substantial base constructed
in Miss Southall's course. She was interested in ideas,
not statistics, in what counted, not how it was counted.
The class that summer was large; and I have no idea how
many, if any others, in the group responded in the manner
I did. No matter. She touched me, really turned me
on to research. She was one I credited when I received
the first NCSS Citation for Exemplary Research in Social
Studies Education. She was not a researcher herself;
but she modeled for us all the scholarly, professional
use and usefulness of research.

Probably most of all for me, she modeled the role of professional leader. Here she was, Miss Elementary Education, a significant, internationally prominent leader and, still, our teacher who met her classes, read papers, wrote comments, attended meetings, and talked to students. Miss Southall just expected that all of us graduate students in elementary education would belong to the Elementary Council. And we did and attended meetings regularly. She encouraged us to go to professional association meetings on the campus and away. I recall how pleased she was to see me at my first ASCD conference in St. Louis while I was still a student. She introduced me to several of her friends, and I was further pleased to learn later that she had served ASCD as an officer for more years than anyone else. Other Peabody professors have been very influential in my professional organization life—Harold Drummond, Bill Van Til, and Bill Alexander in ASCD and Jack Allen in NCSS—but Maycie Southall has played an important role, perhaps more than I've thought.

I have always been impressed by Miss Southall's intense loyalties—to children, to Peabody, and to students. She believed in us all. And, as I've told my own sons, how can you let someone down who believes in you? She is distressed now because of the miscalled "merger" of Peabody with Vanderbilt. Her loyalty to the College never wavered over the years, but now she must think custodians of the College's future have abused her loyalty and that of thousands of us by their action.

Certain it is that the Peabody which nurtured our Miss Southall and which enabled her to enjoy such widespread recognition lives only in memory. The new Peabody, to be worthy of its rich heritage, must recognize that a college, especially for teachers, is never narrowly conceived, never provincial. The future Peabody could be informed by knowing the great teachers of Peabody past. One of these is Maycie K. Southall.[151]

The final letter selected for inclusion in this portion of the study was contributed by Felix C. Robb, executive director of the Southern Association of Colleges and Schools. He was serving as president of George Peabody College for Teachers at the time of Maycie Southall's retirement in 1964.

---

[151]O. L. Davis, Jr., personal letter, May 18, 1979.

In retrospect, he credited his colleague of twenty years with having contributed to the prestige accorded the educational institution:

I was once, for a year, a graduate student at Peabody. I never had a class with Dr. Southall; but I stood in awe of her tremendous accomplishments, her world-wide fame, her driving energy, and her reputation. The mantle of the fabled elementary education professor, Miss Lucy Gage, had fallen upon her capable shoulders; and for decades she was one of that bright group of stellar professors who made Peabody College both famous and great.

Maycie Southall is an exemplar of able teaching. She knows and understands children. And she has the gift of imparting knowledge and challenging the best in her students. That she cared personally for her students was manifest by her famous and lovely dinners held at her handsomely furnished apartment. Invitations to those dinners were much coveted, and the occasions were unfailingly rewarding to the students and to faculty colleagues. Food was always the very best of fine southern cooking, and conversation was on a level to match the food. Dr. Southall made certain that cronies did not spend the evening talking to each other; so at intervals she would announce a "fruit basket turnover," to have everybody in the group move around and become acquainted before the party was concluded. This very special, informal contact with her graduate students was something they carried with them as a moment of high privilege.

Few professors have directed more or better doctoral studies than Dr. Southall, but it was commonplace for her students to be exhausted by her demands for high quality in writing and re-writing of manuscripts. Her schedule of speaking engagements took her all over the United States; and this, coupled with a heavy teaching schedule and the help of only a part-time student, caused her at times to delay completion of her critique of a doctoral study. No one did a "quickie" doctoral program with Dr. Southall. She was thorough and seemed best satisfied when the student had been tested to his or her limit. Her office was usually filled with mountains of papers, and where things were was one of her best-kept secrets.

The national and international influence of her distinguished career has been strong and widely felt. Her students came from all over the world, many from

Asian countries. As the president of ACEI, Dr. Southall
held a pivotal position in education, had an important
platform for her views, and used it as a means of contact with the greatest teachers of young children in the
world. All of her expertise and reflected glory re-
dounded to Peabody College's benefit.

I have always regarded Dr. Maycie Southall as a
kind of epitome. She was and is an elegant lady, very
attractive, always stylishly and expensively dressed.
She has a fierce and demanding side. She does not suffer fools gladly and never had patience with sloth or
incompetence. She was a model of the beautiful, caring,
demanding, highly professional teacher of teachers.

If there were a Hall of Fame for elementary education, Maycie Southall would be in it. My hat is off
and doffed to this great lady, this master teacher, and
this personal and professional guide to thousands of
students who found their way to her classroom.[152]

---

[152]Felix C. Robb, personal letter, February 25, 1980.

The red rose is the flower of Delta Kappa Gamma. It symbolizes mature womanhood; it also suggests beauty of both mind and spirit exemplified by the teacher who is truly a friend of youth.

The cultivation of roses has for many years been one of Dr. Southall's favorite pastimes. A rose from her garden graced her classroom desk almost daily.

When I see a rose, I think of Dr. Southall. Each phase of her life unfolds, as does the rose, into a lovelier stage of mature womanhood.

Lois Jones
Interview
Sewanee, Tennessee
June 13, 1980

CHAPTER IV

DELTA KAPPA GAMMA SOCIETY ACTIVITIES

Preliminary Plans from Which Xi State Emerged

During 1929, the same year in which Maycie Southall accepted a full-time teaching position at George Peabody College
for Teachers, another event was taking place quite removed
from her locality that would loom large a few years later in
her educational career.

Annie Webb Blanton, who had served as state superintendent of public instruction prior to accepting a teaching position at the University of Texas and completing a Ph.D. degree
at Cornell University, recognized the need for an honorary
organization composed of key women educators; through unified
efforts, the members could work toward the needs of women
educators and the betterment of education. Later to become
known as The Delta Kappa Gamma Society, the organization was
founded by twelve women educators; the first initiation was
held on May 11, 1929, in Austin at the Faculty Women's Club
near the University of Texas.[1] The purpose of this study is
not to provide a history of the Society; two compilations
entitled Our Heritage by Eunah Temple Holden serve as excellent references for the organization. This chapter presents

---

[1]Rogers, Light from Many Candles, p. 17.

some of the major aspects of Maycie Southall's work at various
levels of leadership within the Delta Kappa Gamma Society.
Thus, only those brief points of reference concerning the history of the organization deemed necessary to the presentation
of major contributions by Maycie Southall are included.

Although later revised on several occasions, five purposes were listed in the 1929 Constitution:

> Section 1. The first purpose of this Society
> shall be to unite women teachers who have achieved
> prominence in the teaching profession; to develop
> among them a feeling of loyalty, one to another, and
> habits of cooperation, one with another; and to main-
> tain ideals of the duty which each woman who achieves
> success in the work of education owes to those who are
> struggling to uphold high standards in the teaching
> profession; and to secure fair conditions under which
> women may work in the schools.

> Section 2. The second purpose of this society
> shall be to confer distinction upon women who are
> recognized as leaders in the profession of teaching.

> Section 3. The third purpose of this society
> shall be to furnish an organization through which
> women teachers may work effectively to secure desir-
> able school legislation for the betterment of the
> schools, and for bringing about just recognition of
> the services of women teachers and just conditions of
> work for women engaged in teaching, to the end of a
> gradual reduction and final elimination of discrimina-
> tions against women, as compared with men, engaged in
> the work of education. It is expressly provided that
> this organization shall not be used for political pur-
> poses.

> Section 4. The fourth purpose of this society
> shall be to afford an organization through which able
> women teachers may work to secure equal representation
> and equal recognition of women with men in professional
> organizations of teachers, whether these associations
> be city, county, state, or national in their range of
> activities.

> Section 5. A fifth purpose of this society shall
> be to form an organization through which women teachers

shall carry on work which shall result in giving financial aid to some of the capable women who are preparing
themselves for the teaching profession.[2]

Membership which began with a total of twelve women educators has, during the ensuing years, burgeoned tremendously.
Jessie Sim, international treasurer and acting executive
secretary, stated that on May 28, 1980, the records showed
150,327 members; the Society had chapters in every state and
would have representation in twelve foreign countries as of
June 20, 1980, upon Costa Rica's affiliation.[3] Membership is
by invitation only which is followed by a vote of approval
among chapter members. In order to meet eligibility requirements, a candidate must have accumulated at least five years
of educational experience. Also, until the 1970s membership
was further restricted by the use of a quota system that allowed only a certain percentage of women educators in a specific locality to be voted into a chapter. In spite of such
restrictions, the Society now has more members on its roll
than any other women's honorary educational organization in
the world.[4]

In addition to the requirements of professional training,
five years of educational experience, and employment or resi-
dence within the chapter locale, members are expected to exem-
plify traits such as, for example, resourcefulness, initiative,

---

[2]Constitution of The Kappa Gamma Delta Society (name
later changed), art. 2, secs. 1-5 (1929).

[3]Jessie Sim, interview held in Sewanee, Tennessee,
June 14, 1980.

[4] Theresa A. Fechek, personal letter, July 2, 1979.

perception, loyalty, participation, and tact that characterize professional proficiency.[5]

In retrospect, the Society's growth has been remarkable; for the fledgling organization had a tremendous task ahead when, in 1929, the members began to work toward one of their first major goals, expansion. The aftermath of the Suffrage Movement, the economic conditions brought about by the Great Depression of 1929 from which the country struggled for many years toward recovery, and widespread discrimination against married women teachers were prevalent forces during the era when the newly organized Delta Kappa Gamma Society was trying to develop support through expansion of membership.

During the first year of the organization's existence, the Texas membership increased from 12 to 431 members and from 1 to 17 chapters.[6] Encouraged by the relatively staunch stronghold in Texas and still demonstrating her belief in the power of united endeavor, Annie Webb Blanton continued to contact key women educators who she thought would be promising members of a group committed to improving education and to advancing women educators. As in the original Texas organization, expansion into other states elicited the membership of women who represented varied educational endeavors such as college professors, principals, and classroom teachers.

---

[5]The Delta Kappa Gamma Society International, Handbook (Austin: Revised under the auspices of an Ad Hoc Committee, Nadine Ewing, chairman; International Headquarters, 1979), p. 17.

[6]Maycie Southall, "Fifteen Years A-Growin'," The Delta Kappa Gamma Bulletin 10 (June 1944):15.

Thus, zealous in her efforts to expand into an ever-widening geographical area, Annie Webb Blanton contacted key women leaders in education to encourage them to organize within their own states. Already known in educational circles, Maycie Southall was a logical contact in Tennessee. In a letter dated September 25, 1935, Annie Webb Blanton wrote to Maycie Southall:

> I am writing you in regard to membership in the Delta Kappa Gamma Society, an honor-fraternity for women teachers. This order begins its organization in each state with the selection and initiation of a group of Founders (twelve to sixteen), who constitute the first State Executive Board. To this board, later on, the chapter presidents are added, as chapters are formed. The State Executive Board acts as an advisory council for the president, and to it are committed all matters relating to the organization within the state.

> Founders are life members of the State Board. They are authorized to organize chapters, but are not obliged to undertake organization unless they choose. The position of Founder is one of increasing prestige and honor as the years pass. . . .

> You have been recommended to our National Membership Committee as one of the State Founders in the State of Tennessee and I am writing to ask you to accept this position.[7]

Approximately two weeks later, Maycie Southall replied to Annie Webb Blanton's letter: "I am very glad to accept your invitation to membership in Delta Kappa Gamma Society and to become one of its state founders in Tennessee."[8] With her characteristic outlook toward the future, Maycie Southall

---

[7]Annie Webb Blanton to Maycie Southall, September 25, 1935, Archives of Xi State, TEA Building, Nashville.

[8]Maycie Southall to Annie Webb Blanton, October 7, 1935, Archives of Xi State, TEA Building, Nashville.

concluded: "The organization seems to have potentialities of great service to the women in our profession."[9]

In subsequent correspondence, the Texas educator emphasized selectivity: "We want to have as Founders sixteen of the best women in the teaching profession in Tennessee."[10] In the same letter, Annie Webb Blanton described an ideal candidate for membership:

> A Founder should be a leader in her line of work, one well known in her own state. She should be a woman of fine personality and character, professional spirit, and good social qualities.[11]

When she had obtained responses from a sufficient number of women who indicated that they were interested in joining such an organization in Tennessee, Annie Webb Blanton sent pertinent information concerning the initiation which included:

> This is the usual formal notice of initiation sent by the Delta Kappa Gamma Society. Initiation of the Tennessee State Founders and members will take place on Saturday, November 30, at 11:00 A.M. at the Hermitage Hotel, Nashville, Tennessee. Initiation will be followed by election of officers.[12]

One of the Xi State founders, Mary Hall, who was initiated during the November 30, 1935, meeting reminisced recently: "I felt that an invitation to join this organization

---

[9]Ibid.

[10]Annie Webb Blanton to Maycie Southall, October 29, 1935, Archives of Xi State, TEA Building, Nashville.

[11]Ibid.

[12]Annie Webb Blanton to Friends, November 1935, Archives of Xi State, TEA Building, Nashville.

was one of the greatest honors that I had ever had."[13] Her
first acquaintance with Delta Kappa Gamma occurred when an
invitation to join the organization arrived at her home
through the mail. Because an enclosed note advised secrecy,
Mary Hall did not reveal her plans to other staff members at
the educational institution with which she was associated.
Early on the appointed Saturday morning, Mary Hall left her
home near Murfreesboro, Tennessee, and boarded a bus to
Nashville; walked to the Hermitage Hotel; found the designated room; entered; and, much to her surprise, found among
the group gathered there several other women educators with
whom she worked daily. They, too, had not revealed their
plans for attendance.[14]

In a recent interview, Maycie Southall reminisced about
the eventful day when Xi State was organized. Seventeen
women educators, from a total of twenty who had been invited,
were receptive to the potentialities afforded by Delta Kappa
Gamma for the improvement of education and the advancement of
women. Thus, Annie Webb Blanton began the day's activities
by introducing herself after which the others followed suit.
The originator of Delta Kappa Gamma explained the purposes,
discussed the role of founders, and distributed copies of
the organization's literature. Then, a very impressive cere-
mony was conducted by the leader who had donned academic

---

[13]Mary Hall, interview held in Murfreesboro, Tennessee,
May 28, 1979.

[14]Ibid.

attire for the momentous occasion; as a result, sixteen women educators became Xi State founders on November 30, 1935. Next, Annie Webb Blanton appointed a nominating committee and charged its members with the responsibility of presenting a slate of officers later in the day. The group had lunch during which the leader encouraged the women to become better acquainted. After lunch, officers were elected; the group chose Maycie Southall to serve as the first president of Xi State. Because seventeen educators were in attendance but the maximum number permitted to become state founders was sixteen, the dilemma was solved by the initiation of one woman not as a founder but as the first state member.[15]

During her reflections about the first meeting, Mary Hall commented concerning Annie Webb Blanton's emphasis on the major task confronting Xi State; that is, the Texas educator challenged the small group of seventeen women to expand the organization throughout the entire state of Tennessee. Plans were not provided for such a monumental undertaking but were to be worked out locally. Also, the leader said that the organization was to embrace all phases of education; and she charged the group to take great care in the screening of potential members. Too, although she pointed out that the Society had been designed as an exclusive organization, the leader warned against snobbishness on the part of the members.[16]

---

[15]Maycie Southall, interview held in Nashville, June 19, 1979.

[16]Mary Hall, interview, May 28, 1979.

The memorable meeting came to a close early in the afternoon. Annie Webb Blanton had to meet a tight schedule in order to return to her home in sufficient time for resumption of her educational duties on the following Monday; therefore, Maycie Southall, the new president, left early in order to take the Texan to the train station.[17]

Mary Hall added that during the ensuing years as Maycie Southall worked closely with Annie Webb Blanton, the two became very good friends. At her death, Annie Webb Blanton bequeathed to Maycie Southall a bracelet she wears frequently.[18] Maycie Southall later disclosed the significance of the bracelet: The members of Delta Kappa Gamma had chosen Annie Webb Blanton to be the recipient of their first national achievement award, and they had selected the piece of jewelry as a symbol of the honor. The bracelet is engraved with this inscription: "Annie Webb Blanton, National Award, 1933."[19]

Mary Hall expressed enthusiasm as she evaluated the progress of the Society since Xi State's first meeting in 1935: "People have always made fun of 'old maid' schoolteachers, but this has changed. In my opinion, Delta Kappa Gamma has done more than anything . . . to raise the status of women teachers."[20]

[17]Ibid.

[18]Ibid.

[19]Southall, interview, June 19, 1979.

[20]Mary Hall, interview, May 28, 1979.

After returning to Austin from her trip to Nashville,
Annie Webb Blanton wrote to Maycie Southall, the new president of Xi State, a letter which included:

> My time was too short. How I did hate to leave!
> But I loved that group of women when I looked at them--
> including the president. I am happy that you were
> elected president. . . . I know how busy you are. I
> hope it won't be too hard on you. Thank you for not
> declining. I can tell you, from my own experience,
> that it is a work well worthwhile. I believe we are
> forming a worthy organization that will <u>live</u>.[21]

Thus began the Xi State presidency of Maycie Southall, a
term that was to continue from her initiation in 1935 until
1938, the year in which she moved into the ranks of national
presidents of Delta Kappa Gamma.

Maycie Southall: Xi State President

During Maycie Southall's term in office as president of
Xi State, expansion of membership was emphasized. Chapters
began to appear in the more heavily populated areas. Annie
Webb Blanton later recognized the work toward expansion fos-
tered by Maycie Southall in these words: "With her capable
band of Founders and state members, she has carried out a
systematic plan of making Delta Kappa Gamma known to the teaching profession in her state and of establishing it firmly in
Tennessee."[22] By the end of Maycie Southall's term as president of Xi State, six chapters had been formed: Alpha Chapter

---

[21]Annie Webb Blanton to Maycie Southall, December 5, 1935,
Archives of Xi State, TEA Building, Nashville.

[22]Annie Webb Blanton, "Pioneers in Delta Kappa Gamma,"
<u>The Delta Kappa Gamma Bulletin</u> 4 (March 1938):22.

in Chattanooga, Beta Chapter in Nashville, Gamma Chapter in
Johnson City, Delta Chapter in Murfreesboro, Epsilon Chapter
in Memphis, and Zeta Chapter in Knox County.[23]

Perhaps the efforts toward expansion of membership in
Xi State during its early years should be viewed within the
context of time and place. The decade following the Great
Depression of 1929 saw many families struggling for a mere
existence; the frugal mode of life necessitated by meager
teachers' salaries frequently failed to allow for luxuries
such as membership in a variety of organizations. The expenses incumbent with acceptance of an invitation to join
an educational organization, regardless of its desirability,
were an important consideration; and the reason often given
for declining an invitation to join Xi State was the cost.
Correspondence pertaining to invitations and accompanying
responses is housed in the Archives of Xi State; a review of
the material clearly showed that the economy played a very
important role in the early expansion of Delta Kappa Gamma
in Tennessee.

Another reason mentioned for declining an invitation to
Xi State membership was responsibility at home including the
care of elderly parents. Illness among family members and
devotion of time to the aged frequently took priority over
other interests. Worthy of note, too, is the fact that it
was not uncommon for women to recognize a general disapproval

---

[23]Mary Hall, interview, May 28, 1979.

of such organizations and thus consider the possibility that
membership might jeopardize their professional positions. Because of anticipated criticism, the original group in Texas
had earlier worked surrounded by a veil of secrecy. A fac-
simile of the original invitation, illustrated in Our Heritage,
includes the admonition: "If you desire to accept this invitation, you are required to give a pledge that . . . you will
never reveal to any one not a member of the order, its purposes or its secret ritual."[24]

Because of her concern about the aspect of secrecy, one
person to whom an invitation to join Xi State was sent replied:

> I appreciate greatly your invitation to join the
> ranks of the Delta Kappa Gamma Society, and I regret
> that I cannot avail myself of this opportunity to be
> associated with the many excellent teachers who will
> no doubt be enrolled in the Tennessee Chapter.
>
> Years ago I formed a resolution never to accept
> membership in any organization in which a pledge of
> secrecy is required, no matter how praiseworthy the
> aims of such a group of congenial persons may be.[25]

Although expansion is one means of measuring effort,
other goals were also stressed from the very early days of
the Tennessee organization. A well-defined program of work
had been established at the national level; and Tennessee
units, both state and chapter, endeavored to follow the
patterns prescribed by the national leaders. The national

---

[24]Eunah Temple Holden, Our Heritage (Austin: The Steck
Company for The Delta Kappa Gamma Society, 1960), p. 12.

[25]Anne Gates Butler to Maycie Southall, March 27, 1938,
Archives of Xi State, TEA Building, Nashville.

themes for the years during which Maycie Southall served as
Xi State president addressed these concerns:

1935-1936
1. Consideration of Teaching and Its Function
   with Respect to a Philosophy of Education
   A. What shall be the objectives of education?
   B. How shall the education aim at being sup-
      ported?
   C. What is the most effective organization to
      attain these objectives?

1936-1937
1. What is a sound Philosophy of Education as a
   component part of the whole theory of democracy
   as contemplated in the American System of
   Government?
2. What, if any, improvements are needed in the
   methods of national, state, or local support
   of education in your state? What, if any,
   revision or modification of your school laws
   are needed?

1937-1938
1. The Improvement of Education--Its Interpretation
2. The Study of Financing Public Education[26]

Mamie S. Bastian, who began her two-year term as national
president in 1936, reviewed the national program of work carried out during her administration: "In our studies . . . we
have concentrated largely upon the problems of school support,
the functions of education in preserving and advancing Democracy, and upon security in the work of the teacher."[27] Maycie
Southall endeavored to carry out the responsibilities of her

---

[26]The Delta Kappa Gamma Society International, _Program
Manual: 1978-79_ (Austin: prepared under the auspices of the
International Program of Work Committees for the 1976-1978
Biennium, Janice Nerem, chairman of the International Program
Committee, 1976-78; International Headquarters, n.d.), pp. 34-
35.

[27]Mamie S. Bastian, "Circular Letter to State and Chapter
Presidents from Past National President," July 1938, Archives
of Xi State, TEA Building, Nashville.

office as Xi State president by adhering to the themes established at the national level; however, her duties also included directing attention to the study of educational needs pertinent to the state and chapter levels. Some of the Tennessean's efforts expended in meeting the educational needs of her own jurisdiction became apparent through a study of correspondence retained from her administration. One example involved a prospective member who had accepted her invitation to membership in Xi State on April 6, 1936.[28] Maycie Southall recognized the new member's exceptional ability to expedite a share of the work facing the members, and thus the former corresponded with the new member during the following October:

> You will recall that the program we outlined for ourselves this year calls for the organization of four study committees to study the following subjects as they pertain to Tennessee and make recommendations at the state convention of Delta Kappa Gamma.
>
> 1. Inequalities in Opportunities for Women Teachers
> 2. Preschool Education
> 3. Teacher Load in Relation to Pupil Growth and Programs
> 4. Teacher Retirement System
>
> You have been selected to be Chairman of the Committee on Preschool Education. We are not trying to honor you but to put this part of the program in hands that will insure all the progress that can be reasonably hoped for.[29]

Materials such as bibliographies and reports pertaining to legislative efforts, stored in the Archives of Xi State,

---

[28]Gretchen Hyder to Maycie Southall, April 6, 1936, Archives of Xi State, TEA Building, Nashville.

[29]Maycie Southall to Gretchen Hyder, October 12, 1936, Archives of Xi State, TEA Building, Nashville.

suggest that much attention was given during the early years
of the Tennessee organization to major educational concerns
contemporary to the era. Two of these concerns were elimina-
tion of discrimination against married women in education and
promotion of kindergartens.

While still serving as Xi State president, Maycie Southall
was already becoming involved in Delta Kappa Gamma at the national level. In 1936 she wrote to a friend:

> I am writing you en route home from the National
> Convention of Delta Kappa Gamma, held in Oklahoma City
> June 5 and 6. I had to take my examination papers for
> the spring quarter with me and return before the Con-
> vention was over in order to get back for the summer
> school registration. But the trip was well worth the
> extra effort. . . .
>
> Under separate cover I am sending you the June
> Bulletin, which contains the plans for the Convention.
> I led the forum discussion, reported the work of our
> state and gave a toast at the birthday luncheon.[30]

The forum, in which five members participated, was a
new feature in the national convention program and was well
received: "The animated discussion of these brilliant women
proved most challenging and stimulated further interest in
the program of work."[31]

Although Maycie Southall had been a member of Delta Kappa
Gamma for only three years before she accepted the presidency
at the national level, the educator had already served in a

_____

[30]Maycie Southall to [Julia] Green, June 7, 1936,
Archives of Xi State, TEA Building, Nashville.

[31]Norma Smith Bristow, "A Brief History of the Delta
Kappa Gamma Society," The Delta Kappa Gamma Bulletin 5
(June 1939):23.

leadership role in Tennessee and had begun to move, at the same time, in national circles. She had been installed, at the beginning of the 1936 biennium, as corresponding secretary of the national organization.[32]

Annie Webb Blanton later summarized some of the progress made during the term of Maycie Southall's service as president of Xi State:

> As a leader . . . in Tennessee, Dr. Southall has been able to arouse for our work the genuine enthusiasm which only really great leaders can insure. . . . In Nashville and in other educational centers of the state, Dr. Southall and her devoted co-workers have drawn to our ranks a large proportion of the leading women educators of the state. . . .

> Not only has Dr. Southall led the way . . . in Tennessee, but her services in the National organization have been invaluable. At the National Convention in Oklahoma City in 1936, she led the Forum on Problems Which Women Face in This Age of Conflict, and at the convention in Chicago in 1937, she presided at the National Founders Day Banquet. Her counsel in meetings of the National Board has been most helpful, and she has given faithful service on a number of committees. . . . In addition to her work at conventions, Dr. Southall has been unusually helpful in aiding new organizations in other states. As she is in demand as a speaker in a number of other educational organizations, she has been pressed into service . . . to give incidental aid to new chapters and new states while meeting her speaking engagements on various occasions.[33]

In the article which Annie Webb Blanton had prepared as a tribute to some of the outstanding leaders in the organization, she averred:

> Maycie Southall's devotion to Delta Kappa Gamma is a part of her unselfish and untiring devotion to the

---

[32]Ibid.

[33]Blanton, "Pioneers in Delta Kappa Gamma," p. 22.

cause of education. In this organization she recognizes another means of helping her fellow teachers, of
fostering professional spirit, of developing social
life among teachers, and of improving schools for the
children of these United States; her enthusiasm for
Delta Kappa Gamma is a part of the selfless flame of
enthusiasm for education that animates her life and
her work. She exemplifies in herself unconsciously
the ideals towards which Delta Kappa Gamma is bending
its best efforts.[34]

Maycie Southall: National President

In 1938, during the same year that she relinquished the
reins as Xi State president in Tennessee, Maycie Southall
accepted greater responsibility as national president of the
Delta Kappa Gamma Society. Of interest is the fact that she
stated in retrospect during an interview many years later:
"I never sought an office. I have always thought, and taught
my students, that one never goes out of a job; he grows out
of it."[35] In 1944, Annie Webb Blanton wrote in regard to six
previous national presidents of the organization, one of whom
was Maycie Southall: "In all cases, the office has sought the
woman, and the nominating committees have made no mistakes."[36]

Of top priority during Maycie Southall's presidency at
the national level of Delta Kappa Gamma was the program of
work. In a 1939 letter of communication to state and chapter
presidents, she emphasized the fact that the program of work
was of utmost importance and urged unity toward a common goal:

---

[34]Ibid.

[35]Southall, interview, April 23, 1979.

[36]Annie Webb Blanton, "Summary of Delta Kappa Gamma
History," The Delta Kappa Gamma Bulletin 10 (June 1944):27.

"Unless each chapter and state organization cooperates in carrying out the program which was adopted at the National Convention, we cannot have a national program."[37]

The national program themes during Maycie Southall's term as national president were:

1938-1939
    1. Study of the Status of the Teaching Profession as compared to other lines of work
    2. "Discrimination against the Married Woman Teacher" and "Scrapping Teachers"

1939-1940
    1. A study in all local areas of the selection of candidates for all teacher training institutions[38]

Maycie Southall stated recently that the first five-year program of work was initiated during her tenure in office, a fact of which she is very proud; during this time, a committee was established and charged with the responsibility of studying and coordinating with other organizations in an effort to remove discrimination against married women in education.[39] The five-year program of work was activated during the second year of Maycie Southall's term as president. In addition to the 1939-40 year as noted above, the five-year plan included:

1940-1941
    2. Unjust discriminations

1941-1942
    3. Tenure and retirement

---

[37]"The National Program of Work," The Delta Kappa Gamma Bulletin 5 (April 1939):11.

[38]The Delta Kappa Gamma Society International, Program Manual: 1978-1979, p. 35.

[39]Southall, interview, December 15, 1979.

1942-1943
    4. Leadership in international crisis

1943-1944
    5. Enrichment of women teachers' personal lives[40]

In a published message to the membership, Maycie Southall emphasized the importance of research pertaining to women educators: "Each state is not only requested but urged to send to the National convention a doll to represent the most outstanding pioneer woman teacher of that state."[41] In explanation of her desire to continue a project that had originated in a previous administration, Maycie Southall wrote: "It is pleasantly surprising to see how . . . much we learn about the outstanding pioneers in different areas through this part of the program."[42] Envisioning long-range needs, she added: "I hope we may soon have a publication which will give the contributions pioneer women teachers have made to the program of education in the various states."[43] In connection with the project on figurines, it is interesting to note that approximately two years earlier Maycie Southall had been instrumental in presenting a replica of a pioneer woman educator who had contributed significantly to education in Tennessee; chosen for the honor was Julia Sears who was described as a valued

---

[40]The Delta Kappa Gamma Society International, Program Manual: 1978-79, p. 35.

[41]Maycie Southall, "Message from the National President," The Delta Kappa Gamma Bulletin 5 (June 1939):2.

[42]Ibid.

[43]Ibid.

member of the faculty at George Peabody College for Teachers
for thirty years.[44]   Concerning her accomplishments, Maycie
Southall wrote: "Hers is a wonderful example of achievement
and vision to all of us who follow in her lead."[45] As Maycie
Southall had been serving as president of Xi State during the
time of the presentation, she charged the members: "May the
next turn of the century find Tennessee with many, not just a
few, women educators of whom it may be proud."[46]

Another project of particular interest to Maycie Southall
during her term as national president was the realization of
a national scholarship. Determined to effect fruition of a
project that addressed one of the purposes of the organization
and that she considered worthwhile, the president appealed to
the Delta Kappa Gamma membership in June 1939, just two months
prior to the tenth national convention which was scheduled for
the last two days in August:[47]

> There is still some hope that we may be able to
> launch our first national scholarship at the tenth
> annual convention. . . . What a fine achievement it
> would be for our tenth birthday if we could achieve
> one of the major purposes for which Delta Kappa Gamma
> was organized--namely, "to encourage higher training
> for women teachers by endowing scholarships to aid
> women teachers in continuing their studies in higher
> institutions."[48]

---

[44]Maycie Southall, "Tennessee," The Delta Kappa Gamma
Bulletin 3 (June 1937):22.

[45]Ibid.

[46]Ibid.

[47]Southall, "Message from the National President," p. 1.

[48]Ibid., p. 2.

Maycie Southall's administration was successful in win-
ning the members' approval in 1939 for the first national
scholarship.[49] The name of the first recipient, Lillian
Minor, was announced at a dinner meeting during the 1940
national convention held in Washington, D.C.[50] Of interest
is the fact that the same Lillian Minor was awarded her Doctor
of Philosophy degree at George Peabody College for Teachers
in 1943; her major professor was Maycie Southall.

An analysis of Maycie Southall's activities and messages
to the membership clearly indicated a strong interest in the
scholarship program. She believed in women's potentiality
for capable leadership in education; scholarships would provide opportunities to obtain training needed to meet the responsibilities of leadership. Maycie Southall said many years
later that her commitment to scholarship programs could be
traced to her own early experience as a scholarship recipient;
she realized the importance of scholarships to students who
wanted to attain an education because she had completed some
of her graduate work at George Peabody College for Teachers
with aid from the General Education Board.[51]

Maycie Southall presided at the two national conventions
held during her term in office. In August 1939, the tenth

---

[49]Blanton, "Summary of Delta Kappa Gamma History," p. 27.

[50]The Delta Kappa Gamma Society, Minutes of the Executive
Board Meeting, March 21, 1940, p. 12; Archives of Xi State,
TEA Building, Nashville.

[51]Southall, interview, April 23, 1979.

annual convention of The Delta Kappa Gamma Society was held
in Asheville, North Carolina; in March 1940, the members
assembled in Washington, D.C. In 1939, thirty-three states
sent a total of 308 members; in 1940, all organized states
but one were represented by a total of 285 members.[52]

Many efforts bore fruition during the biennium that
began in 1938. Maycie Southall's administration has been
credited with: heartily encouraging research; completing
the first national scholarship; appointing the first art
committee which resulted in the adoption of an official
brass bowl, vase, and tray; expediting the arrangements for
construction of a national headquarters building; and gaining approval to pay the executive secretary a half-time
salary.[53] Additional action taken during Maycie Southall's
presidency resulted in: giving an annual honorarium to the
national treasurer; presenting to Annie Webb Blanton a sum
sufficient to pay a noted artist for painting a portrait of
her suitable for permanent display later in the new headquarters building; and surprising the originator of Delta
Kappa Gamma with a car to replace one that she had used extensively in her travels in behalf of the organization.[54]

At the close of Maycie Southall's term of office as
national president, Annie Webb Blanton summarized and

---

[52]Holden, Our Heritage, pp. 107-8.

[53]Blanton, "Summary of Delta Kappa Gamma History,"
pp. 28-29.

[54]Holden, Our Heritage, pp. 107-8.

evaluated the Tennessean's leadership activities in Delta
Kappa Gamma; as executive secretary, she was in a prime
position to observe the efforts of Maycie Southall's administration. Included in her report was an itinerary of
the national, state, and local meetings that Maycie Southall
attended between 1938 and 1940 during which the latter represented the organization. The president's extensive travels
carried her to widely scattered geographic areas:

> Any work which Maycie Southall would undertake
> would be outstanding in its results, because she is
> a person of extraordinary executive ability, unusual
> intellectual powers, untiring industry, rare talent
> as a speaker, and charm of person that instantly at-
> tracts and arouses enthusiasm.

> The Delta Kappa Gamma Society was, therefore,
> peculiarly fortunate, when, at the Denver convention
> in 1938, Dr. Southall accepted the presidency of the
> organization. For two years, she has led us most
> effectively in the ways we should go.

> Probably her greatest service during the past
> two years lies in the development of unity, of a bet-
> ter understanding of the purposes for which we stand,
> and in the growth of what we call "National spirit."
> She has been herself the embodiment of this spirit,
> and she has given to us a personal leadership which
> it is difficult adequately to evaluate.

> We actually reach people, not so much by written
> messages and obvious precepts, as by personal contacts
> and glowing words proceeding from heart to heart.

> And these Maycie Southall has given to Delta Kappa
> Gamma. No night was too cold and no day too stormy,
> for her to board a plane for what might have been a
> perilous flight across the continent to keep a distant
> engagement. No trip by bus, automobile, or train was
> too rough, even though on some of the adventures she
> was supported by crutches. The following is a summary
> of the various meetings which she attended, at which
> she spoke for Delta Kappa Gamma:

DELTA KAPPA GAMMA MEETINGS
ATTENDED 1938-1940

I. National Meetings (6)
   A. Delta Kappa Gamma Conventions
      1. Tenth National Convention, Asheville, N.C.,
         August 1939
      2. Eleventh National Convention, Washington,
         D.C., March 1940
   B. Other National Meetings
      1. Detroit, Mich.--Progressive Education
         Association, February 1939
      2. Cleveland, Ohio--National Education Assn.,
         Feb. 1939
      3. Atlanta, Georgia--Association for Childhood
         Educ., 1939
      4. Milwaukee, Wis.--Assn. for Childhood Educ.,
         1940

II. State Conventions (19)
    1. Ohio, Columbus
    2. Indiana, Indianapolis
    3. California, Los Angeles
    4. Arkansas, Little Rock
    5. Georgia, Atlanta
    6. Texas, Dallas
    7. Tennessee, Monteagle
    8. Alabama, Birmingham
    9. Iowa, Des Moines
   10. Louisiana, Alexandria
   11. Nebraska, Grand Island
   12. Mississippi, Biloxi
   13. Missouri, Joplin
   14. Illinois, La Salle
   15. Maryland, Baltimore
   16. Pennsylvania, Harrisburg
   17. New Jersey, Trenton
   18. Tennessee, Chattanooga
   19. South Carolina, Columbia

III. Other State or District Meetings (9)
    1. Kentucky, Louisville--State Teachers Meeting
    2. Texas, Bryan--State Supervisors Meeting
    3. Tennessee, Nashville--District Teachers Meeting
    4. Georgia, Atlanta--State Teachers Meeting
    5. Georgia, Milledgeville--Summer Conference
    6. Virginia, Norfolk--District Teachers Meeting
    7. North Carolina, Greensboro--District Teachers
       Meeting
    8. Oklahoma, Muskogee--District Teachers Meeting
    9. Oklahoma, Oklahoma City--State Teachers Meeting

IV. City Meetings (6)
    1. Cincinnati, Ohio
    2. Birmingham, Ala.
    3. Denton, Texas
    4. Chattanooga, Tenn.
    5. Nashville, Tenn.
    6. Raleigh, N.C.

V. Summary
    A. 42 Different Groups
        1. Two National Delta Kappa Gamma Conventions
        2. Four other National meetings
        3. Nineteen State Delta Kappa Gamma Conventions
        4. Nine other State and District meetings
        5. Six City meetings
        6. Two college groups (Summer meetings of Delta
           Kappa Gamma at Peabody College)

When we remember that, while doing this work, Dr. Southall filled a full-time teaching position at Peabody College, we can only add ourselves to the enthusiastic members in her audiences everywhere who felt the marvelous influence of her eloquence and her unequaled poise, but feared for her physical endurance.

Dr. Southall takes Delta Kappa [Gamma] seriously. She believes in its purposes and its powers. She recognizes the organization as one of the means of building up the teaching profession through study by teachers of their own profession and of their own powers in the betterment of education. Perhaps, her second great accomplishment has been the expansion and improvement of the Delta Kappa Gamma program of work. She has appointed capable committees, and with their aid she has set up and carried out the best plans of work that we have ever undertaken. She approves of the social aspects of Delta Kappa Gamma life for she recognizes the fact that this is a type of enrichment of our lives that teachers need if they are to do their best work. But she has been able to make each organization realize that the program of work must be the center of our main activities.

It was under Dr. Southall's leadership that our first National Delta Kappa Gamma scholarship was completed, and the first recipient selected to receive the award. When the Scholarship Fund lacked several thousand dollars of the necessary $20,000, she had the courage to propose to add what was needed from the available fund which that year, was unusually plethoric from extraordinary expansion. A timid woman might have feared censure if a possible deficit should occur the next year;

but our president's quiet courage led her on without hesitation, and now the coveted scholarship is an accomplished fact, one in which all of us feel pride.

It was also largely through her support and assistance that plans for a foundation for an Educators Award were incorporated into the Constitution.

The great expansion of Delta Kappa Gamma in the past two years has been largely due to the enthusiasm resulting from her personal leadership and her untiring work. Her prominence in other educational organizations and the devotion to her of members of these organizations, has served Delta Kappa Gamma well. She has been in constant demand as a speaker, and whenever other organizations have paid her expenses to serve on their programs, she has used the opportunity to visit Delta Kappa Gamma, to solve our problems, and to give us comfort and encouragement. Women who know her in educational associations have accepted our invitations because they thought, "If Dr. Southall directs Delta Kappa Gamma, it must be worth joining." She systematically studied the unorganized states and frequently sent to the organizers, addresses of prospective members which she had obtained from friends in these states. . . . In the two years Delta Kappa Gamma gained 188 chapters and 5,681 members, a total gain, in this biennium of 80 per cent, on the membership of 6,979 of the year preceding her administration.

Throughout her administration Dr. Southall has shown fairness and consideration to all and an utter selflessness rarely seen. No complaint was too trifling for her consideration, yet she was firm in demanding of all that they should hew to the provisions of the Constitution. When members of the committee would have bestowed upon her the achievement award, she stated that the president, while she is in office, should not be considered for the award, and firmly eliminated herself from consideration.

At both of the conventions at which she has presided, Dr. Southall has shown her great ability as an executive. She has exhibited in the appointment of committees, both discrimination as to ability and skill in satisfying the many interests and claims in every large organization. Her programs have been among the best that we have had, and have given opportunity for thought, fun, and fellowship. Her performance at the last National convention in Washington was absolutely heroic. In an automobile accident, three weeks previously, she had suffered a broken knee. She attended

this convention with her knee in a cast. Yet her smile
was as ready and as sweet, her command of every situation as perfect as if she had not been hampered in this
tragic way--and her brave spirit, her gay comradeship,
and her charming personality, captured every heart.

As her chief lieutenant during the past two years,
the writer would like to add, "She is good to work with."
In my own work I have committed errors and made mistakes.
Her comment has always been, "It's a wonder you don't
make more!" She has never said, "You must do this and
that," but always "Would you like to do this?" I have
been able to respect her thinking, to admire her sense
of justice and fair play, and to appreciate the rare
privilege of the close and friendly association of the
past two years. We do not lose Maycie Southall, now that
we have gained Emma Reinhardt. Both are ours for aye in
Delta Kappa Gamma.[55]

During an interview held on December 15, 1979, at her
home, Maycie Southall substantiated the record compiled in
Our Heritage which credited her with having organized the
states of Connecticut, Vermont, Massachusetts, and West
Virginia.[56]

Outstanding Honors

The Achievement Award is considered to be the highest
honor that can be bestowed upon a member; such recognition
was begun in 1933, and only one member is awarded the honor
in any given year. Although Maycie Southall firmly refused
to be considered for the coveted Achievement Award during
her term as national president, the members did not soon forget her efforts in behalf of the organization. Her term as
national president had expired in 1940, and it was during

---

[55]Annie Webb Blanton, "An Outstanding Administration,"
The Delta Kappa Gamma Bulletin 7 (November 1940):12-13.

[56]Holden, Our Heritage, p. 304.

the national convention held in 1941 that Maycie Southall
was presented the organization's national Achievement Award.[57]
Thus, she became the ninth recipient of the emblem which sig-
nified distinguished service to the Delta Kappa Gamma Society.
Presenting the citation was Eula Lee Carter; known affection-
ately among the members as the Texas Skipper, the author's
personality becomes apparent in the presentation delivered
in 1941:

> It is not always that a piece of committee work
> brings such quick returns in the way of exquisite pleas-
> ure as has the chairmanship of the National Achievement
> Award Committee brought this year. Today it becomes my
> privilege to announce to you the winner of the National
> Achievement Award, and to present to her in behalf of
> the National Organization this emblem of distinguished
> service.
>
> But before I announce her name, I shall draw her
> picture in terms of Delta Kappa Gamma dimensions. When
> I finish, you may call with me her name.
>
> In Delta Kappa Gamma STATURE she is tall--very tall.
> Her shadow, and it is a goodly one, stretches across the
> entire continent. We think up whenever we hear her name.
> She moves rapidly in her seven league boots from place
> to place and from state to state. There is no place too
> small, and no job too hard for her.
>
> Her Delta Kappa Gamma EYES are farseeing. She sees
> beyond state boundaries and sectional horizons to a new
> day and to a new tomorrow. She marches fearlessly into
> that new unity of "all for each, and each for all." Her
> banner is Delta Kappa Gamma.
>
> Her Delta Kappa Gamma VOICE is soft and low, yet
> vibrant with enthusiasm. It bids us go forward, and
> again, when the going is too hard or even impossible, it
> bids us wait and be patient in the waiting.
>
> Her Delta Kappa Gamma EARS are attuned to the signs
> of the time. She is able to disregard the raucous noises

---

[57]"The National Convention," The Delta Kappa Gamma
Bulletin 8 (November 1941):6.

of the rabble and to pick up the slightest undercover rumor that bespeaks danger. Like a deer--spelled <u>deer</u>-- she has stalked the enemy and warned us of its nearness. She has advised us when to come out into the open and when to lie low.

Her Delta Kappa Gamma HEART and HEAD work fearlessly, relentlessly for her beloved organization. There has never been any apparent conflict between these two vital organs.

You will notice that I have used the present tense throughout. It is my belief that her continuous service to Delta Kappa Gamma will always bear a vital relationship to the present. I cannot think of her work in terms of past tenses. Her name--her name is synonymous with charm. Her name is Maycie--Dr. Maycie Southall--past National President of Delta Kappa Gamma.

Dr. Southall, in behalf of the National Organization, I present to you this National Achievement Award for 1941.[58]

Again, some two decades later, the organization bestowed an outstanding honor upon Maycie Southall. As a token of appreciation for her many contributions, the Society established in Maycie Southall's name a fifth international scholarship in 1962.[59] Of interest is the fact that she was selected as the recipient of this particular honor for it was during her term as national president that the first national scholarship had been finalized; completed in 1939 and awarded the following year, the first scholarship had been named in honor of Annie Webb Blanton, the originator of Delta Kappa Gamma.[60] Awarded annually, the fifth scholarship is entitled The Maycie K. Southall Scholarship.

---

[58]Eula Lee Carter, "Presentation Speech of the National Achievement Award," <u>The Delta Kappa Gamma Bulletin</u> 8 (November 1941):30.

[59]Dorothy L. Johnson, personal letter, May 1, 1979.

[60]Holden, <u>Our Heritage</u>, p. 221.

Then, in 1974, Maycie Southall and Mary Hall became the first recipients of the Xi State Achievement Award. It recognized their distinguished service to the organization.[61]

Additional Activities

Termination of office at the national level in 1940 by no means meant the end of Maycie Southall's participation in many activities of the organization at all levels.

Maycie Southall became a charter member of Beta Chapter of Xi State on March 23, 1937.[62] A past president of Xi State who has shared membership for many years with Maycie Southall in their chapter which is located in Nashville volunteered that the latter has served their members well in a variety of capacities.[63]

Relics housed in the Archives of Xi State such as yearbooks and programs from past conventions indicate that on many occasions throughout her years of membership Maycie Southall has participated in meetings and conventions at all levels of the organization; she has served in such varied capacities as toastmistress, speaker, consultant, discussion group leader, moderator, and both chairman and member of standing and ad hoc committees. Not intended to be all inclusive, a few random samples of her leadership activities

---

[61]Mary Hall, interview held in Murfreesboro, Tennessee, July 2, 1979.

[62]Nell Parkinson, "Beta Chapter, Nashville," _The Delta Kappa Gamma Bulletin_ 5 (June 1939):82.

[63]McDonald, personal letter, May 9, 1979.

garnered from various sources are presented merely in order to indicate their diversity and continuation over a period of years. She served as chairman of the national committee on membership during 1940-42.[64] She was selected as chairman of the national scholarship committee for a two-year term beginning in 1950.[65] According to a record of business items credited to the 1950-52 biennium, a plan was ". . . outlined for granting a Silver Anniversary Scholarship to each state in 1954."[66] Eula Lee Carter, whose distinguished record in the Society for more than fifty years includes leadership that bore fruition of scholarships for each state in 1954, stated that Maycie Southall is quite well known for her support throughout many years of the scholarship program.[67] Phyllis Ellis, past director of the organization's southwest region, shared: "We always knew we could count on Maycie for help as she was very interested in establishing scholarships for the members."[68] Zora Ellis provided information about more recent activities: "When I was international president (1960-62), she was a member of the Scholarship

---

[64]Maycie Southall, "Report of National Membership Committee," The Delta Kappa Gamma Bulletin 8 (November 1941):35.

[65]Holden, Our Heritage, p. 318.

[66]Eunah Temple Holden, Our Heritage, 2 vols. of which the first is not numbered (n.p.: Steck-Warlick Company for The Delta Kappa Gamma Society, 1970), 2:151.

[67]Eula Lee Carter, telephone interview, Ft. Worth, Texas, September 27, 1980.

[68]Phyllis Ellis, telephone interview, Ft. Worth, Texas, September 27, 1980.

Committee."[69] She continued by noting that Maycie Southall
has in still later years participated in committee work concerned with expansion ". . . as the Society effected organization in other countries."[70] Specifically, "Maycie was a member of the first Delta Kappa Gamma Ad Hoc Advisory Committee
on Foreign Expansion within Scandinavia."[71] Her interest in
the promotion of international education was widely known.
The expansion into Scandinavia was significant to the Society;
that is, "On April 3, 1970, the first Delta Kappa Gamma Chapter
abroad was installed at Oslo, Norway."[72] In 1978, the inveterate traveler attended the Society's Seminar in Purposeful
Living held in Stockholm, Sweden, in order to become acquainted
with key women teachers in Scandinavia and to learn of their
philosophy and research in child development.[73] In 1978, she
spoke at a leadership conference held for chapter presidents
in Tennessee. She has continued to the present time to participate in a variety of activities. In April 1979, she
addressed a Xi State legislative seminar held in Nashville;
and two months later she participated in the annual Xi State
convention, an outstanding assembly for the membership as
much attention was directed toward a celebration of the fiftieth anniversary of Delta Kappa Gamma.

---

[69]Zora Ellis, personal letter, April 26, 1979.

[70]Ibid.

[71]Holden, Our Heritage, vol. 2, pp. 143-44.

[72]Ibid., p. 87.

[73]Southall, interview, December 15, 1979.

Delta Kappa Gamma: In Retrospect

Compilation of this particular chapter of the study was begun during 1979, fifty years after the first organizational meeting of Delta Kappa Gamma in May 1929. It is unlikely that Annie Webb Blanton, in her most vivid imagination, could have envisioned that during the first fifty years the organization would increase in membership and progress through the multiplicity of activities as is now evident. Too, it is highly improbable that Maycie Southall would have dared to dream in 1935, when one of her first goals was expansion of membership through selection of key women educators, that in 1979 Xi State would include a total of sixty-two chapters across Tennessee.

The years have brought changes, and some of the changes will be touched upon briefly; for example, membership in the organization is no longer shrouded by a veil of secrecy. Women feel the freedom of both joining and acknowledging membership in the Society without the fear of such action meeting with disapproval. Too, the affluence currently experienced by this nation permits women educators to affiliate with organizations of their choice more readily than during the early days of Delta Kappa Gamma; thus, expansion of membership within the Society is no longer a primary goal.

Since its inception, Xi State has continued to work within the guidelines of each international program theme. In addition, as in the early years, Xi State leaders are continuing to address local educational concerns; for example, during the past two years the Tennessee unit has directed a tremendous

amount of attention toward a state-adopted project entitled
The Improvement of Literacy. Innumerable individual, committee, and chapter efforts have been evidenced as a result
of adoption of the state project.

The purposes are now seven in number:

    1. To unite women educators of the world in a
genuine spiritual fellowship;

    2. To honor women who have given or who evidence
a potential for distinctive service in any field of
education;

    3. To advance the professional interest and posi-
tion of women in education;

    4. To initiate, endorse, and support desirable
legislation in the interests of education and of women
educators;

    5. To endow scholarships to aid outstanding women
educators in pursuing graduate study and to grant fellow-
ships to women educators from other countries;

    6. To stimulate the personal and professional
growth of members and to encourage their participation
in appropriate programs of action;

    7. To inform the membership of current economic,
social, political, and educational issues to the end
that they may become intelligent, functioning members
of a world society.[74]

Maycie Southall recently shared ruminations about the
progress of Delta Kappa Gamma. Reflecting upon two important
aspects of the organization, the purposes and the programs of
work, she mused:

    My disappointment in the Delta Kappa Gamma Society
has been the fact that we have not had more action to
improve education and the role of women in education that
I had anticipated. We have been giving too much time to
programs that result in purpose No. 7. We have done well
by purpose No. 1, 2, and purpose No. 5 to the neglect of

[74]The Constitution of The Delta Kappa Gamma Society,
art. 2 (1972).

No. 3, 4, and the last part of No. 6. If we are to improve the education of children and youth and improve
the role of women in education, we need programs of action versus study; for example, before I was national
president, most of the efforts of the three first presidents had been given to organizing states and increasing
membership. As a great deal of this had already been
done, I felt that the greatest need was a dynamic program that would further the purposes for which we had
been organized; and I appointed a program committee to
set up a five-year program which would involve all the
states that were then organized and the chapters in a
united effort. Our five-year goal was to remove discrimination against married women because at that time
many of the best teachers were being lost to the service
by the denial of married teachers a right to teach.

In a period in which national programs of action
were carried on, the programs seemed to become more and
more a study rather than a study and action program.
There is a saying, "Study without action is futile, but
action without study is fatal," and therefore both are
essential.[75]

Delta Kappa Gamma has, during its first fifty years,

become international in scope. Maycie Southall's well-known

interest in international education is reflected in her views

concerning expansion into foreign countries:

In retrospect, our expansion committee should have
continued the work of the subcommittee in recognizing key
teachers at each professional level in all the countries
as an aid to fulfilling our purpose of uniting teachers
of the world in spiritual fellowship and also as an aid
to the organization of those countries at a later date.
While I approve our present organization taking the
leadership in organizing other countries, I feel that
this present approach is very expensive and much slower
than necessary if we had some kind of recognition of
each country's leaders, using them to aid and guide in
the country's organization because each country knows
its own leaders. This was the plan we used in the
United States, and I see no reason why it would not work
better than the present plan as we expand into other
countries.[76]

---

[75]Southall, interview, June 19, 1979.

[76]Ibid.

In characteristic style, Maycie Southall preferred to
look toward the future rather than reflect about the past;
thus, she suggested structural changes that should be considered:

> Furthermore, I believe that we have outgrown our
> present organizational structure and need to have not
> only chapter, state, and international organization but
> have chapter, state, national, and international with
> each country having its national organization unified
> through a world society of key women teachers. This
> structure combined with the present would mean that we
> would have regional conventions one year, national an-
> other, and international every third year.[77]

Contributions to Delta Kappa Gamma

In an attempt to derive evaluations of Maycie Southall's
contributions to education through her efforts in The Delta
Kappa Gamma Society International, requests for information
were sent to many leaders including the present and past
national/international presidents and the present and past
Xi State presidents.

Numerous responses were received immediately; both the
promptness and content of the replies indicate enthusiasm
concerning the fact that a study is being made of Maycie
Southall's contributions to education and that it embraces
her efforts in Delta Kappa Gamma.

An analysis of the replies revealed that the leaders of
Delta Kappa Gamma readily acknowledge an extraordinary amount
of influence exerted by Maycie Southall upon the membership
of the organization. The most frequently mentioned ways in

---

[77]Ibid.

which her leadership has been felt centered around her promotion of the scholarship program; her image as a woman educator exemplified through attire; her personal attributes;
and her commitment to the improvement of education. Selected
comments from the communications are included in this study.

Scholarships

A past president at the international level described
Maycie Southall's initiation of action:

> She recognized the importance scholarships could
> play in making possible a teaching career and had the
> courage to complete the first scholarship in Delta
> Kappa Gamma. Her influence has been a driving force
> in the development of our present scholarship program.[78]

Another leader recalled ". . . that during the 1958 convention . . . it was Dr. Southall who prodded us to embark
upon the . . . program which resulted in the awarding of 57
Special Scholarships . . . in 1960."[79] Still another observer remembered Maycie Southall's participation at conventions when the latter had ". . . spoken strongly in favor of
scholarship projects and urged action on legislative matters
affecting education and the status of women."[80] Another
previous officeholder indicated her awareness that the promotion of scholarships was one of the subject's chief contributions, ". . . and she has done much along this line."[81]

---

[78]Parker, personal letter, May 17, 1979.

[79]Dorothy L. Johnson, personal letter, May 1, 1979.

[80]Hiller, personal letter, May 2, 1979.

[81]Nell McMains, personal letter, May 14, 1979.

From the vantage point of Xi State, a past president wrote:
"She led the Society to implement the Scholarship Program;
she led Tennessee to be a leader in scholarship programs."[82]
In conclusion, the international president during the 1978-80
biennium reviewed Maycie Southall's efforts in behalf of the
scholarship program:

> There is documented evidence that Dr. Southall's
> foresight and courage in giving impetus to the scholar-
> ship program on all levels of the Society place her in
> a unique position in our organization. It was during
> her biennium as president that the first national
> scholarship . . . was awarded to Miss Lillian Minor of
> Norfolk, Virginia. This began an impressive movement
> which has touched the lives of hundreds of women among
> our membership. The vitality of the program has in-
> creased through the years to enrich the Society, the
> members, and the profession.[83]

Grooming, A Professional Responsibility

A past leader vividly described a particular incident
that occurred at a meeting she had attended:

> Dr. Southall is always beautifully dressed. At one
> conference I recall her giving some homely and heartfelt
> advice, even some scolding, to professional women about
> their personal appearance and how they should manage
> their wardrobes in relation to their professional duties.
> Her points made with vehemence were: (1) Every profes-
> sional woman owes it to herself, her position, and to
> women to be well-dressed and well-groomed; (2) A profes-
> sional woman should so plan her activities that she does
> not fritter away an undue amount of time shopping; (3)
> A woman teacher who plans her wardrobe well can get her
> shopping done in two major efforts in summer vacation
> and Christmas vacation and thus have time for profes-
> sional meetings and obligations on many weekends. I have
> never forgotten her speech which apparently reflected her
> personal habits and may have indicated how she had time

---

[82]Oakley, personal letter, May 23, 1979.

[83]Bernice Conoly, personal letter, May 14, 1979.

for all the professional duties while also presenting a fashionable appearance.[84]

Maycie Southall saw the opportunity to utilize her natural attractiveness as one means of upgrading the image of all women educators:

> I have admired her greatly for her meticulous attention to good grooming. She has excellent taste in clothes, both as to style and color, and always presents a most attractive image of a woman educator.[85]

Still another incident, shared by a past president of Xi State, provides an example of Maycie Southall's influence:

> Dr. Southall cared about her personal appearance. One young teacher told me, in the days when white gloves were important in the social world, that she had always had an extra pair of clean white gloves ready for any occasion because of Dr. Southall's example of a meticulous appearance.[86]

A retired educator who served as president of the unit in Tennessee during the 1940-42 biennium wrote: "I consider Maycie Southall the flower of Southern womanhood--lovely to look at, attractively and suitably dressed, gracious, cultured, highly intelligent."[87] A more recent past president shared similar views:

> We have been proud to claim her as a Xi State member when we have been with her at regional and international meetings. She is always beautifully dressed and expresses her opinions well and forcefully. The Society owes her much, at both the state and international levels.[88]

---

[84]Edna McGuire Boyd, personal letter, May 4, 1979.

[85]Hiller, personal letter, May 2, 1979.

[86]McDonald, personal letter, May 9, 1979.

[87]Mildred Dawson, personal letter, May 23, 1979.

[88]Eleanor C. Osteen, personal letter, May 11, 1979.

Personal Attributes

A past president of Xi State remembered in particular
Maycie Southall's keen sense of humor.[89] Another contributor
who had often sat near Maycie Southall at head tables during
conventions wrote: "She is a good conversationalist and
talks her _profession_. Her life has been wrapped up in it."[90]
The same observer continued by noting that Maycie Southall
possesses the flexibility required to mix easily among groups
of varied personalities: "In recognition given to her in
many areas, she never assumes an egotistical attitude. She
does not put herself on a high plane. She mixes well."[91]

Determination and persistence are words frequently used
in the evaluations of Maycie Southall's efforts pertaining
to Delta Kappa Gamma. After careful consideration, if she
deems a project or activity to be worthy of the investment of
time and effort requisite to fruition, she works relentlessly
toward effecting the best possible results. A past president
of Xi State remarked: "When Dr. Southall believes in a given
project, she works tirelessly for its completion and insists
that her friends and co-workers do likewise."[92] She added:
"Dr. Southall has worked diligently for the advancement of
women in education. She is a living example of what capable

---

[89]Gertrude Michael, personal letter, May 24, 1979.

[90]Zora Ellis, personal letter, April 26, 1979.

[91]Ibid.

[92]Alyse Morton, personal letter, June 7, 1979.

and dedicated women can achieve when they put minds and hearts into their work."[93] Another contributor addressed the same personal attribute when, in describing Maycie Southall, she wrote that ". . . persistence against odds is one of her fine characteristics."[94]

Maycie Southall's personality fascinated and attracted friends from various age groups. A past president who served at the national level during the 1940s shared her memories:

> I remember Maycie Southall as a very attractive lady who possessed a dynamic personality. She had very high professional standards and always attracted young people so that they responded with enthusiasm and gained professionally from her philosophy.
>
> Dr. Southall's collaboration and cooperation were always excellent in our work for the Society, and Delta Kappa Gamma members responded eagerly to her spirit and sparkle.[95]

Several contributors of information mentioned Maycie Southall's futuristic outlook; for example, one wrote: "I believe that one of Maycie's strongest traits is creative vision."[96] Continuing the same train of thought, she added:

> I believe Maycie epitomizes some of the qualities which will be necessary in education in the future-- indomitable enthusiasm and optimism, great flexibility and adaptability, a world view of education and of human beings, and a feeling that a worthwhile goal is more important than rules or regulations which may impede the achieving of a goal.[97]

---

[93]Ibid.

[94]Parker, personal letter, May 17, 1979.

[95]Catherine Nutterville, personal letter, May 5, 1979.

[96]Parker, personal letter, May 17, 1979.

[97]Ibid.

Another contributor perceived Maycie Southall's ability to think in terms of long-range plans in regard to education: "She is progressive in views and sees the long-range picture as it affects the total education program."[98] In the same letter, the contributor extended her thoughts:

> A lady and educator of high standards for herself and others, she demands the respect of others by her demeanor, her manner of expressing ideas, her ability to challenge others to produce. Her thoughts stimulate need for clear thinking before decision-making in Delta Kappa Gamma and always awaken the need for long-range plans, not impulsive action.[99]

Activities Exemplifying
Commitment to Education

Maycie Southall has attended conventions, conferences, workshops, and regular meetings of the organization; but, even more, she has participated in countless activities in a variety of ways. One member expressed: "Dr. Southall frequently makes very sage comments in our International Executive Board meetings."[100] Another contributor penned: "She goes to conventions and urges women to prepare for and seek leadership positions."[101] Still another member observed:

> At the national convention held in Denver, I had close opportunities to admire her friendly charm and her leadership qualities. Later as I served on the board of AAUW at the same time as did Dr. Southall, I

---

[98]Esther H. Strickland, personal letter, May 1, 1979.

[99]Ibid.

[100]Birdella M. Ross, personal letter, April 27, 1979.

[101]Ival Aslinger, personal letter, May 25, 1979.

came to realize the wide range of her knowledge and
her influence as an educator.[102]

One letter writer emphasized Maycie Southall's ability
to communicate effectively:

> Dr. Southall has been a distinguished and out-
> standing leader in Delta Kappa Gamma. From her posi-
> tion as first state president of Tennessee and soon
> after national president, she worked closely with
> Dr. Annie Webb Blanton so that she has been able to
> communicate to those of us who came later the inspira-
> tion and aspirations for the Society which she re-
> ceived from our Founder.[103]

Maycie Southall's activities extended far beyond the
floor of the convention halls. The manifestations of her
service become evident through reading about her efforts;
for example, one contributor remarked:

> Many superintendents received letters from
> Dr. Southall to make known to them outstanding work
> performed by Delta Kappa Gamma members, and I doubt
> that any woman ever received a promotion that she did
> not congratulate her superintendent on his wisdom in
> making the appointment.[104]

One of the early leaders in Xi State expressed appreciation for help provided by Maycie Southall:

> Dr. Southall was professor at Peabody; I, at the
> University of Tennessee. She was the first state
> president of Delta Kappa Gamma while I was the first
> president of the new chapter at Knoxville. I later
> became the third state president. We always worked
> professionally and personally with complete coopera-
> tion and mutual respect.
>
> Dr. Southall took time to hold a conference with
> me to orient me in the conditions I would meet in be-
> coming the third Delta Kappa Gamma state president.

---

[102]Rawls, personal letter, May 11, 1979.

[103]Parker, personal letter, May 17, 1979.

[104]McDonald, personal letter, May 9, 1979.

So I knew where to move ahead at once, what problems
to face and how, the responsibilities I would have to
assume as state president in an organization with national objectives and programs. She was my backer in
heading up the state organization.[105]

The same contributor included a comprehensive evaluation

of Maycie Southall's contributions to education: "In my es-

timation--past and present--Dr. Southall is and has been the

leading woman educator in the South."[106] In reference to

Delta Kappa Gamma efforts, the same professor evaluated:

Without doubt, Dr. Southall has been outstanding
in Delta Kappa Gamma. . . . Whatever she espoused, she
worked at endlessly, fearlessly, effectively. There
has never been any doubt about where she stood on any
issue as she expressed herself clearly and forcefully
in both word and action.[107]

A past president of Xi State who was initiated into the

Society in 1936 reviewed Maycie Southall's efforts:

She has always been interested in higher education
for women; in equal pay for equal work; in getting women
to accept positions of leadership; and in getting women
to perform at a high level of efficiency.

Dr. Southall has been interested in Delta Kappa
Gamma doing worthwhile projects rather than busy work
and strictly social functions. She has sought to make
Delta Kappa Gamma members something special. . . .

I wish Dr. Southall's dedication to learning, to
worthwhile projects in education, and to Delta Kappa
Gamma could fall like a mantle onto many young members.
I shudder to think of our Society when our great leaders
leave us, but surely the Lord will raise up some who
will carry on the great work she has thus far so nobly
advanced.[108]

---

[105]Mildred Dawson, personal letter, May 23, 1979.

[106]Ibid.

[107]Ibid.

[108]Oakley, personal letter, May 23, 1979.

This portion of the study is concluded with a pertinent comment provided by Margaret Sherer, president of Xi State during the 1977-79 biennium: "We must continue to help educate all members of Xi State that they should strive to be educators emulating the stature of Dr. Southall."[109]

What If . . . ? or Epilogue

Maycie Southall remembers well the day in 1935 when she received the invitation from Annie Webb Blanton to become a member of Delta Kappa Gamma. She had mixed reactions; but because she was already a member of other honor societies, Maycie Southall immediately wrote a note in which she courteously but firmly declined the invitation and started toward the post office to drop the letter in the mail. Before she reached her destination, however, Maycie Southall reassessed the potentiality of the organization; and, realizing that in it lay a genuine opportunity for a group of key women educators to work together toward the improvement of education, she tore the note into shreds and then, on October 7, 1935, mailed her acceptance of the invitation to Annie Webb Blanton.[110]

What if Maycie Southall had mailed in 1935 the letter of refusal? Would some other leader have risen to the occasion and accepted the responsibilities of presidency at both the state and national levels? If so, would the ensuing progress have been different? And, if different, in what respects? Of

---

[109]Margaret Sherer, personal letter, May 22, 1979.

[110]Southall, interview, June 19, 1979.

course, speculation as to what might have occurred instead of what did does not fall within the major area of concern of this research project. The major area of concern within this chapter has been that of recording some aspects, not all by any means, of Maycie Southall's association with, and contributions to, Delta Kappa Gamma. From all indications, a major conclusion to be drawn from the study may be stated as follows: The membership is indeed fortunate that in 1935 Maycie Southall paused and, apparently displaying the futuristic outlook frequently attributed to her, decided to replace her earlier letter of refusal with one of acceptance of Annie Webb Blanton's invitation to join The Delta Kappa Gamma Society.

Dr. Southall is in the "top few" outstanding educators of this century.

Rodney Tillman
Personal letter
July 11, 1979

CHAPTER V

OTHER ORGANIZATIONAL SERVICES AND HONORS

Self-Imposed Responsibilities

In a 1934 letter addressed to President Bruce R. Payne,
George Peabody College for Teachers, Maycie Southall wrote:

> In my own thinking I have used the following three
> criteria as fair measures of the success of a department
> in a teachers' college, namely: (1) how many students
> it draws; (2) how many students it holds to graduation;
> and (3) what type of positions its majors fill. . . .
>
> Some figures compiled by Dr. Garrison . . . show
> that more students took courses in elementary education
> than in any other department of the college last year.
>
> The number taking a master's degree in elementary
> education has increased in spite of the depression. In
> fact, . . . I discovered that as many students have taken
> the master's degree in elementary education at Peabody
> since 1930 as had taken the degree in this department,
> including both the primary and intermediate, in all of
> the previous years put together.
>
> Regarding the third point, . . . practically ninety
> per cent of my majors are holding supervisory positions.
>
> As I see it, there are five types of professional
> activities for which teachers in a graduate school should
> be responsible. . . .
>
> 1. Teaching load or the proportion of the student
>   body taught.
> 2. Number of research studies supervised.
> 3. Extra-mural services rendered.
> 4. Participation in the work of national groups
>   and organizations.
> 5. Contributions to educational literature.[1]

---

[1] Maycie Southall to Bruce R. Payne, October 19, 1934,
Private Files of Maycie Southall.

Although Maycie Southall displayed creditable effort in fulfilling all five of her self-imposed responsibilities, the fourth professional activity is the one to which she devoted an extensive amount of zeal because she earnestly believed that education could be enhanced through participation by teachers in meaningful organizations at local, state, and national--as well as international--levels. Many of her former students attested to Maycie Southall's exceptional participation and expressed appreciation for her encouragement of their involvement as student members in professional organizations during their years of training for leadership positions in education. Maycie Southall recently commented:

> I advised all of my Peabody students to join, as student members, one of the national professional organizations of their choice. I was able to get the Association for Childhood Education International, the Association for Supervision and Curriculum Development, and the Association for Student Teachers to give a student rate. Many of those who joined as students have become national officers and leaders. I believe in professionalizing while still students--begin young and bring them up in the way they should go.[2]

Maycie Southall joined, participated in, and served as a leader of numerous organizations that were related to educational improvement. She did not join any organization simply for the sake of belonging to a group, and she was reluctant to affiliate with any group that did not emphasize education. An analysis of the yearbooks published by George Peabody College for Teachers indicated that she did not sponsor strictly social organizations such as sororities.

---

[2]Southall, interview, June 5, 1979.

She gave of her own time and abilities and encouraged her
students to utilize their time, talents, and energy effectively by working with other members in professional organizations for the betterment of education. The Personal Data
Sheet that Maycie Southall prepared in 1977 for the Office
of Development and Alumni Affairs, George Peabody College
for Teachers, revealed some of her services to education
through extensive involvement in professional organizations:

PERSONAL DATA SHEET

Dr. Maycie Katherine Southall, 1977

Preface: My special interest throughout my professional career has been the improvement of
educational opportunities for all children
everywhere. Since educating children is
society's most indispensable service, educating good teachers for all children is
an educational imperative.

My interest in the education of children
and teachers has been deepened by four
years' experience in teaching children,
eight years of supervision or the in-
service education of teachers, and thirty-
five years in the pre-service education
of teachers and administrators from every
state in the United States and fifty-two
foreign countries. The breadth of my
interest and central concern has led me
to participate in the activities of many
different professional and community service organizations and to work zealously
for legislation to improve education at
the state and national levels, especially
for public kindergartens for all of
Tennessee's five-year-olds.

Realizing that the defenses of world peace
must be built in the minds of children and
youth, my present goal is to develop a
"Children's International Intercultural
Education Center" in Nashville with the
hope that this unique pilot project may be

extended to other parts of the state and
the nation.

Present
Position: Professor Emeritus of Education, George
                 Peabody College for Teachers, Nashville,
                 Tennessee.

Education: B.S., M.A., Ph.D. George Peabody College
                 for Teachers. Visiting student at the
                 University of Chicago and Teachers College,
                 Columbia University as part of doctoral
                 program.

Professional
Experience: 1. Rural and city elementary teacher in
                 Georgia and Tennessee.
             2. County Supervisor, Elementary Schools
                 of Pitt County, N.C., 1920-1924.
             3. State Supervisor of Elementary Instruc-
                 tion, Raleigh, N.C., 1924-1928.
             4. Professor of Elementary Education,
                 George Peabody College for Teachers,
                 1929-1964.
             5. Member of the U.S. Office of Education,
                 Washington, D.C., on leave of absence
                 from Peabody College to set up child
                 development centers in war-impacted
                 communities during World War II.
             6. Distinguished Visiting Professor,
                 University of Southern Illinois, Carbon-
                 dale, Illinois, 1964-1965.
             7. After retirement I (a) participated in
                 Workshops at the University of North
                 Carolina, the University of Texas, the
                 University of Alabama, and George Pea-
                 body College for Teachers; (b) served as
                 Curriculum Consultant for several city
                 and county school systems; (c) helped
                 launch the National Head Start Programs
                 for which I received a certificate of
                 appreciation from President Kennedy.

Organization
Membership   1. American Association of University Women
and Services: (AAUW): Member of National Board of
                 Directors, 1958-1963, and of the Educa-
                 tional Foundation, 1960-1963; Chairman,
                 National Elementary and Secondary Edu-
                 cation Committee, 1958-1963; Active
                 Member of local branch and member of
                 the Tennessee State Board.

2. Association for Childhood Education International (ACEI): National President, 1946-1948; State President, 1931-1932; Member of the Advisory Board, 1948-1964: and member of the ACEI Advisory Council, 1964 to present.

3. Association for Student Teachers: State representative and organizer of the State of Tennessee group, Member of Commission on In-service Education of Supervising Teachers.

4. Association for Supervision and Curriculum Development (ASCD): Field Secretary; Member of Executive Committee of the Board of Directors, four terms; Chairman, Structure and Organization Committee; Member of Appraisal and Plans Committee and the Constitution Committee.

5. Delta Kappa Gamma: National President, national Secretary-Treasurer; Chairman, Scholarship Committee; State Founder and State President.

6. National Education Association: Member of the Departments of Elementary School Principals, Higher Education, Rural Education, and Elementary-Kindergarten-Nursery Education.

7. National Society for the Study of Education: Contributing member to publications.

8. Peabody College Alumni Association: National President and Vice-president and Alumni representative on the Peabody College Board of Trustees.

9. Protestants and Others United for Separation of Church and State: Member of the Original Advisory Council.

10. Southern Association for the Education of Children Under Six: Founder and Life Member.

11. U.S. Teacher Exchange Program: Chairman of the Southeast Regional Interviewing Committee, eighteen years.

12. United States Committee of the World Organization for Early Childhood Education (OMEP): Charter Member and Member of the Governing Board.

13. United Nations Organization: Charter Member of the U.S. Commission for UNESCO; Member of the Executive Committee of the U.S. Commission for UNESCO; and Charter

Member of the Nashville Chapter of the
UNA.
14. Life Member of: Association for Childhood Education International, Associa-
tion for Supervision and Curriculum
Development, Nashville Council for the
Education of Children under Six,
National Education Association, Peabody
Aid, and the Young Women's Christian
Association.
15. Active member of several other local
and state service organizations includ-
ing: Belmont Heights Baptist Church,
Cheekwood, Common Cause, Coordinating
Council on Legislative Concerns, Demo-
cratic Women's Committee, Friends of
the Public Library, James K. Polk
Society, Ladies Hermitage Association,
League of Women Voters, Peabody Women's
Club, Rose Society, Symphony Guild,
Tennessee United Organization for Edu-
cation, and Tennessee Historical
Society.

Honors and
Awards:

National 1. General Education Board Fellowship for
advanced graduate study, 1928-1929.
2. Delta Kappa Gamma: Achievement Award in
1941 and the Maycie K. Southall Scholarship, $2,500 annually, set up in 1963.
3. Charter Member of the United States
Commission for UNESCO and Educational
Consultant to the Sixth General UNESCO
Conference, Paris, France; and Represented the U.S. Office of Education in
securing UNESCO Aid to the education of
all children vs. just those handicapped
by World War II.
4. Honorary Committee of the National
Council of Women of U.S.A.
5. Honorary Membership of the Kiowa Indian
Tribe of Oklahoma City and given the
name, Saun-Tah-Tho-Mah, meaning "Woman
Who Helps Children."
6. Member of Educational Policies Commission, two terms.
7. Member of Honor Societies: Pi Lambda
Theta, Pi Gamma Mu (member at large),
Delta Kappa Gamma, and Kappa Delta Pi
(received Honor Key, 1963; elected to

membership in the Laureate Chapter, 1964).

8. Member of the White House Conference on Women in Policy Making; three White House Conferences on Children and Youth (1940, 1950, 1960); The White House Conference on Rural Education.

9. Listed in Who's Who in America 1943 until retirement, Who Knows and What, and Who's Who in Education.

10. Biographical data given in three books, Light from Many Candles, Our Heritage, Volumes I and II, publications of The Delta Kappa Gamma Society.

State and
Local

1. The Governor of Kentucky's appointment to the "Honorable Order of Kentucky Colonels."

2. Middle Tennessee State University's "Distinguished Alumni Award."

3. Tennessee's Delta Kappa Gamma Society's "Achievement Award."

4. Tennessee Division of the American Association of University Women's Named Gift to the AAUW Foundation and this year a named "Endowment Unit" of the Research and Projects Endowment.

5. Business and Professional Women's "Good Neighbor Program."

6. WLAC's "First Lady of the Day."

7. Emma's Salute "An Orchid to You!"

8. Nashville's YWCA's recognition as "Outstanding Leader in Community Affairs."

9. The Peabody Reflector, "The First Lady of Childhood Education."

10. Several individuals have sent gifts honoring me to the educational foundations of the Association for Childhood Education International, the Delta Kappa Gamma Society, and George Peabody College for Teachers.

Publications:

Books

Direct Agencies of Supervision as Used by General Elementary Supervisors, Contributions to Education No. 66, Nashville: George Peabody College for Teachers, 1929.

Chapters in National Yearbooks and Other Books

"Educational Opportunities for Young Children," Ch. II, The Expanding Role of Education, Twenty-sixth Yearbook, American Association of School Administrators, Washington: National Education Association, 1948, pp. 32-54.

"Providing for the Care and Training of Pre-school Children," American Education in the Post-War Period, Forty-fourth Yearbook, Part II, National Society for the Study of Education, Chicago: University of Chicago, 1945, pp. 23-29.

"Supervisory Techniques Adapted to Newer Teaching Practices," Newer Instructional Practices of Promise, Twelfth Yearbook, The Department of Supervisors and Directors of Instruction, Washington: National Education Association, 1939, pp. 328-52.

"Supervisor's Relation to Materials of Instruction," Ch. VIII, Materials of Instruction, Eighth Yearbook, Department of Supervisors and Directors of Instruction, Washington: National Education Association, 1936, pp. 149-83.

"Special Features and Agencies of Elementary Supervision," The Superintendent Surveys Supervision, Eighth Yearbook, Department of Superintendence, 1930, pp. 65-85.

"Education for All the World's Children," Ch. II, Great Human Issues of Our Times, Nashville, Tennessee: George Peabody College for Teachers, 1955, pp. 15-32.

Bulletins

Value of Supervision in Consolidated Schools. Educational Publication No. 106, Raleigh: North Carolina State Department of Education, 1926.

Direct Means Used by Rural Supervisors to Improve Teachers in Service. Pamphlet No. 9, Washington: U.S. Office of Education, 1930.

Modern Trends in Teacher Education.
Washington: Association for Childhood
Education, 1932 (one section).

Children's International Education.
Washington: Association for Childhood
Education International, 1970 (one
section).

Other Publications

Member of the Educational Policies Commission responsible for preparing the
book Education for All American Children
and the bulletin Educational Services
for Young Children.

Several articles pertaining to the
education and welfare of children were
published in national magazines.[3]

International Influence

The accomplishments of Maycie Southall constitute an
extensive list, and an adequate presentation of her multi-
tudinous endeavors defies condensation into the brevity required within the confines of this study. Descriptions of
her leadership in selected organizations are presented, however, in an effort to reveal the influence of her participation and service.

Maycie Southall has served in a leadership capacity in
four organizations that dealt with education at the international level. They are The Delta Kappa Gamma Society
International; the Association for Childhood Education International; the United States Commission of the United Nations

---

[3]Maycie Southall, "Personal Data Sheet, Dr. Maycie
Katherine Southall, 1977," record in personnel file of
Maycie Southall, Office of Development and Alumni Affairs,
George Peabody College for Teachers.

Educational, Scientific, and Cultural Organization; and the
United States Committee of the World Organization for Early
Childhood Education (Organisation Mondiale pour L'Education
Prescholaire).[4] Her affiliation with each of the four organi-
zations is touched upon briefly:

The Delta Kappa Gamma
Society International

The Delta Kappa Gamma Society was organized in 1929 in
Texas. Six years later Maycie Southall participated in the
organizational meeting of the Tennessee unit at which time
she was elected president; upon completion of her term, she
accepted the same office at the national level. Her efforts
did not cease with the termination of her responsibilities
as state and national president. She has continued in the
forefront of leadership throughout ensuing years implementing
the purposes of the Society.[5] Chapter IV of this study is
devoted to a description of her major services to the organization.

Some of the women in Maycie Southall's classes were, or
later became, members of Delta Kappa Gamma and consequently
have been susceptible to her influence from two vantage
points; for example, Allene Jones knew her at George Peabody
College for Teachers: "I took a course with her just to see
if she was as great as I had heard. She was."[6] The 1979-81

---

[4]Southall, interview, December 15, 1979.

[5]Helen Zuccarello, personal letter, May 22, 1979.

[6]Allene Jones, personal letter, February 20, 1980.

treasurer of Xi State continued: "After teaching many years and becoming active in Delta Kappa Gamma, I have had an opportunity to see her at work in that organization. Her contributions . . . on local, state, and international levels have been as great as her teaching."[7]

Because Maycie Southall served as a leader in Delta Kappa Gamma, she touched the lives of many educators who were not in her classes. A significant way in which she served as a role model for the members was through her willingness to speak out, with wisdom and courage, during meetings when she thought the occasion necessitated constructive criticism.[8]

Delta Kappa Gamma members who shared impressions for this study wrote enthusiastically of their respect for Maycie Southall. The high esteem accorded her was perhaps most succinctly expressed by Patricia Pope, a recent Xi State leader: "She is truly an unforgettable Delta Kappa Gamma member. . . ."[9]

Association for Childhood Education International

Maycie Southall played an exceptionally active leadership role in the Association for Childhood Education International. During a recent interview, she summarized the

---

[7]Ibid.

[8]Pearl Cross, personal letter, February 22, 1980.

[9]Patricia Pope, personal letter, February 29, 1980.

historical development of the organization and recalled some
of the activities in which she had participated. Briefly,
the International Kindergarten was organized in 1892; the
National Council of Primary Education was organized in 1915;
and the two groups merged to form the Association for Childhood Education in 1930 at Memphis. Maycie Southall was a
charter member of the latter organization; and, as president
of the Primary Department of the Tennessee Education Association, she helped to organize the Tennessee Association for
Childhood Education and became its second state president.
In 1936-38, she served at the national level as secretary-
treasurer.[10]

By 1945, Maycie Southall's efforts had included membership on the national executive and editorial boards and participation in organizational programs in many states. During
that year, she was chairman of the national teacher education
committee.[11]

When Maycie Southall served as national president, during
1945-47, the Association consisted of approximately 38,000
members.[12] The last word of the current name, Association for
Childhood Education International, was officially added while
she was in office--an accomplishment of which she is genuinely

---

[10]Maycie Southall, interview held in Nashville,
November 11, 1980.

[11]Margaret Hite Yarbrough, "With the A.C.E. in
Tennessee," The Tennessee Teacher 13 (September 1945):30.

[12]"Childhood Education Leader to Address Florida
Teachers," Tampa Sunday Tribune, February 14, 1946, p. 3-C.

proud. Also, the organization was extended to include inter-
mediate grades, thereby providing services from nursery school
through the elementary grades.[13] According to a co-member,
such actions were a result of Maycie Southall's ". . . sound
leadership, vision, and clear philosophy as to the continuity
in education and international cooperation for children."[14]

Alberta Meyer, ACEI executive director emeritus, advised
that Bernice Baxter, Dorothy Koehring, and Rosamond Praeger
are the living members who served on the Association's executive boards during Maycie Southall's presidency.[15] From
Piedmont, California, Bernice Baxter wrote:

> As president of the Association for Childhood
> Education, Dr. Maycie Southall gave creative and in-
> spiring leadership to the Board. A person of ideas
> and of sufficient insight and determination to imple-
> ment and develop those ideas into policy, she made a
> significant contribution to the organization's program
> for children's education. I found Maycie Southall to
> be aware of the soundest ways to influence opportu-
> nities for childhood development.[16]

Rosamond Praeger, who formerly served as director of
kindergartens for the public schools in Syracuse, New York,
recalled leadership responsibilities shared with Maycie
Southall:

> I was a vice-president of the Association for
> Childhood Education International when she was presi-
> dent. It was a very happy assignment.

---

[13]Southall, interview, November 11, 1980.

[14]McMahan, personal letter, May 5, 1979.

[15]Alberta Meyer, personal letter, May 22, 1979.

[16]Bernice Baxter, personal letter, June 3, 1979.

Dr. Southall was that fortunate combination of
a beautiful lady and a very competent professional
person. Those were some of the best years of our
organization under her leadership.[17]

Frances Mayfarth, retired from her positions as an

editor, university professor, and college president, de-

scribed some of Maycie Southall's leadership activities in

the Association for Childhood Education International:

> My first introduction to Dr. Southall was shortly
> after I became assistant editor of Childhood Education
> in September, 1934. Later, in 1936, I became editor
> of all ACEI publications and thus knew Dr. Southall
> for a total of sixteen years, from 1934 until 1950, as
> an ACEI associate in several capacities: president,
> committee chairman and member, and personal friend. I
> have seen her and heard her public addresses infre-
> quently in subsequent years.
>
> It was always a joy just to look at and be with
> her because of her responsive, warm, outgoing friend-
> liness; her physical beauty; her impeccable and always
> appropriate style in dress; her excellent posture and
> graceful movements--all were pleasing and inspired con-
> fidence. Her keen and perceptive mind--creative, ana-
> lytical, and practical--stimulated all of us privileged
> to work with her. As ACEI president, she was an out-
> standing leader, courageous, yet modest and always
> optimistic, graciously extending herself in helping
> others and in promoting the work of the Association.
> As chairman of the ACEI International Relations Com-
> mittee, she made the Association truly international.
>
> Dr. Southall was of inestimable help in planning
> and producing ACEI publications. Always full of ideas
> about their content, timeliness, and pertinence to the
> philosophy and programs of the organization, she au-
> thored many articles, sponsored many of the bulletins,
> and suggested other authors and their fields of compe-
> tence in preparing publication materials. Her judgment
> was infallible in this respect as it was in everything
> else she did.
>
> During President Truman's administration, and at
> his request, I believe, the Association prepared a
> report on "The Nation and Its Children." Dr. Southall

---

[17]Rosamond Praeger, personal letter, June 5, 1979.

chaired this committee and with members of the committee presented it to Mr. Truman. Never shall I forget the repartee between them. "We present this report to you, President Truman, as citizens concerned for our nation's children, and not as politicians seeking favors," said Dr. Southall.

"My dear Dr. Southall, you are a politician whether you want to be or not," replied the President.

She made a witty reply, sending all of us into gales of laughter, after which she said, "We are willing to be called politicians if you so desire and if you will see fit, as an avowed politician, to carry out our recommendations in this report."

"I'll certainly give them serious consideration and see what action can be taken," he promised.

It would be difficult to credit what influence this report had on subsequent action taken by him and his successors, but these things happened: the budget for the Children's Bureau was increased; the [permanent instead of year-to-year] school lunch program was inaugurated [National School Lunch Act, July 1, 1946]; the Social Security [Administration, as an operating branch of the Federal Security] Agency, was established [July 16, 1946]; and the Department of Health, Education, and Welfare came into being [April 11, 1953], thereby consolidating and extending their individual responsibilities into a more effective and efficient federal agency concerned with all our citizens.

During the war--World War II--the Association decided to hold its annual convention in Washington; and, at the invitation of Mrs. Roosevelt, it was held in the White House. I have forgotten who was the Association president, but on the platform in the East Room . . . were seated: Dr. Southall, Dr. Jean Betzner [president], and Miss Jennie Wahlert. Dr. Margaret Mead [introduced by Eleanor Roosevelt] was to be the speaker at this general session. . . . I had been delegated to serve as Dr. Mead's hostess and was seated beside her. She turned to me, at one point, and whispered, "I am sure we shall never again see such a combination of feminine beauty and brains as personified in those three women. The women leaders of tomorrow may have the brains but not the physical beauty or charm of personality or the selfless dedication to the cause of children."

In later years, I asked Dr. Mead if she still felt she had made an accurate prognosis in terms of the current women leaders and "libbers." She replied, "I think the brains are there, but they are lacking in know-how, and their faces look hard-boiled; their actions are often arrogant and tend to denigrate men and anyone who disagrees with them. I saw no such symptoms in the three women in the White House that day!"

May I insert a personal anecdote which . . . reveals a sensitive quality in Dr. Southall:

Following a national ACEI convention in a place I do not remember, I was to visit the New Orleans ACE branch. A tea and reception had been planned to precede my talk. Quite casually, Dr. Southall asked me if I had a long dress to wear at this afternoon event. "No, I do not. Should I have one for an afternoon affair?"

"Yes, I think you should since long dresses are usually worn in the South for afternoon teas and receptions. Maybe I have one with me that you might like to wear. I believe it will fit and be becoming to you," she replied.

Her dress, a long chartreuse chiffon, fitted me perfectly; and so did her gold slippers to wear with it. Perhaps I may be forgiven for feeling I was Maycie Southall for one delightful afternoon.

I have always loved, admired, and respected her, not only for her beauty and brains, but for her innate humaneness and concern for others--a quality much too rare in these days of hurry, scurry, and greed. Education, as I see it, has three major reasons for being: to make us more human, to help us fulfill the great potentials every individual has, and to learn how to use them for the greater good of mankind. Maycie Southall, by precept and example, helped all privileged to know and work with her to grow in these three ways.[18]

Maycie Southall's efforts in behalf of the Association for Childhood Education were extensive, and her reputation for support of the organization was not confined to any particular section of the nation. From Galveston, Texas, for example, came comments from Alma Hegar, a retired elementary school teacher: "I have seen Dr. Southall at many

---

[18]Frances Mayfarth, personal letter, June 1, 1979.

conventions--especially ACEI. I always enjoyed seeing her
at meetings. She was so sincere in her work; and she really
supported ACEI."[19] From Midvale, Utah, came opinions shared
by Alta Miller, a retired supervisor:

> I first met Maycie Southall years ago during an
> ACEI conference in St. Louis, Missouri. At that time
> I was very impressed with her great ability for friend-
> ship, creative thinking, good common sense, and dedi-
> cation to the well-being of human beings.
>
> Throughout the years, I have observed her in
> active participation. Whenever a crisis arose in any
> of the meetings, Maycie waited until all sides of the
> question had been discussed; then she always quietly
> arose to her feet and proceeded to "save the day."
> This happened many times during my association with
> her in ACEI.
>
> I have always loved her lovely southern "accent"
> and her great ability to express in words the thoughts
> of her mind and heart.
>
> She has always been an inspiration to me, and
> when I think "ACEI" I think Maycie Southall. I feel
> that she is one of the great educators of America, and
> I am proud to have been associated with her.[20]

Maycie Southall utilized her leadership experiences in
national organizations as tools for training her students in
Nashville. She brought firsthand information home to share
with her students; she took many of them to conventions and
introduced them to prominent educators; and she supported local affiliations of educational groups. In 1961, for example,
a student publication reported that George Peabody College
for Teachers' Elementary Council was the oldest student branch
among the two hundred units that operated under the auspices

---

[19]Alma Hegar, personal letter, April 16, 1980.

[20]Alta Miller, personal letter, October 17, 1979.

of the Association for Childhood Education International.[21]
The campus group claimed Maycie Southall as a sponsor for
many years during which she worked diligently to help the
students in their professional growth. William Theo Dalton,
who was awarded the Doctor of Philosophy degree in 1945 and
subsequently served as a professor in three southern universities, recalled his term as president of the student
branch:

> From my enrollment in summer school in 1940 to my
> graduation in the summer of 1945, I observed and expe-
> rienced the influence this professionally dedicated
> scholar had on education in the South and the nation.
> Her influence reached many foreign countries through
> those she prepared for educational work in their home-
> lands. Her influence in preparing her students to
> accept the contributions to be made by intercultural
> relationships was substantial. It was in one of her
> classes that I came to appreciate opportunities to
> share with foreign students.
>
> Dr. Southall introduced me to ACE and ACEI. I
> served as president of the campus branch under her ad-
> visory counsel. The branch was called the Elementary
> Council at that time. During 1945-47, she was national
> president and was greatly influential in getting the
> word "international" included in the title (ACEI).
> Several of the officers and members attended national
> meetings as a result of her encouragement and plan-
> ning. I have since attended a number of ACEI Study
> Conferences where Dr. Southall was a prominent figure
> in board meetings and interest groups. She has been
> a keynote speaker more than once. Always, her former
> students "sat at her feet" and went home with inspira-
> tion and information on innovations in education. When
> Maycie Southall spoke, everyone listened whether she
> was speaking from the stage or from the floor.
>
> Her dedication to the educational cause was such
> that she rarely refused an invitation to travel many
> miles to serve as consultant to important state and
> regional--as well as national--conferences.

---

[21]"'Today's Child, Tomorrow's Adult' Theme of ACEI
Gathering in Omaha," The Peabody Reflector 34 (March-April
1961):51.

Dr. Southall was a leader in every sense of the word. She wanted those who followed to have professional and personal credit. She often drew her illustrations, while speaking and writing, from the classrooms of her graduate students. Dr. Susan B. Riley, professor of English at Peabody, observed when serving as president of AAUW at the national level, "Maycie Southall has had national and international recognition which few of us have enjoyed." The high esteem with which her colleagues recognized her was the absence of jealousy. Dr. Windrow, director of Peabody Demonstration School, depended a great deal on her professional advice. In fact, she taught many of the faculty members of the "Dem" School. They frequently took refresher courses and seminars under her direction. . . .

Her contributions to education included: emphasis on human relationships; improvements in young childhood education; integration of educational disciplines; inspiration to higher standards for all teachers; sound evaluation of educational innovations; development of concepts that placed educational supervision in proper perspective; recognition and implementation of the ideas of others; promotion of the self-discipline concept as a means to responsible freedom; recognition and promotion of research as the foundation of progress; and enthusiasm for balance between theory and practice.[22]

Many contributors to this study expressed appreciation for the opportunity to participate in the project. In his letter, William Theo Dalton included an aside: "It is a great privilege to have a part in this (long-overdue) undertaking."[23]

Maycie Southall both trained and motivated students to become potential leaders of the ACEI through her work on campus. Verna Chrisler, for example, recalled:

Dr. Southall is a very good friend of mine. She was my major professor when I was in Peabody during 1936-37. I was an older student working on my M.A. . . .

That year . . . she spent many weekends traveling to many places where she had been asked to speak to various

---

[22]William Theo Dalton, personal letter, February 25, 1980.
[23]Ibid.

groups on different phases of education. She was a popular speaker--one of the best, I thought. . . .

She was always doing nice things for her students.
I cherish the memories of meetings in her home, drives
in the country, the Association for Childhood Education
meetings, and her interest in that group. She was one
to realize how important it is for students to have many
experiences. She saw to it that students met the educators of importance who visited the campus. . . .

After I left Peabody, I went back to Arkansas and to
what was then Arkansas State Teachers College in Conway.
Arkansas State Teachers College is now the University of
Central Arkansas.

There were several ACE branches in Arkansas but no
state organization. In the fall of 1937, a large group
interested in ACE met in Little Rock; and the state
branch was organized. I was elected the first state
president.

It was during this time that Dr. Southall was most
helpful. She came to several state education meetings
and was often the main speaker. She visited me in Conway
and was helpful in many ways. What we gave her in pay,
she turned in to ACEI Headquarters.

She was responsible for my spending 1941-42 at ACEI
Headquarters in Washington, D.C. I was the fellow from
this southwest area.

Through those busy years, I had much contact with
her in ACEI work and in conferences. She has been responsible for my making many lasting friendships that I
have cherished through the years.

I know that this does not do justice to the works
and life of a great lady, an educator par excellence,
and a dear friend.[24]

Mary Browning, a former member of the student branch,

is another example of a potential leader whose later service

to ACEI was influenced by Maycie Southall's campus efforts.

She wrote from Kentucky:

---

[24]Verna Chrisler, personal letter, March 1, 1980.

During my supervisory days in Louisville, I invited
Dr. Southall to come [here] to help me organize the ACE
group . . . in our fair city. She had served as president
of this illustrious organization; and when her term ended,
she left a very inspiring memory of her versatility.[25]

Dell Kjer, who later served as international president
of the organization, stated that he joined ACEI as a result
of Maycie Southall's influence.[26] An active member of the
Elementary Council, he recalled that her efforts with the
campus group were ". . . aimed at making the programs professional. . . ."[27] He recognized the extent of her influence:

Dr. Southall's students have spread out over the
United States for years (even the world) taking an ac-
tive part in ACEI at local, state, and national levels.
I have met hundreds of such students--all who were at
Peabody would mention their allegiance to Dr. Southall
and ACE. I don't know how many, but again, I'm sure,
hundreds have become officers or college sponsors of
ACEI branches because of Dr. Southall.[28]

United States Commission of the
United Nations Educational,
Scientific, and Cultural
Organization

In 1946, Maycie Southall was appointed by Secretary of
State James F. Byrnes to the United States Commission of the
United Nations Educational, Scientific, and Cultural Organization (UNESCO). She was later reappointed to the same position by Secretary of State George C. Marshall.[29]

---

[25]Mary Browning, personal letter, May 15, 1979.

[26]Kjer, personal letter, August 8, 1979.

[27]Ibid.

[28]Ibid.

[29]Nigh, "Dr. Maycie K. Southall," p. 3.

Members of the Commission first convened in Washington, D.C., during September 23-26, 1946.[30] At that time, Maycie Southall became one of two women elected to serve on the Executive Committee; the other woman was Katherine McHale, director general of the American Association of University Women.[31] An article revealed that among the Commission's one hundred members Maycie Southall was the ". . . only elementary education expert. . . ."[32] The Commission was designed ". . . to serve as a direct and permanent link between United States citizens and the American delegation to the United Nations Educational, Scientific, and Cultural Organization. . . ."[33]

Maycie Southall's private files contain her personal invitation, issued by the Department of State, United States of America, to a dinner honoring the Commission members; it was held in the East Room of the Mayflower Hotel, Washington, D.C., on September 15, 1946. The dinner program, a copy of which is also retained in her private files, revealed that the speakers for the occasion were Ambassador Henri Bonnet and Archibald MacLeish.

----

[30]"Dr. Maycie Southall," The Peabody Reflector 19 (November 1946):386.

[31]Ibid.

[32]Clarissa Start, "Education's Role in Fight to Win Peace," St. Louis Post-Dispatch, April 24, 1948, p. 1-B.

[33]"Dr. Maycie Southall," The Peabody Reflector 19 (November 1946):386.

U.S. National Committee, A Unit
of Organisation Mondiale pour
L'Education Prescolaire (OMEP)

Maycie Southall became a charter member of the U.S.
National Committee of the World Organization for Early Childhood Education. Another charter member recalled mutual activities:

> I've known Dr. Southall through my connections with
> the Association for Childhood Education International
> and with OMEP for more than forty years. She is a great
> lady with a deep commitment to children as exciting, de-
> veloping human beings and to the philosophy and methods
> of their education. She is strong, very well organized,
> discreet, and an excellent administrator which she has
> shown in her work at George Peabody College for Teachers,
> as the president of ACEI and a member of its Board for
> many years, and in her devoted work to the concept of
> the United Nations.
>
> I think Dr. Southall and I are the only charter
> members of the U.S. National Committee of OMEP who are
> still members of the association and are working ac-
> tively as of now for the International Year of the Child
> with UNICEF. I met her at the organizational meeting
> of the U.S. National Committee of OMEP in our mutual
> effort to reach out to the new international movement
> in 1949. We had both learned of the dedicated action
> of Lady Allen of Hurtwood, England, Dr. Alva Myrdal of
> Sweden, and Madam Suzanne Herbiniere-Lebert of France
> who were the initiators of OMEP and who were working
> closely with the United Nations. Dr. Southall was then
> the president of ACEI, and the interrelationship was
> important and natural.
>
> Dr. Southall's charm and wisdom are proverbial with
> all of us who have known her. She is a superb hostess.
> Her tact and clarity of mind always ensure the success
> of any project in which she is involved.
>
> We touch base very rarely but always with pleas-
> ure and respect for the projects in which we are work-
> ing. . . .[34]

---

[34] Sadie D. Ginsberg, personal letter, May 24, 1979.

Leadership in National Associations

Maycie Southall's educational activities have included leadership in several national associations. Numerous persons who contributed impressions for this study associated her name particularly with the American Association of University Women and the Association for Supervision and Curriculum Development:

American Association of University Women

The American Association of University Women, which is currently planning its centennial convention to be held in June 1981, emphasizes the advancement of women through the united efforts of alumnae from various colleges and universities. Membership is available to any woman who has been awarded a baccalaureate or higher degree from an accredited institution. Approximately 190,000 women are members of the organization, according to Mary A. Grefe, 1979-81 national president.[35]

Mary K. Jordan, librarian and archivist of the Association, wrote in 1979: "Dr. Southall became a member of AAUW in 1934-35. She is still a member."[36] Enclosed in the same letter were copies of vitae from the Association's files pertaining to Maycie Southall's service to the organization. A 1964 version revealed that her leadership at the national

---

[35]Mary A. Grefe, personal letter, March 31, 1981.

[36]Mary K. Jordan, personal letter, June 12, 1979.

level had included chairmanship of the Elementary and Secondary
Education Committee during 1958-63 and membership on the Board
of Directors during the same years as well as on the Educational Foundation during 1960-63. A 1962 record showed that
she had served as legislative chairman at the state level during 1957-59 and as education chairman of the Nashville branch
during 1956-57.[37] Honors bestowed upon Maycie Southall by
the Tennessee State Division included a "named gift" to the
AAUW Educational Foundation and a named "unit" of the General
Research & Projects Endowment.[38]

Association for Supervision and Curriculum Development

The Association for Supervision and Curriculum Development was created in the early 1940s (as the Department for
Supervision and Curriculum Development with name changed in
1946) by a merger of the Department of Supervisors and Directors of Instruction, NEA, and the Society for Curriculum Study.
Maycie Southall served on the executive committee of the first
Board of Directors.[39] According to one source, she ". . . was
active in the new organization from the beginning and served
as an elected officer longer than any other person."[40]

---

[37]Ibid.

[38]Southall, interview, November 11, 1980.

[39]Ibid.

[40]O. L. Davis, Jr., "Symbol of a Shift from Status to
Function: Formation of the Association for Supervision and
Curriculum Development," _Educational Leadership_ 35 (May 1978):
613.

Robert R. Leeper, associate secretary and editor of ASCD
publications for many years, corresponded with Maycie Southall
in 1972; his letter addressed some of the reasons for the
organization's bestowal of life membership upon her:

> I appreciate very much your kind letter of July 3
> in acknowledgment of receipt of the life membership sta-
> tus from ASCD. I can think of no person who more richly
> deserves such status in the Association which you have
> served so well and faithfully through the years since
> its founding.
>
> The wise counsel and the sound work which you have
> contributed to the Association, especially in its forma-
> tive years, have helped signally toward its survival and
> growth. Your very special efforts in relation to the
> early constitution of the Association were of special
> benefit. So many of the provisions you inserted have
> proved to be both wise and prudent. . . .[41]

Testimony of Maycie Southall's commitment to professional improvement was provided by Hollis L. Caswell, president emeritus of Teachers College, Columbia University, and
former colleague at George Peabody College for Teachers:

> In the early forties a movement was developed to
> combine the Department of Supervisors and Directors of
> Instruction of the NEA and the Society for Curriculum
> Study. I was active in developing and supporting this
> idea. Several members of the Department who had been
> closely identified with supervision resisted the combi-
> nation. Professor Southall was one of this group. A
> great deal of feeling developed on the part of leaders
> in both groups. The combination was approved, and the
> present ASCD was the resulting organization.
>
> After the combination, some of the leaders who op-
> posed the action withdrew from active work in the new
> association and did all they could to discredit it.
> Professor Southall followed a diametrically opposed
> course of action. She continued to work in the new or-
> ganization with just as much enthusiasm as she had shown

---

[41]Robert R. Leeper to Maycie Southall, July 14, 1972,
Private Files of Maycie Southall.

in the older Department. In fact, she established a
major position of leadership in the Association's program.

Her action in this situation gave me a lasting
deep respect for her both as a person and an educator.
Her devotion to professional improvement was so strong
that she would not permit an issue of organization to
keep her from doing whatever she could to improve education.[42]

Congressional and Governmental Interests

Maycie Southall participated in a variety of congressional and governmental endeavors that addressed educational
concerns. Examples selected for inclusion are presented in
chronological order:

With the U.S. Department of Education

Maycie Southall was granted a leave of absence from her
professorship at George Peabody College for Teachers for the
1943 winter quarter in order to accept an assignment with the
United States Department of Education. She was one of six
educators in the nation appointed to the Extended School Program for Children of Working Mothers; as senior specialist,
her responsibilities included doing ". . . extensive field
work in the Southwest area organizing plans and procedures
protecting the welfare of children in those areas most seriously affected by war industries."[43] With headquarters in
San Antonio, her territorial assignment included Texas,

---

[42]Hollis L. Caswell, personal letter, May 20, 1979.

[43]"Dr. Maycie Southall," The Peabody Reflector 16
(February 1943):65.

Louisiana, and New Mexico where she helped establish child
care programs in war-impacted centers.[44]

Federal Aid to Education

Maycie Southall believed that the federal government
should accept part of the responsibility for financing education. She thought that federal aid could be made available
without federal control.

According to an article written in 1945, "Dr. Southall
was called to Washington recently . . . to testify at the
hearings of the House education committee on the Ramspeck
bill for federal aid to education."[45] The article continued:

> For these hearings, she used data collected from a
> study of "What is Happening to Children" in the south-
> eastern states, which she has just completed, with the
> cooperation of the state departments of education of
> the ten southeastern states.[46]

Meeting of the Women's Joint Congressional Committee of Washington, D.C.

In March 1946, Maycie Southall attended a meeting of
the Women's Joint Congressional Committee of Washington, D.C.
Her private files contain her personal invitation to a din-
ner given by the organization in honor of Eleanor Roosevelt,
United States delegate to the General Assembly of the United
Nations. The March 14 dinner was held in the Grand Ballroom

---

[44]Maycie Southall, interview held in Nashville, July 3,
1979.

[45]Yarbrough, "With the A.C.E. in Tennessee," p. 30.

[46]Ibid.

of the Mayflower Hotel. A newspaper reported that Eleanor
Roosevelt addressed her remarks to ". . . more than 1,300
women gathered to honor her."[47] National presidents of numerous women's organizations were among the invited guests.
In her speech, Eleanor Roosevelt advocated international co-
operation: "She emphasized the need to build a collective
force which could be used by all nations."[48]

Seated at the head table with this country's only woman
delegate to the General Assembly of the United Nations was
another former United States president's wife: "The presence
of Mrs. Woodrow Wilson at the head table prompted Secretary
[of Commerce] Wallace to comment that the two widows of war
presidents together 'represent in a unique way the cause of
world peace.'"[49]

The leadership exemplified by Eleanor Roosevelt and
other women appointed to international posts was recognized
by one of the speakers:

> Hailing Mrs. Roosevelt as "the first lady of the
> world," Mrs. Louis Ottenberg, vice chairman of the
> Women's Joint Congressional Committee, who presided
> said the efforts of the 10,000,000 women represented
> by the committee had been stimulated by the appointment
> of Mrs. Roosevelt and other women to international
> posts.[50]

---

[47]"Churchill Proposal Bars Vital Peoples, Says
Mrs. Roosevelt," _Washington_ (D.C.) _Evening Star_, March 15,
1946, p. B-6.

[48]Ibid.

[49]Ibid.

[50]Ibid.

Potpourri

Maycie Southall's preeminence extended beyond the realm of her peers in local educational circles. Selected examples of outstanding appointments and honors are included in an attempt to disclose the recognition given to some of her contributions and service to education.

Educational Policies Commission

The leadership qualities exemplified by Maycie Southall did not go unnoticed by other educators. A December 1943 article included an announcement of import to education:

> Dr. Maycie K. Southall was elected a member of the Educational Policies Commission at a joint session of the executive committee of the American Association of School Administrators and the National Education Association, held at the Hotel Statler in Cleveland, Ohio, October 18, 1943.[51]

In 1945, Maycie Southall was elected to a second term of membership on the Educational Policies Commission.[52] She served in that capacity until the completion of the term in 1948.[53]

Although the Commission has long since ceased to function, it wielded considerable influence for many years. In 1961, Lawrence A. Cremin penned: "Since its creation in 1936 the Commission had spoken boldly and authoritatively as

---

[51]"Dr. Maycie K. Southall," The Peabody Reflector 16 (December 1943):427.

[52]"Dr. Southall Reelected to Educational Policies Commission," The Peabody Reflector 18 (January 1945):25.

[53]Southall, interview, December 15, 1979.

the responsible voice of the teaching profession."[54] During the years in which Maycie Southall served as a member, the organization issued a series of publications which included Education for All American Youth in 1944, Educational Services for Young Children in 1945, and Education for All American Children in 1948. She worked specifically on the bulletin Educational Services for Young Children and the book Education for All American Children.[55] In regard to the Commission's pronouncements, often referred to as statements, Lawrence A. Cremin commented:

> Once they appeared, they were quickly incorporated into education syllabi across the nation. In retrospect, there is little doubt but that they summed up as well as any contemporary publications the best-laid plans of the teaching profession for American education in the postwar decades.[56]

According to a list published in 1945, Maycie Southall was one of five women among a total of twenty-one members serving on the Commission at that time. Included were such notable leaders as, for example, the presidents of Harvard University, Cornell University, University of Louisville, American Association of School Administrators, National Education Association, Department of Classroom Teachers of the National Education Association, and American Council on Education (advisor); also listed among the members were the

---

[54]Lawrence A. Cremin, The Transformation of the School (New York: Alfred A. Knopf, 1961), p. 329.

[55]Southall, interview, December 15, 1979.

[56]Cremin, The Transformation of the School, p. 332.

U.S. Commissioner of Education (advisor), a state commissioner of education, and several superintendents as well as
assistant superintendents of school systems throughout the
nation.[57] Lawrence A. Cremin recognized the esteem accorded
the organization by the teaching profession during the mid-
1940s:

> Anything these people had to say would undoubtedly
> have been of interest, but their formulations as members
> of the Commission took on added weight because of the
> high prestige that body had come to command in the coun-
> cils of American teachers."[58]

White House Conferences

Outstanding honors that came to Maycie Southall included
invitations to attend influential White House Conferences in
the 1940s, the 1950s, and the 1960s. Listed on her Personal
Data Sheet, some of the conferences that she attended focused
directly on the concerns of children. They continued the
precedent that had been set by President Theodore Roosevelt
who initiated the first White House Conference on Dependent
Children in 1909. President Woodrow Wilson called the second
White House Conference pertaining to the welfare of children
in 1919. President Herbert Hoover was instrumental in incor-
porating and enlarging upon the efforts of the first two conferences through his 1929 call for a White House Conference

---

[57] A. J. Stoddard and others, "An Open Letter to Members
of the American Delegation to the United Nations Conference
on International Organization," The Journal of the National
Education Association 34 (May 1945):99.

[58] Cremin, The Transformation of the School, p. 329.

on Child Health and Protection which was scheduled to meet in
1930.[59]

Also listed on Maycie Southall's Personal Data Sheet was
her membership in the White House Conference on Rural Education which addressed, as had four earlier conferences, the
well-being of children. President and Mrs. Franklin Roosevelt
issued invitations to two hundred persons, selected for their
leadership and work in rural life, to participate in the 1944
meeting. In his address to the members, President Roosevelt
endorsed federal aid without federal interference to education.[60] A participant later evaluated the effectiveness of
the assemblage: "Probably no other conference in this generation has given so much hope, stimulation, and guidance to
rural life as this White House Conference on Rural Education."[61]

Earlier in the same year, Maycie Southall had been
invited to attend a June 14 gathering called by President
Franklin Roosevelt. Entitled the White House Conference on
Women in Policy Making, she considered it to be probably the
most significant of the White House Conference listing shown
on her Personal Data Sheet.[62] According to one source, it
brought together the presidents of seventy-three nationally

---

[59]S. L. Smith, "The White House Conference on Rural
Education," The Peabody Reflector 18 (February 1945):50.

[60]Ibid., p. 51.

[61]Ibid.

[62]Southall, interview, November 11, 1980.

recognized women's organizations.[63] Discussions held during
the meeting were designed to prepare women for a greater and
more effective role in policy making at local, state, and
national levels. Maycie Southall is of the opinion that the
Conference ". . . stimulated what is now called the Women's
Movement."[64]

Honorary Committee of the
National Council of Women
of the United States

Maycie Southall's outstanding career garnered for her
a distinguished appointment:

> Dr. Maycie K. Southall, professor of elementary
> education, has been honored by being named a member
> of the Honorary Committee of the National Council of
> Women of the United States, which is an affiliate of
> the International Council of Women. The committee is
> headed by Mrs. John Kennedy, wife of the President of
> the United States, and its membership includes distin-
> guished women in government, ambassadors' wives, presi-
> dents of member organizations, and outstanding women in
> local communities. This committee has been organized
> in preparation for the 75th anniversary meeting of the
> International Council of Women in Washington June 19-30
> [1963].[65]

Laureate Chapter
of Kappa Delta Pi

Kappa Delta Pi is the name of an honor society in education. Founded in 1911, the organization currently consists of approximately 60,000 members. The Laureate Chapter,

---

[63]"Dr. Maycie K. Southall," The Peabody Reflector 18
(May 1945):183.

[64]Southall, interview, November 11, 1980.

[65]"Faculty Notes," The Peabody Reflector 36 (March-
April 1963):56.

which is composed of highly select members, was installed on
February 23, 1925. According to J. Jay Hostetler, executive
secretary of Kappa Delta Pi, "Membership in the Laureate
Chapter is the highest honor which Kappa Delta Pi bestows on
an individual, and . . . the members are certainly a very
elite group in education. Dr. Southall was . . . elected to
the chapter in 1964."[66]

Membership in the Laureate Chapter is limited to sixty
living persons:

> The selection of laureate members is made on recom-
> mendations of chapters and the membership of the Laureate
> Chapter. This year [1964] the Executive Council takes
> pleasure in announcing the election of five new laureates.

> The laureates announced during the Twenty-fourth
> Biennial Convocation are Paul Robert Hanna, Lee L. Jacks
> Professor of Child Education, Stanford University;
> Francis Keppel, U.S. Commissioner of Education and for-
> merly Dean of the Graduate School of Education, Harvard
> University; Ralph Emerson McGill, Editor and Publisher
> of the Atlanta Constitution; Maycie Katherine Southall,
> Professor of Elementary Education, George Peabody College
> for Teachers; and Harold Taylor, formerly President of
> Sarah Lawrence College, and currently Vice Chairman of
> the National Committee for the Support of the Public
> Schools.[67]

Prior to 1964, when Maycie Southall joined the exclusive
group, more than 120 persons had been elected to the Laureate
Chapter.[68] Of those chosen, fewer than twenty were women.
Among many prominent names placed on the membership roster
throughout the years may be found, for example, Jane Addams,

---

[66] J. Jay Hostetler, personal letter, May 30, 1979.

[67] "Laureates for 1964," The Educational Forum 38, Part 2
(March 1964):384m.

[68] Ibid.

William M. Alexander, William C. Bagley, George W. Carver,
Hollis L. Caswell, James B. Conant, Lawrence A. Cremin,
John Dewey, Albert Einstein, James William Fulbright, John W.
Gardner, Henry H. Hill, Patty Smith Hill, Robert M. Hutchins,
William Heard Kilpatrick, Walter Lippman, Margaret Mead,
Jean Piaget, Eleanor Roosevelt, Lewis H. Terman, and Edward
Lee Thorndike.

Of interest is the fact that both Maycie Southall and
Katherine Vickery were elected to membership in the Laureate
Chapter. They were the only two women awarded doctoral de-
grees in 1929 by George Peabody College for Teachers.

Saun-Tah-Tho-Mah

Selected for the last example presented in this chapter
was a title accorded Maycie Southall in April 1947. It was
bestowed upon her during the national conference of the
Association for Childhood Education in Oklahoma City.[69]

Saun-Tah-Tho-Mah was the name given to Maycie Southall
by the Kiowa Indian Tribe of Oklahoma City; honorary membership was also conferred upon her.[70] According to one source,
a handmade bracelet was presented by Anna Sue White Horse
who paid tribute to Maycie Southall's service to education:

> We feel that it is a great honor to present this
> remembrance of the Indians of Oklahoma to Dr. Southall.
> She has done much in the field of education and in so
> doing has helped untold numbers of children to get a
> better education and to prepare themselves for a better

[69]Southall, interview, November 11, 1980.

[70]Ibid.

living. As I place this bracelet upon her arm, I wish
to bestow upon her the Indian name, SAUN-TAH-THO-MAH,
which translated means, "Woman who helps children."[71]

In a 1970 published article which carried the subtitle
"A tribute to a Peabody teacher and alumna in the semi-
centennial year of her undergraduate class," Etha Green commented about the Indian name given to Maycie Southall:

> Even "Woman Who Helps" would have been appropriate.
> "Woman Who Helps"--in education, religion, international
> affairs, civic programs, professional organizations, and
> welfare efforts. "Woman Who Helps"--her thousands of
> students, colleagues in college classrooms and else-
> where, her alma mater and long-time professional home,
> George Peabody College for Teachers, personal friends,
> overseas students, and strangers. . . .
>
> Many are recipients of her counsel, her professional
> help, her financial generosity, her gracious hospitality,
> her carefully tended flowers, and her unending thought-
> fulness.[72]

In the same article, Etha Green characterized her friend,
Maycie Southall:

> Her accomplishments may be listed in black and white
> in important books and she likely is known to someone in
> most of the many countries in which Peabody has alumni,
> but few persons are close enough to know the deepest--the
> sacrifice, the dedication, the patience, and the nobility
> which are Maycie Katherine Southall.[73]

---

[71]"Annual Study Conference of the Association for Childhood Education," The Peabody Reflector 20 (June 1947):221.

[72]Green, "The First Lady of Childhood Education," p. 130.

[73]Ibid.

        Dr. Southall continues not only to support but
initiates action.

                                        Margaret Sherer
                                        Personal letter
                                        May 22, 1979

CHAPTER VI

THE RETIREMENT YEARS

Widening Horizons

Fifteen years after Maycie Southall's retirement, a past president of an international educational organization wrote: "I am an admirer of Dr. Southall who, in my opinion, is the epitome of a vital older woman who grows in stature, knowledge, interest, and concern for others with each year."[1] In June 1964, Maycie Southall retired from her position as professor of elementary education at George Peabody College for Teachers; but she did not retire from her commitment to educational endeavors. The formalities of retirement barely interrupted her busy schedule of educational activities, projects, and speaking engagements. A close friend recently commented: "I think Maycie has been just as busy since her retirement as before--or, if possible, more so."[2]

When Maycie Southall retired from her professorship at George Peabody College for Teachers, her annual salary was $9,000; it had been raised to that level in January of the same year.[3] Although she had throughout many years been

---

[1]Nadine M. Ewing, personal letter, June 10, 1979.

[2]Brannon, interview, May 8, 1979.

[3]Southall, interview taped by Davis, April 20, 1979.

227

offered choice positions with enticing salaries by other educational institutions, her loyalty to George Peabody College for Teachers and her belief in its mission prompted continuation of her work there.[4]

A Visiting Professor

During an interview at her home on December 15, 1979, Maycie Southall verified a record which stated that upon her retirement she had accepted a position as a Distinguished Visiting Professor of Elementary Education with Southern Illinois University at Carbondale for the ensuing academic year.[5] The salary offered her for a period of nine months was $1,350 per month.[6] Elmer J. Clark, dean of the College of Education, evaluated her performance by stating: "You may be assured that we were pleased to have Dr. Southall on our faculty, and we believe she made outstanding contributions here."[7] He disclosed that during her assignment, from September 23, 1964, through June 15, 1965, ". . . Dr. Southall taught courses in her area of specialization and was active in other professional activities."[8] Extracts from a record showing some of her activities while teaching there indicate that her commitment to educational endeavors had by no means been truncated concomitant with her earlier retirement:

---

[4]Brannon, interview, May 8, 1979.

[5]Holden, Our Heritage, vol. 2, p. 143.

[6]Elmer J. Clark, personal letter, September 13, 1979.

[7]Elmer J. Clark, personal letter, July 16, 1979.

[8]Ibid.

PROFESSIONAL ACTIVITIES, 1965

Maycie K. Southall
Visiting Professor, Dept. of El. Ed.

A. National Activities

1. Spoke at the general session of the Laboratory School Administrators Association, Chicago, February 10.

2. Presided at the general session of the Association for Student Teaching, Feb. 12, Chicago, and attended meetings of the Commission for the In-Service Education of Supervising Teachers, February 12-14, Chicago.

3. [Was] presented . . . [as a] Laureate Chapter member of Kappa Delta Pi at the annual convocation, Chicago.

4. Attended the annual meeting of the Scholarship Committee of Delta Kappa Gamma, Feb. 26-27, Chicago.

5. Served as reactor at one of the assemblies of the Association for Supervision and Curriculum Development Convention and as a member of the seminar for the Education of the Culturally Deprived Children, Chicago, Feb. 28-March 3.

6. Elected to membership in the International Platform Association, March 1.

. . . .

B. State, Regional, and Local Activities

1. Spoke at the annual dinner meeting of the St. Louis Association for Childhood Education International, Jan. 26.

2. Spoke at the luncheon meeting of the Regional Association for Supervision and Curriculum Development, East St. Louis, Jan. 27.

3. Spoke at a dinner meeting of the Regional Association for Childhood Education, Carbondale, Jan. 29.

4. Addressed two sessions of the Southeastern Missouri Education Association, Cape Girardeau, March 12.

5. Served as a panel member at the meeting of the
   Southern Illinois Reading Council, Carbondale,
   March 18.

. . . .[9]

According to the same record, Maycie Southall made plans
to ". . . speak at the monthly meeting of the American Association of University Women on 'Some Educational Problems
Common to the Occident and the Orient', April 13, Carbondale,
Ill."[10] Too, her itinerary indicated plans to participate in
the National Study Conference of the Association for Childhood
Education International to be held in New York during the
latter part of April by attending ". . . joint meetings of
the Advisory Committee and the Executive Committee, and . . .
meetings of the Nominating Committee"; chairing ". . . meetings of the Gifts and Bequests Committee"; leading a Special
Problems Group concerned with "Potential Drop Outs"; and being
". . . a platform guest at the last General Meeting."[11] Her
New York itinerary included attendance at the yearly ". . .
meetings of the U.S. National Committee of the World Organization for Young Children, April 20. . . ."[12] Upon her return
to Carbondale, Maycie Southall made plans to ". . . speak at
a joint meeting of the two local chapters of Delta Kappa Gamma
on 'The Unique Role of Educated Women', May 15."[13]

---

[9] Ibid.

[10] Ibid.

[11] Ibid.

[12] Ibid.

[13] Ibid.

Educational Activities Expanded

At the termination of her assignment at Southern Illinois University at Carbondale, Maycie Southall returned to Tennessee and to the apartment that she had retained across the street from the campus of George Peabody College for Teachers. She continued to live in the spacious apartment, her home for more than forty years, until the building was razed in the 1970s.[14] The close proximity to the educational institution provided her an opportunity during retirement years to keep in touch with its personnel and stay abreast of its progress. Thus, the retired professor had no sooner than settled again in Nashville until she plunged into efforts in behalf of George Peabody College for Teachers and education in general. She conducted, for example, a workshop on the campus after her retirement.[15] Too, following her year in Illinois, she was employed as a curriculum consultant to the Southeastern Head Start Program; her assignment included a two-week stay on the Seminole Indian Reservation in Florida.[16]

On November 22, 1966, officials representing the alumni of George Peabody College for Teachers counted the votes which resulted in an announcement of Maycie Southall's election as national president of the Peabody Alumni Association. Her

---

[14]Maycie Southall, interview held in Nashville, August 7, 1980.

[15]Southall, interview, December 15, 1979.

[16]Ibid.

1967-69 term of office would become effective at the first of the year.[17]

As alumni president, Maycie Southall automatically became a member of the educational institution's Board of Trustees. In 1946, approximately twenty years earlier, Eleanore Meade had been ". . . elected . . . the FIRST woman member of the Board of Trustees of Peabody College in all its one hundred and sixty-one years of history."[18] In a 1980 communication, Henry H. Hill, president emeritus of George Peabody College for Teachers, recalled that he had recommended Eleanore Meade of New Orleans for membership as well as Ruth F. Peabody who became a member in the early 1960s because he thought that interested women should have an opportunity to serve in such positions of responsibility; in the same letter, he stated: "Dr. Southall is the third woman to serve on the Board of Trustees."[19]

Maycie Southall's administration effected several constitutional changes in the Peabody Alumni Association. She endorsed, for example, a plan whereby the number of Association members serving on the Board of Trustees would be increased to two, the president and immediate past president, because she thought additional representation would enhance communication

[17]"Alumni Elect Dr. Southall President," The Peabody Reflector 39 (November-December 1966):269.

[18]Board of Trustees, "Tribute to Eleanore Meade," The Peabody Reflector 43 (Summer 1970):97.

[19]Henry H. Hill, personal letter, November 1, 1980.

regarding the desires of the alumni. As a member of the Board of Trustees, Maycie Southall worked for an increase in the number of women; she also advocated more representation by members from outside of Nashville because she considered the educational institution to be national in scope and service.[20]

"She was elected president of the Peabody Women's Club for 1966-67. . . ."[21] At the October 21, 1967, meeting, during Maycie Southall's administration, the members were advised that the organization had a total of 171 women on its roll, the highest number in several years.[22] Maycie Southall described a special project undertaken while she was president of the group: "We preserved a little of Peabody's history by removing former [Peabody] President Philip Lindsley's mildewed desk from a damp basement, having it beautifully restored, and placing it in the home used by the College's presidents."[23]

1968: A Typical Year

Maycie Southall continued to spend much of her time working in various ways for George Peabody College for Teachers and education in general. Her years of extensive travel laid the foundation for many activities during retirement years. To her, education still meant, in part, the art of persuasion;

[20]Southall, interview, December 15, 1979.

[21]"News of Emeritus Professors, Faculty Wives," The Peabody Reflector 39 (November-December 1966):276.

[22]"Women's Club Marks Increase in Membership," The Peabody Reflector 40 (September-October 1967):247.

[23]Southall, interview, December 15, 1979.

thus, she utilized her ability to influence others through
sharing ideas as a participant at numerous educational functions. Examples taken from one year indicate her indefatiga-
bility; the year selected was 1968.

On March 14, 1968, Maycie Southall ". . . addressed the
Peabody Alumni Breakfast . . . during the Mississippi Education Association meeting at Jackson, Miss."[24] She then spoke
during the Friendship Hour at the meeting of the Alabama
Education Association held in Birmingham.[25] On March 15-17,
she ". . . attended the meeting of the International Expansion Committee of Delta Kappa Gamma in Dallas, Texas . . ."[26]
before returning to her home in Nashville.

Maycie Southall ". . . met with the Peabody Alumni and
the Delta Kappa Gamma State Scholarship Committee during
the Tennessee Education Association meeting in Chattanooga,
Apr. 4-5."[27] During the same period of time, ". . . she was
a guest at the Tennessee Supervisors Luncheon and the Association for Childhood Education Lunch. . . ."[28]

On May 4-5, the seasoned traveler ". . . attended a
conference of educational consultants for the Head Start
program in Atlanta, Ga. . . . She served as a consultant,

---

[24] "Faculty News," The Peabody Reflector 41 (March-
April 1968):99.

[25] Ibid.

[26] Ibid.

[27] Ibid.

[28] Ibid.

May 21, for the DuPont Elementary School, Old Hickory, Tenn."[29]
Between these two engagements, she found time to attend, on
May 10, the regular meeting of the Board of Trustees of George
Peabody College for Teachers.[30]

On June 1, Maycie Southall participated in the festivities
traditionally associated with Commencement Day on the campus
of George Peabody College for Teachers. On behalf of the
Peabody Alumni Association, she, as national president, ". . .
welcomed the graduates into the ranks of the alumni and issued
a cordial invitation to them to become members of the association."[31] Next, she became actively involved ". . . in the
Summer Conference of the Tennessee Association for Childhood
Education, June 6-7, and presided at the luncheon on June 15
during the state meeting of the Delta Kappa Gamma Society."[32]
Then, she participated as a leader during a two-week workshop
in North Carolina.[33]

Maycie Southall's continuing interest in education led
her to Washington, D.C., where, during late July and early
August, she was involved in the Fifteenth World Assembly of

[29]"Faculty News," The Peabody Reflector 41 (May-June
1968):170.

[30]"Board of Trustees Hears President Report on College's
'Pressing Needs,'" The Peabody Reflector 41 (May-June 1968):
134.

[31]"192nd Commencement," The Peabody Reflector 41 (May-
June 1968):150.

[32]"Faculty News," The Peabody Reflector 41 (May-June
1968):170.

[33]Ibid.

the World Organization for Early Childhood Education.[34] During the group's first meeting in this country, childhood education leaders ". . . from 37 countries attended. Earphones
and instant translation in three languages were provided
throughout the week."[35] A conscientious steward of her time,
intellect, and speaking ability, Maycie Southall frequently
planned her itineraries so that when possible she would meet
with more than one organization per trip; thus, she traveled
directly from Washington, D.C., to New York where she ". . .
attended the meetings of the executive board and served as
discussion leader at the Delta Kappa Gamma National Convention in New York City, Aug. 6-11."[36]

Her advice still sought by educational leaders, the
retired professor ". . . served as consultant to a parent
education experiment . . . in Florence, Ala., Sept. 6."[37]
A short time later, Maycie Southall worked as an ". . . elementary curriculum consultant for the schools of Leflore
County in Greenwood, Miss., Sept. 23-24, and evaluated the
elementary curriculum of the Sheffield, Ala., schools,
Sept. 25-Oct. 1."[38]

---

[34]Southall, interview, December 15, 1979.

[35]"Faculty News," The Peabody Reflector 41 (July-
August 1968):234.

[36]Ibid.

[37]"Faculty News," The Peabody Reflector 41 (September-
October 1968):277.

[38]Ibid.

Maycie Southall participated in the evaluation of Dupont Elementary School in Old Hickory, Tennessee, during the middle of October.[39] She served as ". . . guest speaker at the 15th Birthday Dinner of the Rho Chapter of Delta Kappa Gamma at the Brentwood (Tenn.) Country Club on Oct. 26."[40]

"Dr. Maycie K. Southall . . . attended the state meeting of the Virginia Alumni Association at Richmond, November 1, and represented the college at the annual meeting of the Louisiana Alumni Association in New Orleans, Nov. 25-26."[41] On November 7-8, she attended ". . . the semi-annual meetings of the Peabody Board of Trustees. . . ."[42] The retired educator ". . . was guest speaker at the meeting of the Cookeville, Tenn., American Association of University Women on Nov. 14."[43] She met with the same organization's ". . . International Affairs Core Committee on Nov. 22-24 to evaluate materials prepared for a portfolio on International Education for Today's Children."[44] On November 15-17, she joined a group of approximately fifty persons who participated in a two-day retreat symposium held at Park Mammoth Resort, Park City, Kentucky; the study, sponsored by George Peabody College for Teachers,

---

[39]Ibid.

[40]Ibid.

[41]"Faculty News," The Peabody Reflector 42 (January-February 1969):40.

[42]Ibid.

[43]Ibid.

[44]Ibid.

focused on program evaluation and self-criticism of the educational institution.[45]

Legislative Efforts

"I know of no one I respect more for her ability and
continuing use of time in promoting worthwhile causes in education."[46] Souci Hall, a retired supervisor of instruction,
continued: "Dr. Southall has worked untiringly to obtain
kindergartens throughout Tennessee. After years of effort
and influence, she is now realizing this dream she had from
her earliest teaching days."[47] In conclusion, she penned:
"Her combination of vision and expertise has influenced countless numbers and will continue to influence the future of
education."[48]

Legislative efforts in behalf of educational causes were
not new to Maycie Southall as she approached retirement; however, her earlier efforts have perhaps intensified during
recent years. Legislation supporting public kindergartens
has been of particular interest to the retired educator.

The promotion of kindergartens in Tennessee has consumed
a sizable share of Maycie Southall's time and effort throughout her professional career. "Peabody College has been involved in and committed to the kindergarten pre-school concept

---

[45]"Retreat Spurs Desire for More Discussions,"
The Peabody Reflector 41 (November-December 1968):316.

[46]Souci Hall, personal letter, July 31, 1979.

[47]Ibid.

[48]Ibid.

from its beginning."[49] So wrote John E. Windrow who was appointed Director of the Peabody Demonstration School in 1937
and remained in that position for a period of ten years; he
added: "During these years an able staff served its kindergarten and nursery school programs supported by such people
as Lucy Gage, Ullin Leavell, Maycie Southall, Irma Fender,
Lela Newman, Gean Morgan, Paul L. Boynton, and others."[50]

One technique that Maycie Southall utilized in promoting
kindergartens consisted of meeting with and persuading the
members of key organizations to work diligently for passage
of supportive legislation. She carried materials to the educational meetings, kept in touch with the legislative chair-
men, and served as a ". . . voluntary coordinator of efforts,
in a sense, in order to keep the organizations interested."[51]
Some of the key organizations through which she worked were
the ". . . Parent-Teacher Association, League of Women Voters,
Association for Childhood Education, Delta Kappa Gamma, and
Department of Supervisors."[52] An educator recalled: "The
Tennessee United Organizations for Education (TUOE) was both
a forum and a vehicle used by Dr. Southall."[53] Also, she
". . . gathered support through contacts at conventions as

---

[49] J[ohn] E. Windrow, "Head Start," The Peabody Reflector
38 (May-June 1965):97.

[50] Ibid.

[51] Southall, interview, August 29, 1979.

[52] Ibid.

[53] Charles Tollett, personal letter, October 31, 1979.

well as through correspondence."[54] Ruth McDonald, retired
director of elementary programs and staff development for the
Metropolitan Nashville Schools, who knew of Maycie Southall's
work in The Delta Kappa Gamma Society offered:

> Public kindergartens in Tennessee owe their exist-
> ence to the persistence of Maycie Southall and Mary Hall.
> Years before other educators were willing to accept them
> and before the public generally had any interest in them,
> they were talking to civic groups, legislators, and gov-
> ernors about them. They were urging that local chapters
> and Xi State actively support the effort to make them a
> part of the educational program. Their success, after
> many years, has great implications for young children of
> the state.
>
> Of great import, too, is their method of attack.
> They used knowledge and research to inform those who
> could influence decisions. They did not let defeat one
> time slow down their efforts or deter them in any way.
> Their work was in behalf of children and the focus was
> kept there. . . .[55]

Perseverance has long been a widely known trait of the
retired educator. Her colleague throughout thirty-five years
at George Peabody College for Teachers recently reflected:
"Maycie was, to a large extent, the key influence in establishing kindergartens in the state; this was accomplished
largely by her tenacity."[56]

Robert S. Thurman, one of Maycie Southall's former doctoral students and currently a professor of early childhood
education at the University of Tennessee, described the
kindergarten promoter's efforts:

---

[54]Southall, interview, August 29, 1979.

[55]McDonald, personal letter, May 9, 1979.

[56]Windrow, interview, May 8, 1979.

She was a prime mover for state supported kindergartens in Tennessee during the mid-1960s. She developed a research paper that had quite an influence on
the state legislature as well as other members of the
educational community. I met with different groups
during that time including state legislators; and when
I said Maycie Southall, these people knew whom I was
talking about.[57]

Charles Tollett, assistant superintendent of the Cleveland
(Tennessee) City Schools, provided:

It was my privilege to work with Dr. Southall in
a number of activities designed to result in the opportunity for all five-year olds in Tennessee to go to
kindergarten. Dr. Southall made a fantastic contribution toward this goal. I especially remember her in
terms of her experience, her expertise, and her enthusiasm. We can add her energy to continue the emphasis.

. . . I recall Dr. Mary Tom Berry of MTSU as a
colleague who worked with Dr. Southall and made a major
contribution to the campaign.[58]

Mary Tom Berry, chairman of the Department of Elementary
and Special Education, Middle Tennessee State University,
shared: "Dr. Southall served with Miss Mary Hall and others
on a Survey Committee that worked diligently in the early
1960s for a state kindergarten program. They gave the primary leadership--and certainly deserve the credit."[59]

Maycie Southall was quoted in a 1963 newspaper article
that featured her educational efforts:

"I have been most interested in public school kindergartens," declared Dr. Southall. "Tennessee being one of
the seven states without this service, I have joined with
AAUW, P-TA and ACE the three organizations that have
worked nationally and locally to further this move."

[57]Thurman, personal letter, June 29, 1979.

[58]Tollett, personal letter, October 31, 1979.

[59]Mary Tom Berry, personal letter, November 7, 1979.

"Kindergarten is a very necessary part of education
for every child of today," declared Dr. Southall, "not
just those who can afford the private ones."

When asked if she thought when public kindergartens
came into being should they be mandatory, without hesitation she said, "By all means." At the present time
attendance is not compulsory in all states where they
are now in effect.[60]

The promoter's efforts found fruition in part, at least,

in the early 1970s. State of Tennessee Representative John T.

Bragg reviewed in 1979 the inception and growth of the kinder-

garten program: "The Legislature passed it as a volunteer

program under Governor [Winfield] Dunn. It started out as a

pilot project and was expanded through the years until we now

have it at every location which the local school systems de-

sire."[61] Maycie Southall recently stated that the reason the

kindergarten program was proposed as voluntary was through

fear of the legislation's defeat if compliance were mandated.[62]

Former Governor Winfield Dunn and Maycie Southall were

both advocates of a publicly supported kindergarten program:

> Dr. Southall is certainly a pioneer in the kinder-
> garten movement in Tennessee. I know of no person who
> did more than she to initiate the program in Tennessee.
> Former Governor Winfield Dunn is, of course, primarily
> responsible for the expansion of kindergarten with his
> unwavering commitment to the provision of support for a
> state-wide program of kindergarten.[63]

---

[60]Virginia Keathley, "Meet Dr. Maycie Katherine Southall:
National and International Educator," Nashville Tennessean,
May 19, 1963, p. 4-E.

[61]John T. Bragg, personal letter, September 12, 1979.

[62]Southall, interview, August 29, 1979.

[63]Tollett, personal letter, October 31, 1979.

Various legislators have become familiar with Maycie
Southall's endeavors. State of Tennessee Representative
Bob Davis accepted responsibilities that placed him in a
prime position to observe some of the retired educator's
activities in behalf of kindergartens during the 1970s:

> I was chairman of the House Education Committee
> during 1973-77. The kindergarten law was passed in
> 1973. During the 1970 campaign, Governor Winfield
> Dunn had pledged full implementation of a state-wide
> kindergarten program by the end of his term. When
> he recommended such to the Legislature, Speaker Ned
> McWherter asked me to take the Education Committee
> for a series of public hearings across the State.
> As I recall, they were held in Jackson, Murfreesboro,
> Athens, and Johnson City. I do not remember if she
> attended all, but I do recall that Dr. Southall tes-
> tified at one or more of them.
>
> The legislation was passed with the provision
> that it be phased in rather than immediately imple-
> mented because we could not immediately provide the
> personnel or physical facilities. . . .[64]

Representative Davis recalled that questions arose
among the legislators concerning the desirability of a
compulsory versus a voluntary program as well as a home-
based versus a classroom program. Ultimately, the decision prevailed to provide a voluntary, classroom program.[65]
Representative Davis concluded:

> At the time of these deliberations, Dr. Southall
> was much in evidence, lobbying hard for enactment of
> a kindergarten program. Her support was both public
> and private and very effective. We were all aware
> that Dr. Southall had devoted a good portion of her
> life to the advocacy of public kindergartens.[66]

---

[64]Bob [Robert C.] Davis, personal letter, November 1,
1979.

[65]Ibid.

[66]Ibid.

State of Tennessee Senator Ernest Crouch, who has served
as a legislator since 1955, reminisced about the retired educator's efforts:

> During my service in the General Assembly, I have
> become acquainted with Maycie Southall. She has been
> very active in helping the cause of education, particu-
> larly the kindergarten programs and helping obtain
> federal funding for our library system. She has cer-
> tainly been one of the most effective lobbyists for
> education. I can say, without reservation, that she
> has been one of the contributing factors that estab-
> lished education as priority in funding of state dol-
> lars. This year we appropriated 48% of the total
> budget to education. This area received more than any
> other in state funding. Miss Southall is certainly a
> pioneer and can be thanked for her efforts that have
> resulted in this type of recognition for the need for
> education and necessary funding.[67]

State of Tennessee Senator Halbert Harvill, who is currently serving as chairman of the Senate Education Committee,
has known Maycie Southall through his former positions such
as state commissioner of education and president of Austin
Peay State College:

> I have known Maycie Southall for many years, through
> both my association with George Peabody College and the
> state Senate. She was such a good teacher and was always
> interested in good quality education. She did a lot in
> working with the legislature to get bills passed that
> would help education.[68]

Maycie Southall reminisced about her efforts at both
state and national levels in behalf of public kindergartens
for all children. During the 1940s, she invested considerable
time and effort in promoting this cause. As she had found
through research that Tennessee was one of few states with

---

[67] Ernest Crouch, personal letter, July 23, 1979.

[68] Halbert Harvill, personal letter, July 23, 1979.

neither permissive nor mandatory laws for public kindergartens,
she worked diligently with others toward influencing legislators who enacted a permissive kindergarten bill in 1945; she
remarked that no state funds were appropriated, however, so
only those areas which received federal funds because they
were classified as war-impacted were able to maintain public
kindergartens. During the same decade, Maycie Southall worked
through her position as ACEI president to promote the education of children under six. Along with representatives of
several national educational organizations, she attended a
conference held in Washington, D.C., where the group sought
the support of President Harry Truman in its request for federal aid. She was somewhat disappointed when the majority of
the representatives decided to seek funding for all grades
from kindergarten through twelve rather than promote the
kindergarten program as a separate entity. Although the
availability of public kindergartens for all children was
delayed in Tennessee, Maycie Southall's enthusiasm was not
diminished; she continued to work during ensuing decades for
the fruition of public kindergartens for all children.[69]

Distinguished Alumna

Not only has Maycie Southall continued during her retirement years to direct her attention and give her time to issues
that she considers important, but she has also continued to be
honored on many occasions as a distinguished educator; that

---

[69]Southall, interview, December 15, 1979.

is, her life has changed very little in many respects from the earlier years when she both gave of her talents to education and received recognition for her services.

On May 5, 1973, Maycie Southall was honored by the Middle Tennessee State University Alumni Association during its annual reunion; she had been chosen as one of three former graduates who were designated "Distinguished Alumni" during the festivities. The selections, which included Brainard B. Gracy, III, and Bealer Smotherman, had been made from names submitted by fellow alumni to a secret committee appointed by the Alumni Association. Maycie Southall and her co-honorees joined the ranks of thirty-nine other persons selected during the preceding fourteen years.[70]

"Dr. Maycie Katherine Southall Day"

Mayor of Metropolitan Nashville Richard Fulton presented to Maycie Southall an official proclamation in his office that designated October 16, 1977, as "Dr. Maycie Katherine Southall Day."[71] It has been described as ". . . a fitting tribute to one of Nashville's distinguished citizens--widely known as an educator whose special interest . . . [for] over half a century has been the improvement of educational opportunities for all children everywhere."[72] A copy of the proclamation follows:

---

[70]"MTSU Names 3 Graduates '1973 Distinguished Alumni,'" Murfreesboro (Tennessee) Daily News Journal, March 25, 1973, p. 10.

[71]Richard Fulton, personal letter, April 5, 1979.

[72]Susan Brandau, "'Day' a Tribute to Dr. Southall," Nashville Tennessean, October 16, 1977, p. 4-E.

Proclamation

WHEREAS, Dr. Maycie Katherine Southall, Professor Emeritus of Education at George Peabody College, has devoted every effort of her professional career, spanning almost half a century, toward the improvement of educational opportunities for all children everywhere; and

WHEREAS, Dr. Maycie Katherine Southall, who served as Professor of Elementary Education at her alma mater, George Peabody College, from 1929 until her retirement in 1964, has been involved in improving educational opportunities for children to the extent that it can truly be said she has exerted an influence on educators throughout the world; and

WHEREAS, Dr. Maycie Katherine Southall's career work has involved her with numerous educational and humanitarian organizations and has earned awards and recognitions too numerous to list in this short space;

NOW, THEREFORE, I, Richard H. Fulton, Mayor of Metropolitan Nashville, do hereby proclaim Sunday, October 16th, 1977, as

"DR. MAYCIE KATHERINE SOUTHALL DAY"

and urge the Metropolitan Nashville community to add our names to those who recognize and honor this woman and the many contributions she has made to help build a better world for all mankind.

IN WITNESS WHEREOF, I have hereunto set my hand on this, the Fourth day of October, 1977.

RICHARD FULTON
MAYOR

Activities of the day included a reception during the afternoon at David Lipscomb College in Nashville. At that time, a plaque was presented to Maycie Southall in recognition of her accomplishments.[73]

Hobbies

Because Maycie Southall had devoted so much of her life to her educational career and related endeavors, one of her close friends good-naturedly teased her by coining a humorous epitaph: "Here lies Maycie K. Southall who was always so busy helping others with their problems that she never took the time to take care of herself."[74] The friend reported: "As a result of my kidding, we went, for a change, on a dove hunt or a fishing trip--I don't remember which particular activity--but it was the first time in quite a while that Maycie had stopped long enough to enjoy such an outing."[75]

In spite of extensive time spent on educational causes during her retirement years, Maycie Southall has still pursued some of her hobbies. An interest in fishing was a carry-over from earlier days. A Nashville newspaper carried in 1963 a human interest story:

> Peabody College teacher Maycie Southall and student Billie Brannon obtained permission from Dr. J. E. Windrow to fish on his Eagleville farm--where there are three ponds.

---

[73]Lois Jones, interview held in Sewanee, Tennessee, June 13, 1980.

[74]Brannon, interview, May 8, 1979.

[75]Ibid.

"One pond has no fish, the other two are well-stocked," explained Windrow.

Several hours later Windrow drove down to see how Maycie and Billie were doing.

"I suppose by now," he told them, "you have discovered you are fishing in the pond--which has NO fish?"

"That may be true," replied Maycie, "but here's what we've caught already."

. . . And she held up a string of 32 fish![76]

Maycie Southall has gained a reputation for her appreciation of fine horses. Accustomed to horses since early childhood, she has, according to a 1963 article in which she was quoted, ". . . always ridden horseback. 'My father raised horses and I have ridden all my life. . . . I find early Sunday morning before church service is my freest time.'"[77] A niece described Maycie Southall's hobbies: "She loves horses, and we frequently rode through Percy Warner Park trails. Our family had walking horses that she rode. She also liked to swim, so we would go to Centennial Park and have a picnic and swim."[78] A close friend related in 1979: "Maycie is an excellent horse person and knows her animals; however, she has not mounted a horse recently because of a hip injury suffered during a fall while working in her flower garden."[79]

---

[76]Red O'Donnell, "'Round the Clock," Nashville Banner, August 8, 1963, p. 1.

[77]Keathley, "Meet Dr. Maycie Katherine Southall: National and International Educator," p. 4-E.

[78]Jean Jones, interview, May 18, 1979.

[79]Brannon, interview, May 8, 1979.

Many of Maycie Southall's friends have received on various occasions exquisite roses and other lovely flowers, the cultivation of which constitutes another of the educator's hobbies. While employed as a professor, she had described herself as a moonlight gardener because although she had a little flower garden, she could find time to cultivate it only at night.[80] One of her former doctoral students remembered that Maycie Southall ". . . tried always to have a flower on the desk in her room. It came from her own garden. . . . She said that many children came from homes in which they did not see beauty, and they deserved to see it at school."[81] The same former student continued: "This I have copied from her, and it has paid off in student interest."[82] In June 1979, another former student reminisced about Maycie Southall's aesthetic expressions: "My classes in 1937-39 were a joy, both in philosophy and her gracious charm. She wore beautiful dresses, usually with gold tones to match her hair. Always she brought a flower to her desk."[83] The same former student, and later colleague whose friendship with Maycie Southall spans more than forty years, described a recent visit with the retired educator: "Her hobby (or one) is her flowers, especially her roses. The last time I was in Nashville she

---

[80]Keathley, "Meet Dr. Maycie Katherine Southall: National and International Educator," p. 4-E.

[81]Ethel B. Miller, personal letter, October 18, 1979.

[82]Ibid.

[83]Rubie E. Smith, personal letter, June 2, 1979.

joined me for lunch . . . laden with roses for me to bring home."[84] Another friend, Frances Ingram, related that Maycie Southall enjoys growing and sharing her roses and that although the latter's religious convictions disallow labor on the Sabbath, she ". . . works in her roses on Sunday--they have the Lord's blessings."[85]

Because of her sensitivity to beauty, an outstanding honor bestowed upon Maycie Southall on November 27, 1977, became especially meaningful. According to a Nashville radio broadcast, a flower shop saluted the retired educator by selecting her as the recipient of an orchid, a token of appreciation for her outstanding contributions. The script began:

> Each week for the past 35 years, Emma's flower and gift shops have selected some person outstanding in the business, cultural, or civic activities of Nashville and saluted him or her with "An Orchid to You." Today we salute Dr. Maycie Katherine Southall, professor emeritus of education, George Peabody College for Teachers.[86]

After summarizing and lauding many of the educator's efforts at the local, state, and national levels, the script concluded:

> We of WSIX Radio and J. Haskell Tidman of Emma's salute Dr. Maycie Katherine Southall, great lady of the world of education whose achievements seem endless. We thank her for the many contributions she has made to our city, state, and our nation. A lovely orchid from Emma's is on its way to Dr. Southall's home.[87]

---

[84]Ibid.

[85]Frances Ingram, personal letter, February 26, 1980.

[86]"An Orchid to You," script prepared for broadcast on Radio Station WSIX, Nashville, November 27, 1977.

[87]Ibid.

Children's International Intercultural
Education Center

"I have never seen anyone do what she does at her age--
and continues to do--and still look like a movie star."[88]
Director Marshall Stewart, Public Library of Nashville and
Davidson County, continued to share his impressions of Maycie
Southall with whom he has worked recently in an attempt to
establish a Children's International Intercultural Education
Center: "I have never known of anyone except her who does
not know defeat. We have gone to the Governor [Ray Blanton]
and on down trying to obtain support. This is a time of tight
budgets, and there seems to be no money available for this
project."[89] Director Stewart concluded: "Everyone suggested
that we try to get a grant. We have applied, and the prospects
look pretty good."[90]

Maycie Southall has been engaged for the past several
years in efforts directed toward realization of a Children's
International Intercultural Education Center to be located in
Nashville. A 1977 newspaper article reported: "Maycie is a
member of a committee seeking federal funds and foundation
grants to establish the proposed center."[91] The retired educator provided a time frame for fruition of the committee's
work when, according to the article, she said the members

---

[88]Marshall Stewart, interview held in Nashville,
July 11, 1979.

[89]Ibid.

[90]Ibid.

[91]Brandau, "'Day' a Tribute to Dr. Southall," p.4-E.

hoped to have the pilot project established by 1979 because of that year's designation as International Year of the Child.[92]

Insight into some of the efforts expended by Maycie Southall in behalf of the project may be gleaned through her January 26, 1979, letter written to State Commissioner of Education Edward A. Cox:

> I am enclosing a copy of a most fitting and valuable project proposed for the celebration of the International Year of the Child, 1979, which I discussed with you by phone. It is not only a unique pilot project, but one which would have lasting and far-reaching value in helping today's children and tomorrow's citizens understand their complex world and billions of world neighbors. . . .
>
> I might add that, while the project originated in the local chapter of the United Nations Association, its committee includes key citizens, children's city and state librarians, and a Metro Supervisor and School Board member. Although this pilot project will only serve one of the seventeen state library centers, we hope it will prove so valuable that it will be extended to the other sixteen library centers in the state and thereby serve all of Tennessee's children through the help of bookmobiles.
>
> As you suggested, I shall try to review the steps that have been taken in trying to secure funds to finance the proposed project.
>
> Since it would serve a state library center, my first step was to ask the late Dr. Oliver Ikenberry, then president of the "Friends of the Library", to go with me to see Commissioner Sam Ingram, head of the state's library system. Dr. Ingram realized immediately that such a center would be a very valuable addition to the state's present library services to children. He said he thought that they had received or were going to receive some federal funds for improving international relations and that he would look into the matter.
>
> In the meantime, Commissioner Ingram and I requested and received a conference with Governor Blanton. He, too, thought it a most worthwhile project and after the Legislature adjourned he could meet with us again.

---

[92]Ibid.

At my next conference with Dr. Ingram, which included Marshall Stewart, Director of the Central Library,
Kay Culbertson, Tennessee State Librarian and Archivist,
and Dr. Ikenberry, Dr. Ingram asked his staff member in
charge of federal grants to research all possible sources
to see what he could come up with. This study revealed
that federal grants were limited to school systems. Then
Dr. Ingram suggested that I ascertain whether Metro or
Murfreesboro would be interested in having this proposed
center.

After some delay in getting a meeting with the committee which Dr. Elbert Brooks appointed, I had a conference with Director Brooks, Assistant Superintendent
Patterson, and the chairman of this committee, Willodene
Scott. Both Dr. Brooks and Mr. Patterson were enthusiastic about having the Children's International Intercultural Education Center. Dr. Brooks suggested, as
the next step, a conference be set up which would include Metro's staff member and the State's staff member
responsible for federal grants to see what could be
cooperatively worked out.

This conference was scheduled and they along with
Mr. Patterson, Mrs. Scott, and I met in the Cordell Hull
Building. Unfortunately, the Metro staff member had,
just the day before, received a notice that Metro's request for an extension of a grant for aid in the teaching
of arithmetic had been granted. Since no school system
may have two federal grants at the same time under the
same title, this information brought an end to this
approach.

After this conference, I went to Dr. Ingram's office
to report to him our disappointment. He was again helpful and said there might be some funds in the Governor's
Discretionary Fund and that he would discuss this with
Dr. Jones, Commissioner of Finance. But he thought it
would be better to wait until after the November election.

Both men were very busy and frequently out of the
city, but their secretaries were able to set up a conference of Commissioner Jones, Commissioner Ingram, and
myself. Commissioner Jones stated that he had children
and recognized that such an international intercultural
center would be a most valuable asset to the state's
education program and that he and Commissioner Ingram
would see what they could do about funding it.

Later, Dr. Ingram reported that they had talked
briefly at the governor's reception before Christmas
and Commissioner Jones told him that he would try to
get funds for our project in next year's budget.

After Christmas, I talked with Commissioner Jones and he said there were still funds in the Governor's Discretionary Fund, but it would not be exactly fair to the incoming governor to leave it empty. He advised that I talk with you as soon as you took office and, as you know, I was one of the first to your doorstep.

I am sending Dr. Ingram a copy of this lengthy summary and asking him to check the accuracy of my re-call. I would be most appreciative for a conference with you at your earliest convenience. I think you understand my haste because "time is of the essence." February 5 is just around the corner.[93]

Former State Commissioner of Education Sam H. Ingram, who had resigned from that position to accept the presidency of Middle Tennessee State University, corresponded with Maycie Southall. The January 31, 1979, letter included:

I have read your summary of our efforts to receive money for the library project which you have been work-ing so long to fund, and I believe it represents an ac-curate description of the steps which have been taken. I wish you the best in your continuing efforts on this particular project. If you are able to get through all the bureaucracy to get this funded, it will be nothing less than a miracle. I hope you accomplish it and if anyone can, I know it is you.[94]

On September 20, 1979, President Ingram shared his im-pressions of Maycie Southall for the purpose of this study:

I am delighted that you are doing your study on Dr. Southall. She has made tremendous contributions to education and continues to be active in the cause of young people in this state. She was one of a small group of people who lobbied intensively for many years until they were successful in getting the kindergarten programs approved for Tennessee. While I was not active at the state level during these years, I was aware of her efforts on behalf of kindergartens.

[93]Maycie Southall to Edward A. Cox, January 26, 1979, Private Files of Maycie Southall.

[94]Sam H. Ingram to Maycie Southall, January 31, 1979, Private Files of Maycie Southall.

I am much more knowledgeable about her more recent efforts in regard to the Children's International Intercultural Education Center. Dr. Southall met with me personally on more than one occasion. She also met with Governor Blanton and me, and with Commissioner Jones and me on this issue.

There are two things that I would like to say in regard to Dr. Southall and her efforts on this and other projects. First, she does not select a project on which to devote her time and energy unless it is one that is worthwhile and in the best interest of the young people of our state. Secondly, she is persistent in her attempt to achieve her objectives. I fully believe, for example, had I continued to serve as Commissioner of Education and had the Governor and the Commissioner of Finance and Administration not changed that Dr. Southall would have been successful in her efforts to obtain some state funding for the . . . Education Center.

Finally, I would like to point out that the kindergarten program and the . . . Education Center are just two of the many projects that she has been interested in and worked toward achieving during her long career in education. Education in Tennessee and Tennessee's youth are much better off today than they would have been without Dr. Maycie Southall. We need more friends like her who will fight for the educational opportunities that our young people need. . . .[95]

On June 18, 1979, Chairman Maycie Southall and her twelve committee members completed the forms requisite to obtaining financial assistance for the proposed Children's International Intercultural Education Center; the application appealed to the U.S. Office of Education under the federal title Citizen Education for Cultural Understanding Program; the request for a one-year grant of $50,000, to be supplemented by local funds totaling $10,500, was submitted by The Urban Observatory of Metropolitan Nashville-University Centers under the signature of Director Ralph E. Balyeat, certifying representative. On the first page of the application, Maycie Southall wrote:

_____

[95]Sam H. Ingram, personal letter, September 20, 1979.

The proposed project for a Children's International Intercultural Education Center grew out of the Nashville Chapter of the United Nations Association's desire to celebrate the International Year of the Child (IYC) by doing something that would be of lasting and far-reaching value to children. Since we were the first chapter of the United Nations Association to be organized in the U.S.A., we wanted to have a project which would help children understand their one world and their responsibility as future world citizens. To expedite matters, the Executive Committee appointed a Children's International Intercultural Education Center Committee. I was made Chairman because I was a charter member of the U.S. National Committee for UNESCO and firmly believe that "Since wars are made in the minds of men, it is in the minds of men (children) that the defenses of peace must be built." The members of the C.I.I.E.C. Committee are all leaders of community-wide organizations.[96]

The application included a rationale for creation of a

Children's International Intercultural Education Center:

As never before today's children are growing up in a world that is dependent on the understanding and co-operation of its many cultural groups. They need to be educated to become knowledgeable and worthy citizens, not only of their local, state, and national communities but of a world community with all its different cultures and diversity of interests. This requires more authentic resource materials than are now available in our best schools and libraries. Furthermore, materials that accurately portray the life of peoples of foreign countries are extremely difficult to find and procure. Foreign students and educators are appalled at the inaccuracies they find in our best reference books and the paucity of material about their country in our most recent textbooks. If a similar center is now available to American children, we have not found any reference to it. The nearest is in the Public Library in Boston to which publishers have given children's books in the native language. Therefore, this would be unique as well as a very valuable project in the U.S.A. Similar intercultural centers for youth and children have been developed in Munich, Germany, and Vienna, Austria.[97]

---

[96]The Urban Observatory of Metropolitan Nashville-University Centers, "Children's International Intercultural Education Center," application for a Federal Grant, June 18, 1979, p. 1.

[97]Ibid., pp. 1-2.

The application explained briefly the purpose for the
proposed undertaking:

> The purpose of the proposed international resource
> center is to provide a service for our community and the
> surrounding area which will bring together all types of
> authentic multi-sensory materials to help children learn
> about their three billion world neighbors, which is a
> practical necessity today and will be even more so to-
> morrow.[98]

After careful consideration of several possible sites,
a decision was reached concerning a suitable location:

> The Committee's choice was the Nashville Public
> Library because the city's sixteen branch libraries
> could make the Center's materials and services more
> accessible to children and their parents and teachers.
> We were fortunate to have the president of the Friends
> of the Public Library, Dr. Oliver Ikenberry, as a member
> of our Committee. He and the Committee Chairman were
> instructed by the local United Nations Executive Board
> to go before the Library Executive Board to seek ap-
> proval of the Committee's plan for a Children's Inter-
> national Intercultural Center located in the Public
> Library. We were pleased to find that the Director,
> Mr. Marshall Stewart, recognized the importance of the
> project and was willing to seek and secure the permis-
> sion of the Library Board to house the Center in the
> Public Library of Nashville and Davidson County. For-
> tunately, the Children's Librarian and the Supervisor
> of the sixteen branch libraries were both enthusiastic
> about the project and willing to work with our Committee
> to its realization.
>
> This strategic location, through its sixteen branch
> libraries, will make it possible for this proposed Chil-
> dren's International Intercultural Center to supplement
> the services of 89 elementary school libraries used by
> 48,335 children and their 2,113 teachers--not to mention
> the thousands of parents who will be accompanying their
> children. Last year's records of the Public Library of
> Nashville and Davidson County show that 467,767 books
> were checked out by children and that 93,585 children
> attended story time, viewed films, or [watched] mario-
> nette shows.[99]

---

[98]Ibid., p. 2.

[99]Ibid., pp. 3-4.

Committee members who supported Chairman Maycie Southall's
efforts were Eleanor Bauer, Gladys Beasley, Pearle Bradley,
George Cate, Helen Clark, Lee Davis, Edwin S. Gleaves, Diane
McNabb, Willodene Scott, Caroline Stark, Alonzo Stephens, and
Olivia Young. According to the application, the members were
already looking toward the future while working specifically
on obtaining funds for the Center's first year of operation:

> If this proposed multicultural center is funded for
> one year, we believe it will be continued and expanded
> because eighteen men and women's civic organizations in
> Nashville have expressed interest in having a C.I.I.E.
> Center. Furthermore, we hope that similar intercultural
> centers will be provided in the other sixteen public li-
> brary centers in the state and through their branch li-
> braries and bookmobiles the lives of all of Tennessee's
> children can be enriched. We are fairly confident that
> this expansion can be effected because the Commissioner
> of Education and key legislators have expressed interest
> and willingness to help work for state funding of this
> and similar projects next year.[100]

Reflections

During the course of this study, letters were sent to key
persons seeking their evaluation of Maycie Southall's effectiveness within the context of her service to education. From
numerous responses, four are included in this chapter. They
were selected because they are typical examples of the letters
received, they refer to various projects and activities in
which Maycie Southall has been engaged during her retirement
years, and they were contributed by persons from diverse walks
of life.

---

[100]Ibid., p. 7.

Former President Henry H. Hill, George Peabody College for Teachers, shared his impressions:

> Before I came to Peabody as president in 1945, I knew and admired Maycie Southall. She was a member of the Educational Policies Commission, a potent body for leadership in education. I recall also how the president of the American Council on Education sought out Dr. Southall to grace the head table at the annual banquet. From the early days until the present, she has always been attractive and is always tastefully and attractively dressed--a really beautiful woman in the best meaning of the term.
>
> She has been outstanding in her devotion to elementary education and to the public schools generally. I still have the vignette in my mind of her seated in the Peabody registration hall before a long line of students waiting to see her. The line was long not because of dilatory action on her part but because she gave each individual registrant her full attention and care. I think this is one source of her well-merited popularity. She never wrote textbooks but spent the time helping students instead.
>
> After retirement from Peabody College--but never from her active interest in Peabody--she accepted a position at Southern Illinois University for a year. Although paid an unusually high salary, she left the position after a year in order to devote more time to her former students and to educational causes and organizations she believed in. She never flinched from a fight in the legislature or in Peabody affairs in general if she believed in the importance of the issues. She spent a lifetime successfully advocating early childhood education. If she lost an early fight for public school kindergartens, to use one example, she made it easier for others to succeed later.
>
> I shall not review all her national and even international honors but summarize her career as one of great service to humankind everywhere. Gifted with a remarkable constitution, she has persisted all her life in innumerable kindnesses to her friends and to those who needed her. Gifts of roses, her own jellies and preserves, and most of all of her own time and energy mark her as a wonderful woman who has lived wisely and well.[101]

---

[101]Henry H. Hill, personal letter, June 18, 1979.

In 1968, Christine Sadler Coe was elected to the Board of Trustees, George Peabody College for Teachers. A woman of distinction within her own rights, she has realized a long and successful career as a journalist and author. Her observations about Maycie Southall included:

I was not a classmate of Miss Southall (I graduated in the August, 1927, class and knew few of my classmates-- so she could have been among them, I suppose), nor have I known her well until recent years--although I have known OF her for a long time, mostly through her former students, who invariably seemed almost to revere her. In the early '30s when I was on The Nashville Banner in the afternoons for one or two years I worked for The Peabody Reflector, then edited by John E. Windrow. It was a pleasure then to see her cross the campus with students always rushing to be with her. She was very beautiful, and still is.

When I went on the Peabody Board of Trustees, she was finishing her term and was delightful to me. My worry was that I never could approach her status in that position. Her brains and understanding of the job were way beyond me! She was not the least intimidated by "all those men" and when she talked up--which never loath to do--they listened. She then lived on 21st Street, just across the road, and her apartment was lovely. Usually one or more of her former students would drop in for advice or just to be near her. She was a marvelous cook and excelled in making jellies and jams. The conversation went in all directions and was very up to date in current and world affairs. Her guests left knowing more than when they came, and in a glow from basking in the radiance of her personality and wisdom.

She moved to another apartment and made her long trip around the world. I lost touch until the MERGER [George Peabody College for Teachers and Vanderbilt University] was imminent. She entered that fray with both feet. . . . She was terribly concerned . . . lest Peabody get the little end of the stick. She wrote and circulated a paper of warnings and suggestions-- based on the experience of Teachers College of Columbia University during . . . earlier merger days. How much it was or will be used, who knows--but it was a masterful presentation.

It seems to me that Dr. Southall owes her reputation as a super teacher to a rare combination of brains and glamour working in tandem--and to her active love of teaching. She never grew tired nor became a whit stodgy in the classroom. Her radiant personality and her growth beyond the classroom spurred her students to look beyond the textbooks, and strive to be at home in the world, to be live activists. Small wonder her students loved her! She gave them so very much. If more teachers really loved their jobs and kept abreast of the world around them, think what a plus that would be for education.

. . . I do know she's a rare person, and I am delighted you are writing about her.[102]

State of Tennessee Senator Douglas Henry, Jr., from the twenty-first senatorial district of Davidson County, evaluated Maycie Southall's recent project:

Thank you for writing me for my impressions of Dr. Southall. We have known each other for several years through her interest in legislation affecting the education of children and the legislative program of the American Association of University Women. It is certainly no exaggeration to say that Dr. Southall is a distinctive blend of energy, intelligence, and informed persistence when she is advocating a proposal in the interest of the children whom she has elected to serve with her career. Although the stated qualities in another could describe a personality which would wear out its welcome with a legislator, Dr. Southall's presence, although always stimulating, is never in any manner burdensome.

As to her most recent venture, the proposed Children's International Intercultural Education Center, there is no doubt but that the emphases which she proposes, if effectively mediated to the children, would not only greatly enhance their lives through exposure to the diversity of other cultures but would be a concrete step toward improved international understanding, upon the children's maturity, with all the benefits in various directions for our State and for our part of the world which that understanding would comport.[103]

---

[102]Christine Sadler Coe, personal letter, May 20, 1979.

[103]Douglas Henry, Jr., personal letter, September 4, 1979.

Horace G. Hill, Jr., former chairman of George Peabody
College for Teachers' Board of Trustees, is a well-known
executive among business circles; he is president of a
Nashville-based firm, H. G. Hill Company. His interest in
and commitment to the educational institution are of long
standing as his father had earlier served for many years
in positions of leadership on the same Board of Trustees.
Horace G. Hill, Jr., expressed his views regarding Maycie
Southall's contributions to education during her retirement
years:

> As a trustee of George Peabody College for
> Teachers (1967-69), Dr. Maycie K. Southall brought
> to the Board the knowledge and the wisdom of a long
> and productive career in education, which was most
> effective in the deliberations and decisions of the
> Board. Her loyal and sincere dedication to Peabody
> College, and to the Peabody mission, in the field of
> teacher education, was an inspiration to me person-
> ally and to the other members of the Board.
>
> It was a rare privilege for me to have served
> on the Board with such an illustrious personality
> and educator. Her warm and gracious manner and her
> keen interest in the world about her "brightens my
> day" and endears her to her host of friends and all
> of her associates.
>
> Dr. Southall is often referred to as "The First
> Lady of Childhood Education" and, perhaps more than
> any other one person, promoted legislation which
> established kindergartens in the State of Tennessee
> under the administration of Governor Winfield Dunn.
> Governor Dunn is a former member of the Board of
> Trustees of Peabody College.
>
> All of us are pleased that her professional and
> educational contributions are being recognized through
> your graduate study. . . .104

104Horace G. Hill, Jr., personal letter, August 28,
1979.

Throughout her years of teaching at Peabody
and even since retiring, Dr. Southall was and is
the image of George Peabody College for Teachers
to many--Peabodians and non-Peabodians--throughout
the nation and the world. She is the exemplar of
Peabody's mission and philosophy, "Education, a
Debt Due from Present to Future Generations."

John Julia McMahan
Personal letter
May 21, 1979

CHAPTER VII

SUMMARY AND CONCLUSIONS, IMPLICATIONS, AND SUGGESTIONS FOR FURTHER RESEARCH

Summary and Conclusions

This study has addressed the life and contributions to education of Maycie Southall. An educator who began her career in the early 1900s, Maycie Southall has been an avid proponent of both supervision of instruction and childhood education; she has been especially interested in improving the education of children from two through twelve years of age with emphasis on the pre-service and in-service training of teachers. Her leadership and influence have not been confined to the educational institution setting but have been exemplified through contributions to educational literature; extensive affiliation with professional organizations; and participation in civic, religious, and legislative affairs. Her life reflects an era of the history of education, particularly in the South.

The following conclusions regarding Maycie Southall's life and contributions to education have been drawn from the information compiled for this study:

1. Maycie Southall has devoted her life to the service of education. At an early age, she was developing a yearning for knowledge that was to culminate later into a respect for, and commitment to, the advancement of education. Her vocation

265

was directed primarily toward teaching others to teach children. In her retirement years, she has continued to work diligently for the cause of education.

2. Maycie Southall taught courses in elementary education for thirty-five years at George Peabody College for Teachers. Her efforts contributed to the esteem accorded the institution as one that emphasized the importance of teacher education; she was instrumental in endeavors that brought to George Peabody College for Teachers recognition as one of the better centers for teacher education not only in the South but in the nation and in the world.

3. As she was accustomed to teaching unusually large classes and advising exceptionally large numbers of students, Maycie Southall had an opportunity to influence directly myriad administrators, supervisors, and classroom teachers. Replies to an inquiry concerning her influence on some of her former students' educational careers attested to the fact that she has been instrumental in causing many others to commit themselves more fully to the betterment of education. Ruth Bowdoin, a consultant for parent education, was one among many former students who replied to the inquiry:

> Dr. Southall's efforts have broad dimensions that have touched the lives of many of us. The spectrum of her accomplishments is deep enough to reach into the understanding of the behavior of children; broad enough to reach educators in many fields of service; and high enough to provide aspirations for those who concern themselves with the education of our youth.
>
> She personally influenced my choice to focus on education of the very young child when I was a student

in her Early Childhood Education class . . . more than
thirty years ago. For this, I shall be eternally grateful to her. Her willingness to work for causes in which
she believed, her indefatigable efforts for the improvement of teacher competencies, and her unfailing support
of kindergarten programs in Tennessee and throughout this
nation attest to her qualities.[1]

4. Throughout her teaching career and since her retirement, Maycie Southall has been an outstanding leader. Typical
of many evaluations contributed to this study was one provided
by Margaret Hopper, a former elementary school principal:

It was Maycie K. Southall who challenged me in my
professional preparation for teaching at Peabody College.

She was a woman of charm and beauty with keen intellect and a great and unique leader for the serious-minded
learner. She was a teacher whose knowledge seemed im-
mense, whose grasp of the past through her pioneer experience was inculcated in the best of the "todays" of the
'30s, whose vision extended beyond the campus to other
cultures, whose energy and time seemed boundless, whose
leadership was nation-wide, whose organizational efforts
were extensive, whose enthusiasm for teaching was caught,
whose courage gave inspiration, and whose services were
dedicated to learning and growth.

Her guidance and stimulation were never easy. Rigorous, hard work and thoroughness were required. I feel
very grateful for her leadership in my past, and I am
thrilled to see her work tirelessly in 1980 with vision
for her present dreams.[2]

5. Maycie Southall possessed the rare ability not only
to ferret out potential leaders but to motivate them to become
leaders. Many of her former students have become outstanding
leaders in a variety of intellectual endeavors. According
to one source, Maycie Southall ". . . was geared to finding
leaders. She was constantly finding scholars, teachers, and

---

[1] Ruth Bowdoin, personal letter, March 1, 1980.

[2] Margaret Hopper, personal letter, April 7, 1980.

administrators of merit and seeing to it that others did not
overlook them and that they did not underrate themselves."[3]
The same observer continued by noting that Maycie Southall
had guided innumerable students toward self-actualization:

> But she did not overlook anyone. She pointed out
> things to do, found complimentary things to say, kept
> probing and challenging gently until the student was
> able to work on his or her own. She knew the value of
> self-esteem and had developed the art of helping stu-
> dents grow until they experienced it.[4]

6. Maycie Southall attracted many students to George
Peabody College for Teachers. Those students, in turn, encouraged others to enroll at the educational institution in
order to study under her guidance. Mable Grey Patterson,
retired from her position as an associate professor of education at the University of Central Arkansas, reminisced about
Maycie Southall:

> Her gracious manner and social poise challenged
> the young woman teacher from the rural South to set
> higher goals and to be a very special teacher of chil-
> dren. (I think she challenged many. I have urged at
> least a dozen young women to go to Peabody and study
> under Miss Southall. They did.)
>
> She brought a wide range of knowledge to the class-
> room. Example: She challenged us to grow. One way to
> grow was by reading. . . . Professional organizations
> offered many specific ways to grow: the publications,
> the conferences, the travel, and the people involved
> in these organizations. Growth came through workshops,
> college classes with the goals for a higher degree, and
> certainly service to others. . . .
>
> As a college teacher . . ., I incorporated many of
> her teaching techniques and even a full course (Research
> in Elementary Education) in our curriculum for graduate

---

[3]J. C. Matthews, personal letter, February 26, 1980.

[4]Ibid.

(MSE) students. The contents of that one course were worth all my efforts in Miss Southall's class--and those efforts were many because Miss Southall was a challenging teacher. . . .

As I observe education and teachers in particular these last few years, it is difficult to find teachers who are as dedicated as Miss Southall, who inspire students as she did, and who show a real concern for professionalism.[5]

7. Maycie Southall has worked diligently for the cause of education and has expected others to do likewise. Although her assignments were rigorous and her expectations high, she was a very popular teacher. Typical of the expressions provided by many former students was one made by Arthuryne J. Taylor:

Dr. Southall commanded the respect of her students because of her personal sense of professionalism and thoroughness in research. I consider it a privilege to be numbered among her many students. She is quite deserving of this study which highlights her professional life.[6]

8. Maycie Southall realized the value of research and taught her students to appreciate the importance of developing a sound knowledge of available research, especially in human development and learning. Jess R. Beard was one among many former students who remembered Maycie Southall's emphasis on research:

The thing I learned from her as an instructor was the importance of knowing the research. Although I had the Master's degree and thirty semester hours beyond when I went to Peabody, no one had ever emphasized knowing the research. . . . I read research studies by the hundreds and never felt that I was keeping up. I think

[5]Mabel Grey Patterson, personal letter, March 16, 1980.

[6]Arthuryne J. Taylor, personal letter, January 7, 1980.

that emphasis on knowing the research followed me, and I used that technique frequently. . . .

I found Dr. Southall to be extremely generous of her time. As I have worked in Higher Education over the years, I keep thinking of how she spent her life in teaching as opposed to those people who seem to emphasize research. I suspect that this may have hampered her own professional career to a certain extent, but it certainly garnered for her many admirers and friends.[7]

9. Maycie Southall cares for other people. Many former students described incidents pertaining to her thoughtfulness and generosity; they were impressed with her sensitivity to their needs that extended beyond the strict confines of the usual teacher-student relationship. Esther D. Schroeder, for example, who later taught at Western Michigan University in Kalamazoo, had come from Minnesota in 1935 to study at George Peabody College for Teachers. Money was scarce during the era of economic recovery from the Great Depression; and as her finances were limited, she, as well as many other students, attended graduate school with the aid of a scholarship. In 1980, after more than four decades, she vividly recalled Maycie Southall's compassion:

Her sensitivity to students' needs was well brought out when she found that I chose the library rather than the cafeteria at noon because I was so short on funds. At graduation time, she loaned me the required long-sleeved white blouse to wear. I was deeply touched.[8]

10. Maycie Southall believed in educating the whole person for the present and throughout life. She thought that learning should extend beyond the classroom and thus initiated

---

[7] Beard, personal letter, November 1, 1979.

[8] Esther D. Schroeder, personal letter, March 2, 1980.

many off-campus activities designed to promote social development and cultural enrichment.

11. Maycie Southall's viewpoint was oriented toward the
future. She envisioned and put into practice several ideas
that were many years later to become considered educational
innovations. She emphasized, for example, the importance of
a positive self-concept in learning and living, parent-teacher
partnerships, and intercultural understanding.

12. Maycie Southall affiliated with numerous educational
organizations. Recognition was soon given to her leadership
abilities, and she began to accept responsibilities that drew
her into educational circles occupied by the intellectual
giants of the day. From her affiliations, benefits were ac-
crued for her students, the educational institution at which
she was employed, and education at large.

Through her connections with national leaders, Maycie
Southall kept abreast of contemporary educational thought.
She traveled extensively to stay in touch with avant-garde
trends in education and brought back from her trips firsthand information from the national leaders which she generously shared with her students and colleagues.

Because of her prominence in educational circles, Maycie
Southall became instrumental in bringing to the campus of
George Peabody College for Teachers many illustrious person-
ages of her era. As a result, she provided exceptional opportunities for her students to become acquainted with notable
leaders and to hear their views on contemporary issues.

Maycie Southall encouraged her students to join educational organizations and to participate in their activities. As a result, several of her former students have become well-known leaders in highly respected educational organizations at levels ranging from local to international. The prestige accorded George Peabody College for Teachers has been, in part, effected by the prominence of Maycie Southall and, ultimately, that of her students in educational organizations.

She used some of the educational organizations as instruments through which she could enlist the help of many persons to gain support for causes in which she believed. She worked avidly, for example, through such groups to call attention of the people and, finally, that of the legislature to the need for public kindergartens in Tennessee.

13. Although she served for many years on the editorial boards of The Peabody Reflector and the Peabody Journal of Education, two publications sponsored by George Peabody College for Teachers, and has contributed substantially to educational literature through articles, bulletins, and yearbooks, Maycie Southall has utilized the spoken word as her major medium of communication. Her charisma and eloquence of speech caused her to be sought frequently as a platform guest. Many of her speaking engagements were recorded in The Peabody Reflector as campus news items. An analysis of the number of trips and frequency of her travels to speak in behalf of the welfare of children indicated that the time and effort she expended were exceedingly extensive. During a recent interview, she stated

that she used the remuneration derived from some of her local
and state speaking engagements to finance her participation
in distant national conferences which contributed to her own
professional growth.[9]

14. Maycie Southall is courageous. She has been forth-
right in espousing educational causes that she considered
worthwhile. Her viewpoints, backed by careful research and
enhanced by a brilliant memory, have been forcefully presented; and she has not yielded from her stand on issues
when principles were involved merely to win the favor of an
audience. An observer described Maycie Southall's courage:

> My predecessor in the presidency at North Texas
> State University said of me: "Matthews does not know
> fear." I am a coward when compared to Dr. Southall.
> She is objective, fair, and long-suffering; but when
> the time comes for someone to stand firm until the
> problem is solved, she has the self-confidence, devo-
> tion, decisiveness, and energy to see it through.[10]

15. Maycie Southall believes in equality in education.
Encompassing many facets of equality, she has included opportunities for the rural student, the deprived student, and
the foreign student. Also, she has advocated termination of
discrimination against elementary school teachers by those
in higher education; women teachers who were married; and,
more recently, women educators who aspire to advancement in
position and equal pay for equal work.

---

[9]Maycie Southall, interview held in Nashville,
October 25, 1980.

[10]Matthews, personal letter, February 26, 1980.

16. Maycie Southall supports the position that women should be encouraged to work diligently, to actualize their potentialities, and to strive for positions of educational leadership. One way of effecting the process is through the provision of opportunities for women to complete their education. Thus, Maycie Southall has encouraged the granting of scholarships by educational organizations to help women who want to obtain advanced degrees in order to qualify for leadership roles.

17. Although Maycie Southall's major efforts have been contained under the expansive umbrella of education, her interests were many within that realm. She was described by Martha D. Bishop, a professor of education at Winthrop College in South Carolina, as ". . . truly a great person and the champion of many causes."[11] Maycie Southall advocated, for example, public kindergartens for all children, leadership of women in education, federal aid without federal control for education, and intercultural as well as international understanding. A colleague who remembered frequent contacts with Maycie Southall in organized movements stated: "Her interests were broad and her commitments were strong on behalf of reform. She could always be found on the humanitarian side."[12]

18. Maycie Southall is committed to the belief that a lasting peace among nations can best be brought about through

---

[11] Martha D. Bishop, personal letter, February 14, 1980.

[12] Norman L. Parks, personal letter, September 24, 1979.

the education of children. Her efforts in this respect have ranged from informal talks to persons at the grass-roots level on the one hand to active participation as a member of the U.S. Commission for UNESCO at the other extreme.

19. Maycie Southall is an exceptionally loyal person. This loyalty has been exemplified particularly in her commitment to her students; to her family, colleagues, and friends; to the promotion of childhood education; to the ongoing of the teacher education process; and to the institution, George Peabody College for Teachers.

20. Maycie Southall is never without an educational project. Although she retired from her professorship at George Peabody College for Teachers in 1964, she has remained active in a variety of educational and community endeavors. She served, for example, on the board of the YWCA in Nashville for six years, during 1966-72. Anne Gulley, who also served on the board during a portion of those years, remarked that Maycie Southall ". . . has certainly had a deep and continuing commitment to the welfare of children."[13]

Maycie Southall's latest, and current, project is the development of a Children's International Intercultural Education Center in Nashville; the only one of its kind in the nation, the Center would provide opportunities for children to learn more about other countries, thus enhancing better understanding and, ultimately, the hope of peace among nations.

---

[13]Anne Gulley, personal letter, January 4, 1980.

Concerning Maycie Southall's commitment to the project, one
of her committee members, Diane McNabb, stated:

> The quality which impressed me most of all about
> Dr. Southall has been the persistence with which she has
> followed all possible . . . sources of support for this
> project. She has no hesitancy whatever about seeking
> appointments with governors, mayors, supervisors, and
> whoever she feels could be influential--and presenting
> the proposal to them. . . . Her determination is diffi-
> cult to ignore!

> It has certainly been impressive to me that a person
> of her age and failing health has still maintained the
> interest in children and the energy required to push such
> a project. . . .[14]

21. Maycie Southall holds a position of high regard among
her former students, colleagues, friends, and acquaintances.
From a retired principal in Tampa, Florida, came the remark:
"I've been a great admirer of Dr. Southall."[15] From a former
student now living in Richmond, Virginia, came the comment:
"Dr. Southall is one I have admired through the years and feel
honored that I had the privilege of studying with her."[16]

22. Maycie Southall is widely known in educational circles. The fact that the letters of correspondence utilized
throughout this study have come from such diverse geographical
locations attests to this conclusion. Extending far beyond a
host of former students, colleagues, and friends who have had
direct contact with Maycie Southall is her reputation as an
educator. Typical of statements made by contributors of

---

[14]Diane McNabb, personal letter, January 9, 1980.

[15]Florence A. Wallace, personal letter, September 20,
1979.

[16]Joella A. Bradley, personal letter, April 10, 1980.

limited acquaintance was one shared by a co-member of an educational organization who lives in Manhattan, Kansas: "I was aware of her great reputation."[17]

23. In spite of her many accomplishments and accolades, Maycie Southall has throughout her career mixed easily with individuals of varied educational, financial, and cultural backgrounds.

24. Numerous persons who shared impressions for this project enthusiastically endorsed Maycie Southall's life and contributions to education as a subject worthy of research. Ella Bramblett, professor emeritus of early childhood education at Towson State University in Maryland, exclaimed: "What a great idea! Certainly Dr. Southall is a worthy subject."[18] Phyllis Shutt, an educational administrator in Nashville who described herself as an admirer and friend, opined: "The contributions and life of Dr. Southall certainly merit such a study."[19] Erick L. Lindman, whose teaching career found fruition in California, expressed: "I am delighted that you are writing about Dr. Southall."[20]

25. Maycie Southall was a friend to her students. In a 1977 letter to Maycie Southall, Hattie J. Johnson, a retired high school counselor, wrote: "You and all you have meant to

---

[17]Mary Frances White, personal letter, June 18, 1980.

[18]Ella Bramblett, personal letter, June 7, 1979.

[19]Phyllis Shutt, personal letter, February 19, 1980.

[20]Erick L. Lindman, personal letter, October 23, 1979.

me have really been a part of my life since 1938."[21] She continued by describing their association: "First, I met you in
. . . Cincinnati. In just a few days, I became your student.
Then, only a short time later, it was you who had charge of
the ritual when I went into Delta Kappa Gamma."[22] She concluded: "What you taught, what you were, and your friendship
were all a part of those rich, good years."[23] Numerous contributors to this study described their former professor as
a friend both during their college days and throughout later
years. The consensus of many former students is reflected in
the candid remark made by Dorris M. Johnson, a retired supervisor of student teachers: "I love and respect her dearly."[24]

26. Maycie Southall's contributions to education are
immeasurable. She served as a role model for those students
whose professional growth and personal development were en-
trusted to her care. To countless students, colleagues,
educators in professional organizations, friends, and acquaintances, Maycie Southall has been the epitome of what an
educator should be. Her influence upon individual lives and,
ultimately, upon education at large cannot be measured until
time is no more; for the benefits each succeeding generation
receives tend, in their turn, to benefit the next generation,

---

[21]Hattie J. Johnson to Maycie Southall, October 16, 1977,
Private Files of Maycie Southall.

[22]Ibid.

[23]Ibid.

[24]Dorris M. Johnson, personal letter, January 16, 1980.

and the next, and the next--similar to the impetus created by a tiny pebble which, when dropped into a brook, gives rise to ripples that flow on and on toward a distant sea.

Implications

Educators who aspire toward improvement or who are responsible for training potential educators may want to consider the following implications:

Maycie Southall served as an example to myriad students, colleagues, and friends. Testimonies contributed to this study indicate that her words and actions left indelible imprints upon the minds of many observers and wielded considerable influence upon her students' later educational efforts. At the time, Maycie Southall probably did not realize the extent of her influence upon the lives of those with whom she came in frequent contact. Educators of today are reminded, through this study, that they too are serving as examples to countless observers and that their words and actions may have a far-reaching influence upon the lives of others.

Maycie Southall has demonstrated that a woman can be an effective educator. She has shown, moreover, that a woman can be a leader among educators. Her achievements suggest that success does not require abrasiveness. Worth pondering is the fact that her influence and power, although remarkable in degree and retrospect, neither overshadowed, competed with, nor diminished to any measurable extent her reputation as a lady in the very best meaning of the word.

Throughout her career, Maycie Southall has eagerly pursued intellectual growth. She has studied, observed, explored new ideas, sought improvement, and interacted at length with her surroundings--and shared her adventures with her students-- thus providing a stimulating classroom environment conducive to learning. Her continuous intellectual growth has enriched her own life as well as the lives of those with whom she has come in contact.

Of significance is the fact that Maycie Southall cared for her students, and she worked diligently at communicating to them her interest in their welfare. She conscientiously rendered the textbooks their due measure of importance, she upheld scholarship, and she adhered to the pedagogical expectations incumbent with her professorship at a renowned educational institution; however, Maycie Southall's genuine caring for her students should be analyzed carefully for it was an effective instrument that attracted students to her in such measure that she could then communicate successfully her larger sense of caring for education. She served as a model of caring--for both her students and education at large--and through this process she motivated an untold number of her students to care, in turn, for their students and for education at large.

Suggestions for Further Research

Research completed during the preparation of this study revealed that Maycie Southall has devoted an extensive amount of time and effort to the Association for Childhood Education International. Although her contributions to several educational organizations were outstanding, she probably touched the lives of more educators through her leadership in the ACEI than through her other affiliations. This study includes an exploration of Maycie Southall's major contributions to The Delta Kappa Gamma Society International; a similar study of her leadership in the ACEI is worthy of consideration.

A second suggestion for a research topic directs attention to the life and educational contributions of Mary Hall as the subject of a worthwhile study. The time and effort necessitated by such a project would most assuredly be well spent if a researcher's pen could capture only a small portion of the energetic forcefulness consistently displayed by "Miss Mary" as she speaks of her dominant interest, the betterment of education.

Mary Hall, whose educational efforts have somewhat parallelled those of Maycie Southall, has experienced a long and impressive career in education. The daughter of a prominent medical doctor, she was encouraged to enter the teaching profession in spite of her earlier resistance to the suggestion. Her educational experiences encompassed employment in a one-teacher school, elevation to a position as an elementary supervisor for middle Tennessee, and finally an illustrious tenure as a staff member at Middle Tennessee State University in Murfreesboro. Although retired from her teaching position, "Miss Mary" is quite active in professional organizations,

religious efforts, civic projects, and social affairs. A
stately campus building which bears her name evidences only
one display of innumerable accolades that have been bestowed
upon a leader who has committed her life's efforts to the
service of education.

Mary Hall and Maycie Southall are two among sixteen
founders of Xi State, the Tennessee unit of The Delta Kappa
Gamma Society International. Both were born in 1895; and,
although they have matured into a ripeness of life during
which repose coupled with ample time for retrospect would be
understandable, both educators are physically active, mentally alert, and much in demand as participants in a variety
of public service concerns because of their boundless enthusiasm, leadership ability, and devotion to causes of educational significance. In the educational history of Tennessee,
there are few female leaders who are more widely known, who
have exerted more influence upon the lives of ensuing generations of teachers, and whose names are more respected than
those of Maycie Southall and Mary Hall. As this project has
addressed the life and contributions to education of the former, the suggestion is made that a similar study be undertaken
about Mary Hall. Future generations will have access only to
the history that has been recorded. As the years are taking
their toll, this pioneer educator's story should be handed
down to posterity through a study made while she possesses
the faculties of a keen mind and vivid memory in order that
it may be written with accuracy of detail.

1979

Maycie K. Southall

APPENDIX

LETTERS OF INQUIRY

May 5, 1979

Dear Former Graduate Student of Dr. Maycie K. Southall:

I am a doctoral student at George Peabody College for Teachers and am working toward completion of a dissertation. Both Dr. Southall and my Doctoral Advisory Committee have approved my topic which is tentatively entitled, "Dr. Maycie Katherine Southall: Her Life And Contributions to Education."

Through my research, I have found that you knew Dr. Southall while you were enrolled in graduate work at Peabody. Consequently, I am writing to you in search of information that would "enliven" and provide authenticity for my study. I shall really appreciate your taking a few moments of your time to reminisce, analyze, and evaluate Dr. Southall's contributions to education.

Also, I shall appreciate your description of classroom incidents, campus activities, or personal observations that would provide "human interest" as well as an account of her ministry to education.

I am attaching a separate page suggesting ideas for responses; however, please feel free to be flexible in your replies.

At this point, I am contacting only the students associated with Dr. Southall at the doctoral and specialist level; however, I realize that many students on the master and bachelor level would be excellent sources for information. Thus, if you have reason to know of additional persons whom you would recommend that I contact, please advise.

I shall appreciate your help. As I am working "around the clock" on this project, I hope to hear from you as soon as your schedule will permit.

Please be objective in your replies. Although "sweetness and light" are flattering, the quality of Dr. Southall's efforts will be reflected most clearly through substance.

Thank you very much for your time, effort, and contribution to this project.

Sincerely,

Louise Brown

(Mrs.) Louise Brown

Please advise if I have permission to quote from you in my project.

SUGGESTED IDEAS FOR RESPONSES

1. In what capacities have you known Dr. Southall? Include time frames, her position, your position, and other pertinent details.

2. Did you have classes with Dr. Southall? If so, describe.

3. Were you active in campus organizations that Dr. Southall sponsored (such as, for example, ACEI)? If so, describe.

4. What was her educational philosophy? Have you kept any notes or records from your Peabody days that would relate some of her thoughts and "teachings"? Please share.

5. How would you describe Dr. Southall's leadership? Was she, for example, forceful? Relate her strengths and/or weaknesses.

6. How would you describe her personality? (Think in terms of class-room, campus, organizations, and home.)

7. Can you describe some incidents or anecdotes (in classroom, for example) that indicate Dr. Southall's teaching methods, rapport between students and teacher, ability to communicate, understanding of and sensitivity to the needs of others, or "love" for teaching?

8. Did Dr. Southall encourage students to improve their own education? Did she influence students to come to Peabody? If you were enrolled at a time prior to working toward completion of your final degree, were you influenced to return to Peabody by Dr. Southall for your additional work or degrees?

9. Has Dr. Southall been influential in education in your opinion? How?

10. Has your association with Dr. Southall influenced your life and sub-sequent efforts in education? Have you made a career of education? What positions have you held? Where? What is your current position?

11. Perhaps most important of all, from your analysis of Dr. Southall's effectiveness in regard to her educational efforts, can you draw any conclusions or determine any implications for education?

12. Please share any pertinent ideas not previously covered.

* * * * * * * *

SIGNATURE: Louise Brown has my permission to use any or all of my responses in a dissertation: _____ (or) _____.
(Yes) (No)

_____
(Please sign your name)

_____
(Street Address)

_____
(City) (State) (Zip)

Dear Friend of Dr. Maycie K. Southall:

I am a doctoral student at George Peabody College for Teachers and am working toward completion of a dissertation. Both Dr. Southall and my Doctoral Advisory Committee have approved my topic tentatively entitled, "Dr. Maycie Katherine Southall: Her Life and Contributions to Education."

As one means of obtaining pertinent information, I sent letters to former doctoral and specialist students of Dr. Southall; in that correspondence I requested that the former students recommend additional sources to whom I should write. As a result of "feedback" from that effort, you have been recommended as a person whose professional association with Dr. Southall and whose knowledge of her educational efforts place you in a prime position to provide substantive analysis of her career.

I would surely appreciate your taking a few moments of your time to share your observations of Dr. Southall's efforts with me. Such comments, that I may use with your permission, should "enliven" and add substance to the project. Please discuss her effectiveness from your vantage point--be it a colleague, a department chairman, a co-committee member, an associate in an educational organization, and/or a personal friend--as well as from the standpoint of education in general. Your inclusion of time frames concerning your mutual work, projects, and endeavors would be helpful.

Of interest, too, would be your inclusion of any anecdotes or incidents (such as campus happenings) that reflect the real Dr. Southall within the context of her service to education.

Also, from your analysis of Dr. Southall's effectiveness, I would appreciate your sharing any conclusions or implications for education that you may draw.

As I am working "around the clock" on this study, I shall appreciate hearing from you as soon as your schedule will allow. Thank you very much for your time, effort, and contribution to this project.

Sincerely,

Louise Brown

(Mrs.) Louise Brown

SIGNATURE: Louise Brown has my permission to use any or all of my responses in a dissertation: _____ (or) _____.

                                           (Yes)   (No)

_____

(Please sign your name)

_____

(Your Position)

_____

(Street Address)

_____

(City)   (State)   (Zip)

SOURCES CONSULTED

Books

Brickman, William W. _Research in Educational History_.
Norwood, Pa.: Norwood Editions, 1973.

Cremin, Lawrence A. _The Transformation of the School_.
New York: Alfred A. Knopf, 1961.

The Delta Kappa Gamma Society International. _Handbook_.
Austin: Revised under the auspices of an Ad Hoc Committee, Nadine Ewing, chairman; International Headquarters, 1979.

Encyclopaedia Britannica, 11th ed. S.v. "Peabody, Elizabeth
Palmer."

Freeman, Jo. "Women on the Move: The Roots of Revolt."
In _Academic Women on the Move_, pp. 1-32. Edited by
Alice S. Rossi and Ann Calderwood. New York: Russell
Sage Foundation, 1973.

George, Carol V. R. _"Remember the Ladies."_ Syracuse:
Syracuse University Press, 1975.

Hillway, Tyrus. _Introduction to Research_. 2d ed. Boston:
Houghton Mifflin Company, 1964.

Holden, Eunah Temple. _Our Heritage_. Austin: The Steck
Company for The Delta Kappa Gamma Society, 1960.

_____. _Our Heritage_. Vol. 2. Two volumes of which
first is not numbered. N.p.: Steck-Warlick Company
for The Delta Kappa Gamma Society, 1970.

Robbins, D. P. _Century Review of Maury County, Tennessee,
1805-1905_. N.p.: published under the auspices of the
Board of Mayor and Alderman of Columbia, 1905; author
later added 1906 Supplement and Corrections; reprinted
by Maury County Historical Society, n.d., p. 323 of
Supplement.

Rogers, Lucille. _Light from Many Candles_. Nashville:
McQuiddy Printing Company for Xi State, Delta Kappa
Gamma, 1960.

Sexton, Patricia. _Women in Education_. Bloomington, Ind.:
Phi Delta Kappa Educational Foundation, 1976.

Smith, George W. _Quantitative Methods of Research in
Education_. Washington, D.C.: College and University
Press, 1975.

Southall, Maycie. "An Appreciation of Lucy Gage." Gage Book of Memoirs. Located in John Stevens Collection (unpublished papers of Lucy Gage). Nashville: George Peabody College for Teachers, 1942. (Handwritten.)

Stuart, Jesse. To Teach, To Love. New York: World Publishing Co., 1970.

Wiersma, William. Research Methods in Education. 2d ed. Itasca, Ill.: F. E. Peacock Publishers, 1975.

Wiggins, Sam P. and others on the Ruml Plan Committee. A Report to the Board of Trustees of George Peabody College for Teachers. Nashville: The College, 1960.

Wilson, Lester M., and Kandel, I. L. Introduction to the Study of American Education. New York: Thomas Nelson and Sons, 1934.

Journals and Periodicals

"Alumni Elect Dr. Southall President." The Peabody Reflector 39 (November-December 1966):269.

"Annual Study Conference of the Association for Childhood Education." The Peabody Reflector 20 (June 1947):221.

Blanton, Annie Webb. "An Outstanding Administration." The Delta Kappa Gamma Bulletin 7 (November 1940):12-13.

_____. "Pioneers in Delta Kappa Gamma." The Delta Kappa Gamma Bulletin 4 (March 1938):22-24.

_____. "Summary of Delta Kappa Gamma History." The Delta Kappa Gamma Bulletin 10 (June 1944):25-29.

Board of Trustees. "Tribute to Eleanore Meade." The Peabody Reflector 43 (Summer 1970):97.

"Board of Trustees Hears President Report on College's 'Pressing Needs.'" The Peabody Reflector 41 (May-June 1968): 133-41.

Bristow, Norma Smith. "A Brief History of the Delta Kappa Gamma Society." The Delta Kappa Gamma Bulletin 5 (June 1939):18-23.

Campbell, Clarice T. "The Historian's Task." The Delta Kappa Gamma Bulletin 32 (Summer 1966):29-34.

Carter, Eula Lee. "Presentation Speech of the National Achievement Award." The Delta Kappa Gamma Bulletin 8 (November 1941):30.

Chapman, Anne. "Women in the History Curriculum." Social Studies 69 (May-June 1978):117-21.

Crabb, A. L. "Statelier Mansions." The Peabody Reflector and Alumni News 5 (August 1932):321-22, 324-26.

Davis, O. L., Jr. "Symbol of a Shift from Status to Function: Formation of the Association for Supervision and Curriculum Development." Educational Leadership 35 (May 1978): 609-14.

Dawson, Mildred. "A Living Pioneer in Tennessee." The Delta Kappa Gamma Bulletin 8 (March 1942):20-22.

"Degrees Conferred by George Peabody College for Teachers, 1915-1967." The Peabody Reflector 40 (November-December 1967):[292-93].

"Dr. Maycie K. Southall." The Peabody Reflector 16 (December 1943):427.

"Dr. Maycie K. Southall." The Peabody Reflector 18 (May 1945):183, 185.

"Dr. Maycie Southall." The Peabody Reflector 16 (February 1943):65.

"Dr. Maycie Southall." The Peabody Reflector 19 (November 1946):386.

"Dr. Southall Reelected to Educational Policies Commission." The Peabody Reflector 18 (January 1945):25.

"Editorial Comment." The Peabody Reflector 23 (July 1950): 202.

"Faculty News." The Peabody Reflector 41 (March-April 1968): 96-99.

"Faculty News." The Peabody Reflector 41 (May-June 1968): 167-70.

"Faculty News." The Peabody Reflector 41 (July-August 1968): 232-34.

"Faculty News." The Peabody Reflector 41 (September-October 1968):277-79.

"Faculty News." The Peabody Reflector 42 (January-February 1969):40-42.

"Faculty Notes." The Peabody Reflector 36 (March-April 1963): 56.

Friedrich, Betty. "Student Organizations." The Peabody Reflector 18 (November 1945):357, 359-60.

"Geographical List of August Graduates." The Peabody Reflector and Alumni News 2 (August 1929):16-18. (Group picture on p. 7 and copy of Commencement Program on p. 10.)

Green, Etha. "The First Lady of Childhood Education." The Peabody Reflector 43 (Fall 1970):130-34.

Howe, Florence. "Sexism and the Aspirations of Women." Phi Delta Kappan 55 (October 1973):99-104.

Jackson, Ruth M. "Values of Research on Pioneer Women Educators." The Delta Kappa Gamma Bulletin 23 (Spring 1957): 47-49.

"Laureates for 1964." The Educational Forum 38, Part 2 (March 1964):384m-p.

Lee, Ruth. "Summer Conferences and Workshops." The Peabody Reflector 23 (April 1950):105-6, 112.

"The National Convention." The Delta Kappa Gamma Bulletin 8 (November 1941):5-8.

"The National Program of Work." The Delta Kappa Gamma Bulletin 5 (April 1939):10-11.

"News of Emeritus Professors, Faculty Wives." The Peabody Reflector 39 (November-December 1966):274-77.

"1929." The Peabody Reflector and Alumni News 2 (January 1929):17.

"192nd Commencement." The Peabody Reflector 41 (May-June 1968):148-64.

"178th Commencement." The Peabody Reflector 34 (May-June 1961):69-88.

Parkinson, Nell. "Beta Chapter, Nashville." The Delta Kappa Gamma Bulletin 5 (June 1939):82.

Payne, Bruce R. "Dreams." The Peabody Reflector and Alumni News 2 (August 1929):[4].

"Peabody Women . . . An Editorial." The Peabody Reflector 38 (March-April 1965):inside front cover.

"Retreat Spurs Desire for More Discussions." The Peabody Reflector 41 (November-December 1968):316.

Robb, Felix [C.]. "President Looks at Peabody's Problems, Needs, Aims, Hopes." The Peabody Reflector 34 (September-October 1961):130-39.

Smith, S. L. "The White House Conference on Rural Education." The Peabody Reflector 18 (February 1945):50-51.

Southall, Maycie. "Fifteen Years A-Growin'." The Delta Kappa Gamma Bulletin 10 (June 1944):15.

_____. "Message from the National President." The Delta Kappa Gamma Bulletin 5 (June 1939):1-2.

_____. "Report of National Membership Committee." The Delta Kappa Gamma Bulletin 8 (November 1941):34-35.

_____. "Tennessee." The Delta Kappa Gamma Bulletin 3 (June 1937):16-26.

Stoddard, A. J. and others on the Educational Policies Commission of the National Education Association and the American Association of School Administrators. "An Open Letter to Members of the American Delegation to the United Nations Conference on International Organization." The Journal of the National Education Association 34 (May 1945):99.

"Summer Officers of Elementary Council with Dr. Hunter, National ACEI Head." The Peabody Reflector, Summer Supplement, 11 (July 28, 1960):[4].

"Summer School Registration." The Peabody Reflector and Alumni News 2 (June 1929):18.

"'Today's Child, Tomorrow's Adult' Theme of ACEI Gathering in Omaha." The Peabody Reflector 34 (March-April 1961):51.

"The Unique Role of Peabody College," including letter from F. Lynwood Wren to Henry H. Hill. The Peabody Reflector 19 (November 1946):363-66, 370.

Windrow, J[ohn] E. "Head Start." The Peabody Reflector 38 (May-June 1965):97-101.

"Women's Club Marks Increase in Membership." The Peabody Reflector 40 (September-October 1967):247.

Yarbrough, Margaret Hite. "With the A.C.E. in Tennessee." The Tennessee Teacher 13 (September 1945):30.

Newspapers

Brandau, Susan. "'Day' a Tribute to Dr. Southall."
Nashville Tennessean, October 16, 1977, p. 4-E.

"Childhood Education Leader to Address Florida Teachers."
Tampa Sunday Tribune, February 14, 1946, p. 3-C.

"Churchill Proposal Bars Vital Peoples, Says Mrs. Roosevelt."
Washington (D.C.) Evening Star, March 15, 1946, p. B-6.

Keathley, Virginia. "Meet Dr. Maycie Katherine Southall:
National and International Educator." Nashville
Tennessean, May 19, 1963, p. 4-E.

"Many Receive Their Diplomas at Peabody." Nashville
Tennessean, June 11, 1919, p. 2.

"MTSU Names 3 Graduates '1973 Distinguished Alumni.'"
Murfreesboro (Tennessee) Daily News Journal, March 25,
1973, p. 10.

O'Donnell, Red. "'Round the Clock." Nashville Banner,
August 8, 1963, pp. 1, 38.

Start, Clarissa. "Education's Role in Fight to Win Peace."
St. Louis Post-Dispatch, April 24, 1948, p. 1-B.

"Vine Hill One of Maury's Oldest, Largest Homes." Columbia
(Tennessee) Daily Herald, July 1, 1971, p. 1.

Correspondence

Alexander, William M. Personal letter, May 23, 1979.

Alford, Arthur S. Personal letter, July 18, 1979.

Anderson, Mary Louise. Personal letter, May 30, 1979.

Aslinger, Ival. Personal letter, May 25, 1979.

Baxter, Bernice. Personal letter, June 3, 1979.

Beard, Jess R. Personal letter, November 1, 1979.

Berry, Mary Tom. Personal letter, November 7, 1979.

Bishop, Martha D. Personal letter, February 14, 1980.

Bowdoin, Ruth. Personal letter, March 1, 1980.

Boyd, Edna McGuire. Personal letter, May 4, 1979.

Bradley, Joella A. Personal letter, April 10, 1980.

Bragg, John T. Personal letter, September 12, 1979.

Bramblett, Ella. Personal letter, June 7, 1979.

Browning, Mary. Personal letter, May 15, 1979.

Bryant, Paul P. Personal letter, May 15, 1979.

Caswell, Hollis L. Personal letter, May 20, 1979.

Cauthen, Harold C. Personal letter, January 12, 1980.

Chrisler, Verna. Personal letter, March 1, 1980.

Clark, Elmer J. Personal letter, July 16, 1979.

_____. Personal letter, September 13, 1979.

Coe, Christine Sadler. Personal letter, May 20, 1979.

Conoly Bernice. Personal letter, May 14, 1979.

Cos, Vergie F. Personal letter, July 6, 1979.

Cross, Pearl. Personal letter, February 22, 1980.

Crouch, Ernest. Personal letter, July 23, 1979.

Dalton, William Theo. Personal letter, February 25, 1980.

Darden, Anna Belle. Personal letter, May 4, 1980.

Davis, Bob [Robert C.]. Personal letter, November 1, 1979.

Davis, O. L., Jr. Personal letter, May 18, 1979.

Dawson, Elizabeth Sutton. Personal letter, October 20, 1979.

Dawson, Mildred. Personal letter, May 23, 1979.

Delk, Paul. Personal letter, May 2, 1979.

Dement, Geraldine B. Personal letter, February 24, 1980.

Drummond, Harold D. Personal letter, June 22, 1979.

Duckworth, Irene. Personal letter, July 8, 1979.

Eady, Vernon. Personal letter, January 11, 1980.

Ellis, Zora. Personal letter, April 26, 1979.

Emmons, Phebe H. Personal letter, June 6, 1979.

Ewing, Nadine M. Personal letter, June 10, 1979.

Farrell, Emma L. Personal letter, May 17, 1979.

Fechek, Theresa A. Personal letter, July 2, 1979.

Fulton, Richard. Personal letter, April 5, 1979.

Gammell, Bertha M. Personal letter, October 23, 1979.

Gilstrap, Robert. Personal letter, January 22, 1980.

Ginsberg, Sadie D. Personal letter, May 24, 1979.

Grefe, Mary A. Personal letter, March 31, 1981.

Grove, Anne. Personal letter, July 30, 1979.

Guess, George T. Personal letter, May 31, 1979.

Gulley, Anne. Personal letter, January 4, 1980.

Hall, Souci. Personal letter, July 31, 1979.

Harvill, Halbert. Personal letter, July 23, 1979.

Hegar, Alma. Personal letter, April 16, 1980.

Heinz, Mamie. Personal letter, May 29, 1979.

Henderson, R. C. Personal letter, May 13, 1979.

Henry, Douglas, Jr. Personal letter, September 4, 1979.

Hill, Henry H. Personal letter, June 18, 1979.

_____. Personal letter, November 1, 1980.

Hill, Horace G., Jr. Personal letter, August 28, 1979.

Hiller, Ola B. Personal letter, May 2, 1979.

Hinson, Barbara J. Personal letter, February 24, 1980.

Hopper, Margaret. Personal letter, April 7, 1980.

Hostetler, J. Jay. Personal letter, May 30, 1979.

Huddleston, Sherian. Personal letter, May 28, 1979.

Humphreys, Clemit O. Personal letter, July 14, 1979.

Hunter, Eugenia. Personal letter, June 3, 1979.

Husk, Mary Jo. Personal letter, February 14, 1980.

Hymes, James L., Jr. Personal letter, June 10, 1979.

Ingram, Frances. Personal letter, February 26, 1980.

Ingram, Sam H. Personal letter, September 20, 1979.

Johnson, Dorothy L. Personal letter, May 1, 1979.

Johnson, Dorris M. Personal letter, January 16, 1980.

Jones, Allene. Personal letter, February 20, 1980.

Jordan, Mary K. Personal letter, June 12, 1979.

Kjer, Dell C. Personal letter, August 8, 1979.

Lindman, Erick L. Personal letter, October 23, 1979.

Martin, Hilda. Personal letter, June 19, 1979.

Matthews, J. C. Personal letter, February 26, 1980.

Mayfarth, Frances. Personal letter, June 1, 1979.

McBride, Otis. Personal letter, July 15, 1979.

McDonald, Ruth. Personal letter, May 9, 1979.

McMahan, John Julia. Personal letter, May 5, 1979.

————. Personal letter, May 21, 1979.

McMains, Nell. Personal letter, May 14, 1979.

McNabb, Diane. Personal letter, January 9, 1980.

Meyer, Alberta. Personal letter, May 22, 1979.

Michael, Gertrude. Personal letter, May 24, 1979.

Miller, Alta. Personal letter, October 17, 1979.

Miller, Ethel B. Personal letter, October 18, 1979.

Millspaugh, Margaret. Personal letter, January 18, 1980.

Morton, Alyse. Personal letter, June 7, 1979.

Morton, Dorothy. Personal letter, April 29, 1980.

Mumpower, D. L. Personal letter, June 9, 1979.

Murdoch, Euleta. Personal letter, October 19, 1979.

Nashville, Tennessee. George Peabody College for Teachers.
    Office of the College Archivist and Historian.
    Personnel File of Maycie Katherine Southall includes:

Thomas Alexander to J. J. Didcoct. May 8, 1920.

Norman Frost to J. J. Didcoct. May 14, 1920.

R. L. Harris to J. J. Didcoct. May 10, 1920.

Bernice C. Reaney to J. J. Didcoct. May 14, 1920.

Nashville, Tennessee. Private Files of Maycie Southall
    include:

Sam H. Ingram to Maycie Southall. January 31, 1979.

Hattie J. Johnson to Maycie Southall. October 16, 1977.

Robert R. Leeper to Maycie Southall. July 14, 1972.

Felix C. Robb to Maycie Southall. January 25, 1965.

Maycie Southall. "Christmas Letter." Correspondence
to friends, 1970. (Duplicated.)

Maycie Southall to Edward A. Cox. January 26, 1979.

Maycie Southall to Bruce R. Payne. October 19, 1934.

Nashville, Tennessee. Tennessee Education Association
    Building. Archives of Xi State, The Delta Kappa Gamma
    Society International. Collection includes:

Mamie S. Bastian. "Circular Letter to State and Chapter
Presidents from Past National President." July 1938.

Annie Webb Blanton to Friends. November 1935.

Annie Webb Blanton to Maycie Southall. September 25,
1935.

Annie Webb Blanton to Maycie Southall. October 29,
1935.

Annie Webb Blanton to Maycie Southall. December 5,
1935.

Anne Gates Butler to Maycie Southall. March 27, 1938.

Gretchen Hyder to Maycie Southall. April 6, 1936.

Maycie Southall to Annie Webb Blanton. October 7, 1935.

Maycie Southall to [Julia] Green. June 7, 1936.

Maycie Southall to Gretchen Hyder. October 12, 1936.

Nutterville, Catherine. Personal letter, May 5, 1979.

Oakley, Louise. Personal letter, May 23, 1979.

Osteen, Eleanor C. Personal letter, May 11, 1979.

Parker, Alida W. Personal letter, May 17, 1979.

Parks, Norman L. Personal letter, September 24, 1979.

Patterson, Mabel Grey. Personal letter, March 16, 1980.

Paxton, Willene. Personal letter, February 21, 1980.

Pledger, Maude Myrtice. Personal letter, May 4, 1979.

————————. Personal letter, May 20, 1979.

Pope, Patricia. Personal letter, February 29, 1980.

Powell, Mary Northcutt. Personal letter, May 30, 1979.

Praeger, Rosamond. Personal letter, June 5, 1979.

Ramsey, Marjorie E. Personal letter, May 9, 1979.

Rawls, Flora. Personal letter, May 11, 1979.

Robb, Felix C. Personal letter, February 25, 1980.

Ross, Birdella M. Personal letter, April 27, 1979.

Schlichter, Carol L. Personal letter, June 22, 1979.

Schroeder, Esther D. Personal letter, March 2, 1980.

Sherer, Margaret. Personal letter, May 22, 1979.

Shutt, Phyllis. Personal letter, February 19, 1980.

Smith, Haidee L. Personal letter, May 17, 1979.

Smith, Rubie E. Personal letter, June 2, 1979.

Snyder, Marjorie S. Personal letter, January 15, 1980.

Sparks, Nona. Personal letter, July 23, 1979.

Strickland, Esther H. Personal letter, May 1, 1979.

Sun Hi Lee Ro. Personal letter, July 23, 1979.

Taylor, Arthuryne J. Personal letter, January 7, 1980.

Thurman, Robert S. Personal letter, May 29, 1979.

_____. Personal letter, June 29, 1979.

Tillman, Rodney. Personal letter, July 11, 1979.

Tollett, Charles. Personal letter, October 31, 1979.

Turner, Virginia S. Personal letter, October 15, 1979.

Van Til, William. Personal letter, January 18, 1980.

Wallace, Florence A. Personal letter, September 20, 1979.

Ward, Frances. Personal letter, January 8, 1980.

Whelchel, Frances S. Personal letter, July 10, 1979.

White, Mary Frances. Personal letter, June 18, 1980.

White, Sue. Personal letter, January 5, 1980.

Whorley, Elizabeth. Personal letter, February 21, 1980.

Wiggins, Sam [P.]. Personal letter, October 15, 1979.

Wilcox, June. Personal letter, April 8, 1980.

Willis, Jack E. Personal letter, May 30, 1979.

Zuccarello, Helen. Personal letter, May 22, 1979.

Interviews

Brannon, Billie. Nashville, Tennessee. Interview, May 8, 1979.

Carter, Eula Lee. Fort Worth, Texas. Telephone interview, September 27, 1980.

Ellis, Phyllis. Fort Worth, Texas. Telephone interview, September 27, 1980.

Hall, Mary. Murfreesboro, Tennessee. Interview, May 28, 1979.

_____. Murfreesboro, Tennessee. Interview, July 2, 1979.

Jones, Jean. Columbia, Tennessee. Interview, May 18, 1979.

Jones, Lois. Sewanee, Tennessee. Interview, June 13, 1980.

Morgan, Mary Harris. Columbia, Tennessee. Telephone interview, May 18, 1979.

Parsons, Virginia. Columbia, Tennessee. Telephone interview, May 20, 1979.

Sim, Jessie. Sewanee, Tennessee. Interview, June 14, 1980.

Southall, Maycie. Nashville, Tennessee. Interview, April 23, 1979.

_____. Nashville, Tennessee. Interview, June 5, 1979.

_____. Nashville, Tennessee. Interview, June 19, 1979.

_____. Nashville, Tennessee. Interview, July 3, 1979.

_____. Nashville, Tennessee. Interview, August 29, 1979.

_____. Nashville, Tennessee. Interview, September 3, 1979.

_____. Nashville, Tennessee. Interview, December 15, 1979.

_____. Nashville, Tennessee. Interview, August 7, 1980.

_____. Nashville, Tennessee. Interview, October 25, 1980.

_____. Nashville, Tennessee. Interview, November 11, 1980.

_____. Nashville, Tennessee. Interview taped by O. L. Davis, Jr., April 20, 1979.

Stewart, Marshall. Nashville, Tennessee. Interview, July 11, 1979.

Windrow, John E. Nashville, Tennessee. Interview, May 8, 1979.

Miscellaneous Materials

Bailey, Carrie. "Life and Work of Lucy Gage, Pioneer Teacher and Leader." M.Ed. thesis, George Peabody College for Teachers, 1960.

Constitution of The Kappa Gamma Delta Society. 1929. (Name later changed.) Headquarters of The Delta Kappa Gamma Society International, Austin, Texas.

Constitution of The Delta Kappa Gamma Society. 1972. Headquarters of The Delta Kappa Gamma Society International, Austin, Texas.

Courthouse Records. "Marriage White, 1873-81; Marriage License Issued: No. 12259." 5:88, Maury County Court House, Columbia, Tennessee.

The Delta Kappa Gamma Society. Minutes of the Executive Board Meeting. March 21, 1940, Archives of Xi State, Tennessee Education Association Building, Nashville.

The Delta Kappa Gamma Society International. Program Manual: 1978-79. Prepared under the auspices of the International Program of Work Committees for the 1976-78 Biennium, Janice Nerem, chairman of the International Program Committee, 1976-78. Headquarters of The Delta Kappa Gamma Society International, Austin, Texas.

Nashville, Tennessee. George Peabody College for Teachers. Office of the College Archivist and Historian. Personnel File of Maycie Katherine Southall includes:

"Application Blank for Scholarship in Peabody College," [1927].

"Memorandum for the Appointment Committee," [1920].

Nashville, Tennessee. George Peabody College for Teachers. Office of Development and Alumni Affairs. Personnel File of Maycie Katherine Southall includes "Personal Data Sheet, Dr. Maycie Katherine Southall, 1977."

Nigh, Sam[uel C.]. "Dr. Maycie K. Southall." Term paper prepared for course in Educational Leadership, George Peabody College for Teachers [1953]. Private Files of Maycie Southall.

Oakley, Louise. "Some Facts about Light from Many Candles." Report prepared for the membership of Xi State, August 1967. Archives of Xi State, Tennessee Education Association Building, Nashville.

"An Orchid to You." Script prepared for broadcast on Radio
    Station WSIX, Nashville, November 27, 1977.

Southall, Maycie. "Response to Award as Outstanding Alumna
    of Middle Tennessee State University." Speech given
    during Alumni Meeting, Middle Tennessee State University,
    May 5, 1973. Private Files of Maycie Southall.

_____. "These Our Founders." Speech delivered at Founders
    Day meeting, George Peabody College for Teachers,
    February 15, 1961. Private Files of Maycie Southall.

The Urban Observatory of Metropolitan Nashville-University
    Centers. "Children's International Intercultural
    Education Center." Application for a Federal Grant,
    June 18, 1979.